A GUIDE TO PROGRAMMING THE

IBM PERSONAL COMPUTER

BRUCE PRESLEY

LAWRENCEVILLE PRESS, INC.

First published in 1982

Copyright ©1982
by

LAWRENCEVILLE PRESS, INC.

ISBN 0-442-26015-6

Educational orders may be placed by writing or calling:

Van Nostrand Reinhold Inc.
76 25 Empire Drive
Attn: Department T
Florence, Kentucky 41042
Telephone 606-525-6600

Van Nostrand Reinhold Company
135 West 50th Street, New York, NY 10020

Van Nostrand Reinhold Ltd.
1410 Birchmount Road, Scarborough, Ontario M1P 2E7

Van Nostrand Reinhold Australia Pty. Ltd.
17 Queen Street, Mitcham, Victoria 3132

Van Nostrand Reinhold Company Ltd.
Molly Millars Lane, Wokingham, Berkshire, England RG11 2PY

16 15 14 13 12 11 10 9 8 7 6 5 4 3

PREFACE

The publication of this first edition of A GUIDE TO PROGRAMMING—IBM PERSONAL COMPUTER represents the latest achievement of faculty members and students at The Lawrenceville School in developing curricular materials to assist students in learning to program computers.

Based on experience gained in our classrooms over the past fifteen years, we are convinced that a structured, concisely written computer manual is invaluable in teaching and learning programming. This latest manual, written specifically to instruct students in IBM BASIC, not only retains but expands on the features which have resulted in the wide acceptance of our previous publications, A GUIDE TO PROGRAMMING IN APPLESOFT and A GUIDE TO PROGRAMMING IN BASIC PLUS.

The production of this manual has involved the cooperation and talents of many individuals. Lester Waters, Robert Lynch, Eli Hurowitz, and Donald Mikan, have all made contributions to this publication which have been invaluable. Each has authored and taken responsibility for specific areas of the manual. The clarity and accuracy of each chapter reflect their considerable effort and expertise. Majorie Vining, of the Rhode Island School of Design, has produced the imaginative cover design, and William Sumfest of Trentypo the art work, while Dr. Theodore Fraser of The College of the Holy Cross has edited the text to ensure that it is both grammatically and stylistically correct. A very special thanks is due Harold Simon and his staff at Trentypo. Their assistance in producing this and our earlier manuals has been invaluable.

To all of these people I am deeply grateful. Thanks to their combined efforts we have produced what I believe to be one of the very finest computer manuals available today.

Bruce Presley

TABLE OF CONTENTS

INTRODUCTION TO PROGRAMMING

To communicate with a computer a special language is required. The language described in this manual is IBM BASIC which consists of simple English words understood by the computer. In this chapter the user will be introduced to the most fundamental statements required to write a program on the IBM Personal Computer.

What Is a Program?

A program is a sequence of instructions that informs the computer of the tasks which the user wants it to perform. From the very beginning, it is important to realize that the user must determine the order in which the computer performs all tasks assigned to it. It is also essential to realize that the computer operates with a limited vocabulary and that it can understand only certain key words which serve as commands. Hence, words which make perfect sense to the user may make no sense at all to the computer if they are not part of its vocabulary. This manual will present one of the special vocabularies of the IBM Personal Computer and will explain how it can be used in a variety of applications.

Line Numbering

To establish the sequence of instructions for any given program, line numbers must be assigned to each line within a program. This operation is essential since the computer reads instructions beginning with the lowest line number, then progresses to the next higher number, and ends with the highest numbered line.

It is permissible to type the program lines out of order because the computer puts them back into their proper order. For example, line 20 may have been typed before line 10; but, when the program is run, the computer automatically reads line 10 first. Such a system has the advantage of allowing any forgotten instructions, say between lines 10 and

20, to be entered later as lines 15, or 12, or 17, etc. For this reason it is best to number the lines of the program in units of ten (10, 20, 30, etc.) since this leaves nine possible line numbers that can later be inserted. It is also important to realize that the capital letter O cannot be used in place of zero.

An error in any instruction may be corrected at any time by depressing the return key and retyping the entire line using the same line number. If two lines are given the same line number, the computer uses only the last one typed and erases the first. By typing only a line number followed by the RETURN key (←┘) the line is eliminated entirely. The highest line number allowed on the computer is 65529.

PRINT

There are two basic types of information which the computer can utilize: numbers and words. What distinguishes one from the other is the fact that a number can be used in a mathematical calculation, whereas a word cannot. The PRINT statement is used to print both numbers and words.

PROGRAM 1.1

This program uses the PRINT statement at each line to print the results shown below.

```
10 PRINT 5 * 3
20 PRINT 12 + 8
30 PRINT 7 / 2
40 PRINT "SAND"
50 PRINT "5*3"
Ok
RUN
 15
 20
 3.5
SAND
5*3
Ok
```

Line 10 instructs the computer to print the product of 5 and 3. Note that an asterisk (*) is used to indicate multiplication. Line 20 adds 12 and 8 while line 30 divides 7 by 2, with the slash (/) indicating division. At line 40 the word SAND is printed. When a word or any set of characters is printed, they must be enclosed within quotation marks. Line 50 prints "5*3" rather than 15 because quotation marks are used. Information enclosed in quotation marks is called a string. Both lines 40 and 50 contain strings. If a printer is available, the command LPRINT, rather than PRINT, will send the output to the printer rather than to the video display.

The command RUN is typed after a program has been entered to execute the program, but it is not part of the program.

Typing Errors

An error in a program can be corrected in one of three ways. First, the program line can be retyped using the same line number. For example,

```
40 PRINT "ROCKS"
RUN
 15
 20
 3.5
ROCKS
5*3
Ok
```

changes only that part of the output which is produced by line 40. The second method of correcting an error involves the use of the key marked (←) which can be employed if the error is detected while the line containing the error is being typed. Each time the (←) key is pressed, it causes the computer to erase one character to the left of the cursor on the screen. The third method of error correction consists in the use of the built in line editor. To learn how to use this feature refer to Appendix A.

LIST

The LIST command is used to print the program currently in the computer's memory. Typing LIST followed by a RETURN will print the entire program, while LIST followed by a line number and a RETURN will cause only that line to be printed. To list portions of a program, type LIST followed by the first and last line numbers of the portion desired, separating the two numbers with a hyphen (-). For example:

```
LIST
10 PRINT 5 * 3
20 PRINT 12 + 8
30 PRINT 7 / 2
40 PRINT "ROCKS"
50 PRINT "5*3"
Ok
LIST 50
50 PRINT "5*3"
Ok
```

```
LIST 20-40
20 PRINT 12 + 8
30 PRINT 7 / 2
40 PRINT "ROCKS"
Ok
```

To send the program listing to a printer, type LLIST instead of LIST.

NEW

Before entering a program into the computer, the NEW command should be used to clear the computer's memory. The use of this command insures that program lines from a previous program do not affect the new program.

```
LIST
10 PRINT 5 * 3
20 PRINT 12 + 8
30 PRINT 7 / 2
40 PRINT "ROCKS"
50 PRINT "5*3"
Ok
NEW
Ok
LIST
Ok
```

Observe that after the NEW command is used, a subsequent LIST shows that no program is currently in the computer's memory.

What Is a Variable?

One of the most useful properties of a computer is its ability to manipulate variables. A variable is a symbol that may assume many different values. The computer uses variables to represent numbers or strings.

Numeric variables are represented by letters or by letters and numbers. A, D, A1, and B1 are all legal names for numeric variables. The computer allows the use of longer names for variables, but for the sake of simplicity only a single letter or a single letter followed by a single digit will be used in the early chapters of this manual.

Variables can change in value as the name itself implies. For example, suppose that program line

$$20 X = 5$$

is typed. When the program is run and reaches line 20, X will be assigned the value 5.

Suppose a later statement such as

$$50 \ X = 7$$

is entered. Then at line 50 the value of X will change from 5 to 7.

Just as in algebra, the computer can have one numeric variable defined in terms of another. For example, when the statement $Y = 4*X$ is executed by the computer, Y will be assigned the value 20 if X=5, or Y will be assigned 28 if X=7, and so on.

It is important to realize that the equal sign (=) is interpreted as "is assigned the value." Therefore, when assigning a value to a variable, the statement must be in the form: 'variable = value', *not* 'value = variable'. Therefore, the statement

$$50 \ 7 = X$$

is invalid.

PROGRAM 1.2

This program assigns values to the variables X and Y, where the value of Y depends upon the value of X.

```
10 X = 12
20 Y = 3 * X + 5
30 PRINT X,Y
40 X = 15
50 PRINT X,Y
60 Y = 3 * X + 5
70 PRINT X,Y
Ok
RUN
 12            41
 15            41
 15            50
Ok
```

The value of X is originally 12 at line 10 and then becomes 15 at line 40. Y changes its value at line 60 because X changed at line 40. Note than when X and Y are printed at line 50, X is now 15, but Y is still 41 because the variable Y is not changed until it is reassigned at line 60. A comma is used in the PRINT statements at lines 30, 50, and 70 to allow the values of X and Y to be printed on a single line. Up to six variables can be printed on a single line of the display by the use of commas to separate each variable name.

String variable names are used in the same way as numeric variable names, except that a string variable name must end with a dollar sign ($). For example, A$, D$, A1$, C5$ all represent string variables. To assign characters to a string variable the characters must be enclosed in quotation marks. For example, the statement

$$10 \ A\$ = \text{``HARRY''}$$

will assign "HARRY" to the string variable A$. At some later point in a program it is possible to assign different characters to the same variable. For example, the statement

$$50 \text{ A\$ = "SHERRY"}$$

will replace "HARRY" with "SHERRY".

PROGRAM 1.3

This program assigns two different sets of characters to the string variable B$.

```
10 B$ = "GEORGE"
20 PRINT B$
30 B$ = "JUDY"
40 PRINT B$
50 PRINT "IT IS NICE TO SEE YOU ";B$
Ok
RUN
GEORGE
JUDY
IT IS NICE TO SEE YOU JUDY
Ok
```

Observe that at line 50 a sentence can be formed from two strings, the first of which in this case is not a variable.

Note that when a semicolon rather than a comma is used to separate items in a print statement, the items will be printed next to each other on the same line.

REVIEW

1. Write a program that will print the value of Y when X=5 and Y=5X+7

2. Write a program that will produce the following output by using string variables for "HARRY" and "SHERRY", but not for the other words.

```
RUN
HELLO HARRY
HOW ARE YOU?
SHERRY IS LOOKING FOR YOU.
```

READ, DATA

A variable may be directly assigned its value not only by a statement such as X = 5, but also by a combination of READ and DATA statements.

PROGRAM 1.4

This program uses READ and DATA statements to assign values to numeric variables.

```
10 READ X, Y, Z
20 PRINT 2 * X + 3 * Y + 8 * Z
30 DATA 3, 2, 0.5
Ok
RUN
 16
Ok
```

The READ statement at line 10 instructs the computer to assign numbers to the variables X, Y, Z. The computer finds these numbers in the DATA statement at line 30 and assigns them in the order listed (X = 3, Y = 2, and Z = 0.5).

In a DATA statement only numbers that are expressed in decimal or scientific form are acceptable. For example, the numbers .0032, -5.78, 1050, 2.9E5, and 4.76 E-12 are acceptable. The E stands for "times ten to the power" (e.g., 5.3 E3 = 5300 and 8.72 E-3 = .00872). However, data such as the arithmetic expressions 15/3, 3*5, and 7+2 are not permitted in DATA statements since, unlike PRINT statements, DATA statements allow for no calculations.

GOTO

Suppose that a student has more than one set of values for the variables X, Y, Z in Program 1.4. To introduce the extra values, line 30 can be retyped as follows:

```
30 DATA 3, 2, 0.5, -7, 2.5, 1E2
RUN
 16
Ok
```

Note that only the first three numbers in the DATA statement are processed, the remaining numbers are not used. To overcome this problem, line 30 could be retyped each time a new set of data is to be run, but this involves unnecessary labor. By including a GOTO statement between lines 20 and 30, the problem can be more easily solved by establishing a loop which allows line 10 to be used over again.

```
LIST
10 READ X, Y, Z
20 PRINT 2 * X + 3 * Y + 8 * Z
25 GOTO 10
30 DATA 3, 2, 0.5, -7, 2.5, 1E2
Ok
RUN
 16
 793.5
Out of DATA in 10
Ok
```

Observe that by typing the command LIST, the computer prints the current version of Program 1.4 including the new line. By running Program 1.4, all of the data presented in line 30 can now be processed. Each time the computer reaches line 25, the GOTO statement causes the computer to return to line 10 where the next set of data is assigned to the variables. On the first pass through the loop $X = 3$, $Y = 2$, $Z = .5$; on the second pass $X = -7$, $Y = 2.5$, $Z = 1E2$. However, on the third attempted pass, no additional data is available for assignment to the variables at line 10 and, therefore, an error message is printed.

The location of the DATA statement within a program is not important. Therefore, it can be placed anywhere. When the computer encounters a READ statement, it makes use of the DATA statement regardless of its location. DATA statements may contain strings as well as numbers and are usually placed at or near the end of a program.

PROGRAM 1.5

This program reads the names and grades of three students and prints the averages of their grades.

```
5 PRINT "NAME", "AVERAGE"
10 READ N$, A, B, C, D
20 X = (A + B + C + D) / 4
30 PRINT N$, X
40 GOTO 10
50 DATA WATERS,83,95,86,80,FRENCH,42,97,66,89,MIKAN,61,83,42,90
Ok
RUN
NAME            AVERAGE
WATERS          86
FRENCH          73.5
MIKAN           69
Out of DATA in 10
Ok
```

Examine this program carefully since it contains a number of important concepts. Line 5 produces the headings for the columns and is placed at the beginning of the program to insure that the headings will only be printed once. Line 10 assigns a student's name to the string variable N$ and the student's four grades to the numeric variables A, B, C, D. Unless the sequence of string variables and numeric variables in the READ statement is the same as the sequence of strings and numbers in the DATA statement, an error will occur. Line 40 returns the program to line 10 to read more data. What would happen if

$$40 \text{ GOTO } 5$$

was substituted for the current line 40?

REVIEW

3. Write a program using READ, DATA statements to evaluate Y where Y = 3X +5 and X = 3, 5, 12, 17, 8.

4. Write a program containing the DATA line in Program 1.5 which prints only the name and first grade of each student

```
RUN
NAME              FIRST GRADE
WATERS               83
FRENCH               42
MIKAN                61
Out of DATA in 10
Ok
```

INPUT

In many instances it is preferable to introduce data from the keyboard rather than placing it in a DATA statement. To do this an INPUT statement is used in place of the READ, DATA statements. When an INPUT statement is executed, the computer prints a question mark (?) and then waits for data to be entered.

PROGRAM 1.6

Data entered from the keyboard is used to assign a value to the variable X in the following program.

```
10 INPUT X
20 PRINT 5 * X * X + 3 * X + 2
30 GOTO 10
Ok
```

```
RUN
? 3
 56
? 6
 200
? 2
 28
?
Break in 10
Ok
```

The GOTO statement at line 30 creates a loop which will continue to run until it is interrupted. To interrupt the program strike the BREAK key while depressing the CTRL key which then causes BREAK IN 10 to be printed. If this is not done, Program 1.6 will continue to run until the computer is shut off.

PROGRAM 1.7

This program is a revision of Program 1.5. Here a student is asked for his or her name and four grades. The computer then prints the name and grade average. It is possible to have the INPUT statement print a question or a remark by enclosing the words to be printed in quotation marks followed by a semicolon and the variable names. Also, note that more than one variable can be entered by using a single INPUT statement.

```
10 INPUT "WHAT IS YOUR NAME"; N$
20 INPUT "WHAT ARE YOUR FOUR GRADES"; A, B, C, D
30 X = (A + B + C +D) / 4
40 PRINT N$, X
50 GOTO 10
Ok
RUN
WHAT IS YOUR NAME? TED
WHAT ARE YOUR FOUR GRADES? 87, 54, 76, 95
TED            78
WHAT IS YOUR NAME? JOHN
WHAT ARE YOUR FOUR GRADES? 98, 96, 47, 84
JOHN           81.25
WHAT IS YOUR NAME? ALBERT
WHAT ARE YOUR FOUR GRADES? 100, 95, 31, 60
ALBERT         71.5
WHAT IS YOUR NAME?
Break in 10
Ok
```

In an INPUT statement if a comma rather than a semicolon follows words enclosed in quotation marks, the question mark will not be printed. For example,

10 INPUT "WHAT IS YOUR NAME", N$

will print WHAT IS YOUR NAME without the question mark and then wait for INPUT when the program is run.

PRINT Formatting

There are a number of ways in which output can be formatted by the use of punctuation. A few of the more important uses of punctuation are demonstrated by the following program.

PROGRAM 1.8

The computer is capable of printing 80 characters on a single line. This line is divided into six printing zones consisting of 14 characters each, except for the last zone which is only 10 characters wide. When commas are used in a PRINT statement, the output is printed in successive zones.

```
5 PRINT "N A M E", "G R A D E S", "AVERAGE"
10 READ N$, A, B, C
20 X = (A + B + C) / 3
30 PRINT
40 PRINT N$, A; B; C, X
50 GOTO 10
60 DATA   SQUEEKY,72,81,78, GRUMPY,74,97,93, DOPEY,69,79,95
Ok
RUN
N A M E         G R A D E S     AVERAGE

SQUEEKY          72  81  78      77

GRUMPY           74  97  93      88

DOPEY            69  79  95      81
Out of DATA in 10
Ok
```

Note the output produced by line 5. Each word begins at the beginning of one of the zones because commas have been used to separate the words. The PRINT at line 30 is used to place a blank line between each of the printed lines. When printing a number, the computer places a single space in front of and behind the number. If the number is negative, the space in front is occupied by the minus (−) sign.

When semicolons (;) are used in place of commas (as in line 40), the output of each variable begins in the next space following the last variable printed.

PROGRAM 1.9

This program demonstrates the difference between commas and semicolons used in a print statement.

```
10 PRINT "ZONE 1", "ZONE 2", "ZONE 3", "ZONE 4", "ZONE 5", "ZONE 6"
20 X = -14
30 PRINT "**"; X; "**"
40 T = 42
50 PRINT "**"; T; "**"
60 A$ = "86"
70 PRINT "**"; A$; "**"
80 PRINT X; T; A$; 99; "Done"
Ok
RUN
ZONE 1          ZONE 2          ZONE 3          ZONE 4          ZONE 5          ZONE 6
**-14 **
** 42 **
**86**
-14  42 86 99 Done
Ok
```

Note how the values −14 and 42 were printed by lines 30 and 50, respectively. Line 70 shows that strings are not printed with a leading and trailing space.

REVIEW

5. Write a program in which you input a value of X and have the computer calculate 5*X and X/5. The printout should appear exactly as shown below.

```
RUN
WHAT IS X? 12
5*X= 60
X/5= 2.4
WHAT IS X? 20
5*X= 100
X/5= 4
WHAT IS X? 64
5*X= 320
X/5= 12.8
WHAT IS X?
Break in 10
Ok
```

6. Write a program which allows you to input your name and the name of a friend and then produces the printout as follows:

```
RUN
WHAT IS YOUR NAME? BRUCE
WHAT IS YOUR FRIEND'S NAME? JUDY
JUDY IS A FRIEND OF BRUCE
```

```
WHAT IS YOUR NAME? DON
WHAT IS YOUR FRIEND'S NAME? SHERRY
SHERRY IS A FRIEND OF DON

WHAT IS YOUR NAME?
Break in 10
Ok
```

Immediate Mode

The computer may perform simple tasks using the immediate mode rather than a program. An immediate mode instruction is typed without a line number. When the computer receives a command without a line number, it recognizes that the command is not part of a program but is to be executed immediately. The following are examples of immediate mode statements:

```
PRINT (3*5)+4
 19
Ok

PRINT 7/9
 .7777778
Ok

A=5
Ok
B=2
Ok
PRINT A + B + 4
 11
Ok

A$ = "BETTY"
Ok
PRINT A$;" BOO"
BETTY BOO
Ok
```

Note that a RUN command was not used in any of the preceding examples. Most commands are permissible in the immediate mode with the notable exception of the INPUT statement. In performing most tasks it is best to write complete programs and to reserve the use of immediate mode for simple calculations.

REM

The REM statement is used in the body of a program to allow the programmer to introduce explanatory remarks. Everything to the right of a REM statement is ignored by the computer when the program is run. For example,

$$30 \text{ REM CALCULATE AREA OF CIRCLE}$$

will be printed only when the program is listed. Remarks placed strategically within a program are useful in explaining the function of various parts of the program.

PART A

1. Write a program which prints the following.

```
            RUN
            A
              B
                C
            ABCD
```

2. Write a program which makes the following calculations. Check the results by hand computation.

    (a) 8 * (19 - 4)
    (b) 1 * 2 + 2 * 3 + 3 * 4 + 4 * 5
    (c) 1 + 1 / 10 + 1 / 100
    (d) 10 - 20 + 30 - 40 + 50 - 60

3. What is the exact output for the following program?

```
10 A = 3
20 PRINT "THE VALUE OF B"
30 B = A + 4 * 4
40 PRINT B
```

4. How many lines of output does the following program produce before an error message appears indicating "Out of DATA in 10"?

```
10 READ A, B, C
20 PRINT (A + B + C) / 3
30 GOTO 10
40 DATA 11,32,43,14,25,36,47
50 DATA 58,39,50,61,22,83,94
```

5. Peter Kolodnigork has loused up once again. Here is a program of his which he says "mysteriously doesn't work". Give Peter a hand and correct this monstrosity for him so that the output looks like the following:

THE SUM IS 20
THE SUM IS 14
OUT OF DATA IN 10

```
10 READ A B
20 PRINT   THE SUM IS   A + B
30 GOTO 12
40 DATA 12,8,3*3,5
```

6. Write the output, and check by running the program.

```
10 READ A$
20 PRINT A$
30 GOTO 10
40 DATA S,I,X!," 6",6
```

7. Write a program in which the price (P) in cents of a loaf of bread and the number (N) of loaves bought are entered from the keyboard. The total spent for bread is to be printed in dollars and cents.

8. Write a program to enter your weight (W) in pounds and height (H) in inches and which then prints the quotient W/H followed by the words "POUNDS PER INCH".

9. Using an INPUT statement, write a program which produces the following output.

```
RUN
? 2,4
X= 2            Y= 4            X*Y= 8
? -8,70
X=-8            Y= 70           X*Y=-560
?
```

10. Predict the output of the following program. Check the answer by running the program.

```
10 P$ = "TOTAL PRICE"
20 P = .89
30 PRINT P$;" = $0";P
```

11. Predict the output, and check by running the program.

```
10 READ A,B,C,D
20 PRINT A,B
30 PRINT C;" ";D
40 DATA 3E2,510,3E-1,.51
```

12. Use immediate mode to print the following numbers.

(a) .05

(b) .005

(c) 123456789

(d) 1234567890

(e) −.065

(f) 4.62E5

(g) .086E-3

(h) −4,900

13. Self-proclaimed computer whiz Cecil Cedric Cenceless has typed the following gibberish in the immediate mode and has challenged anyone to guess the output correctly before he or she presses the RETURN key. Put Cecil in his place and correctly predict the answer.

```
PRINT "AAA";111,222;"AAA","333";"   ";16-3*2
```

14. Write a program which will add the numbers 3, 5, and 7.

PART B

15. What is the exact output for the following program?

```
10 A$ = "ABCD"
20 B$ = "XYZ"
30 F = 7
40 G = −4
50 PRINT A$;B$
60 PRINT A$;F
70 PRINT F;B$
80 PRINT G;B$
```

16. Write a program to evaluate each of the following expressions for A = 10 and B = 7.

$(7A + 10B)/2AB$ 　　　　　　　　　 $(1/2)A/(A—B)$

17. In the first week of the season the cross country team ran the following number of miles each day: 2, 3, 4, 3, 5. Write a program to calculate and print the total mileage for the week.

18. A piece of pizza normally contains about 375 calories. A person jogging one mile uses about 100 calories. Write a program that asks a person how many pieces he or she wishes to eat and then tells him/her how far they must run to burn up the calories they will consume.

```
RUN
HOW MANY PIECES DID YOU EAT? 4
YOU MUST RUN 15 MILES.
```

19. Have the computer evaluate the expression 12x + 7y for the following data:

x	3	7	12
y	2	9	–4

20. The art of thinking up good insults can be enormously aided by the computer. To test an insult, have a computer program ask for the victim's name and the insulting word which should then be attached to the suffixes "breath" and "head". For example, given "Gary" as the victim's name and "bone" as the insulting word, the program should print:

GARY IS A BONE-HEAD
or
GARY IS A BONE-BREATH

21. Using an INPUT statement, write a program that will compute the volume of a room given its length, width, and height.

22. Write a program to compute the areas (cm²) of circles with radii 5.0 cm., 3.0 cm., and 8.0 cm. Have the output in the form "AREA OF CIRCLE =" with two spaces between each of the printed lines.

23. Just as three-dimensional objects are measured by volume, so four-dimensional objects are measured by tesseracts. Have your program ask for the dimensions of a four-dimensional object, height, width, length, and "presence" and print the object's tesseract.

24. With the equation $E = MC^2$, Einstein predicted that energy could be produced from matter. If the average human hair weighs a tenth of a gram and the town of Woodsylvania uses 2×10^{11} units of energy in a day, find out how many hairs from Einstein's head would be required to supply the town for a day ($C = 3 \times 10^{10}$).

25. Use the computer to calculate your library fines. Enter the number of books you have borrowed and how many days late they are. Have the computer print the amount of your fine if you are charged 10¢ per day per book.

26. The perimeter of a triangle is equal to the sum of the lengths of the three sides of the triangle. The semiperimeter is one-half of the perimeter. A triangle has sides of lengths 13 cm, 8 cm, 11 cm. A second triangle has sides of 21 ft, 16 ft, 12 ft. Write a program that reads these measurements from a DATA statement and then prints the semiperimeter of each triangle showing the correct units. The output should look like this:

SEMIPERIMETER OF FIRST TRIANGLE 16 CM.

SEMIPERIMETER OF SECOND TRIANGLE 24.5 FT.

27. Professional athletes have succeeded in making staggering sums of money through careful negotiations. Of course, the real winner is Uncle Sam who does not negotiate at all. Write a program which asks for a player's name and salary and then prints the player's name, take-home salary, and taxes if the tax rate for his income bracket is 44%.

```
RUN
WHAT IS THE PLAYER'S NAME? JUGGIE RACKSON
WHAT IS JUGGIE RACKSON'S WAGE? 150000
JUGGIE RACKSON WOULD KEEP $ 84000
HE WOULD PAY $ 66000 IN TAXES.
Ok
RUN
WHAT IS THE PLAYER'S NAME? DOPEY
WHAT IS DOPEY'S WAGE? 4200
DOPEY WOULD KEEP $ 2352
HE WOULD PAY $ 1848 IN TAXES.
```

28. Sale prices are often deceptive. Write a program to determine the original price of an item, given the sale price and the discount rate.

```
RUN
SALE PRICE? 3.78
DISCOUNT RATE? 10
THE ORIGINAL PRICE WAS $ 4.2
```

29. The area of a triangle can be found by multiplying one-half times the length of the base times the length of the altitude (A = .5 x base x height). Write a program that allows the user to enter from the keyboard the base and altitude of a triangle and then skips a line before printing out the area of the triangle.

```
RUN
WHAT IS THE BASE? 10
WHAT IS THE ALTITUDE? 5

THE AREA IS 25
```

30. A state has a 7 percent sales tax. Write a program that will allow you to INPUT the names and prices (before taxes) of different items found in a department store and then print the item, tax, and the price of the item including tax.

```
RUN
ITEM'S NAME? COAT
WHAT IS ITS PRICE? 65.00
COAT HAS A TAX OF $ 4.55 AND COSTS $ 69.55
ITEM'S NAME? TENNIS RACKET
WHAT IS ITS PRICE? 23.00
TENNIS RACKET HAS A TAX OF $ 1.61 AND COSTS $ 24.61
ITEM'S NAME?
Break in 10
Ok
```

31. In an election in Grime City, candidate Sloth ran against candidate Graft for mayor. Below is a listing of the number of votes both candidates received in each ward. What total vote did each candidate receive? What percentage of the total vote did each candidate receive?

Candidate	Sloth	Graft
Ward 1	528	210
2	313	721
3	1003	822
4	413	1107
5	516	1700

32. A Susan B. Anthony dollar of diameter 2.6 centimeters rests on a square postage stamp as shown. Have the computer find the area in square centimeters of the part of the stamp not covered by the coin.

33. Given the assumption that you sleep a healthy 8 hours a night, have the computer print the number of hours of your life which you have spent sleeping. Input the date of your birth and today's date in numeric form (e.g., 6, 4, 62). Use 365 days in each year and 30 days in a month.

34. Using an INPUT statement, write a program which averages each of the following sets of numbers: (2, 7, 15, 13); (8, 5, 2, 3); (12, 19, 4); (15, 7, 19, 24, 37). Note that the sets do not contain the same number of elements.

DECISIONS AND LOOPS

The statements presented in Chapter One allow the user to perform routine calculations and to print numbers or strings in different formats. The higher capabilities of a computer are not called upon, however, until the computer is used to make decisions or to carry out a process many times. This chapter presents the conditional statement IF . . . THEN . . . ELSE which allows the computer to make simple decisions, and also the statements FOR . . . TO . . . STEP, NEXT which allow loops to be established in a convenient manner.

IF . . . THEN

The statements introduced in Chapter One (GOTO, PRINT, etc.) are called unconditional because the computer will always execute them. In contrast, the IF . . . THEN statement is conditional because the action taken depends upon whether the conditonal statement is found to be true or false.

The simplest form of the IF . . . THEN statement is:

IF <condition> THEN <line number>

The 'condition' portion of the statement compares two quanities which must be separated by one of the symbols indicated in the table below:

SYMBOL	MEANING
=	equal to
>	greater than
<	less than
>=	greater than or equal to
<=	less than or equal to
<>	not equal to

An example of an IF . . . THEN statement is:

$$20 \text{ IF } X>5 \text{ THEN } 60$$

When the condition in line 20 (X is greater than 5) is true, the computer jumps to line 60. When the condition is false, as when X is less than or equal to 5, the computer proceeds to the next line of the program.

PROGRAM 2.1

This program determines whether the value entered for X is the solution to the equation $2X - 18 = 0$. The computer decides which of two messages is to be printed.

```
10 INPUT X
20 IF 2*X - 18 = 0 THEN 50
30 PRINT X; "IS NOT THE SOLUTION."
40 GOTO 10
50 PRINT X; "IS THE SOLUTION"
Ok
RUN
? 15
 15 IS NOT THE SOLUTION.
? 4
 4 IS NOT THE SOLUTION.
? 9
 9 IS THE SOLUTION
Ok
```

Note the necessity of line 40. Without it, the program would print "IS THE SOLUTION" even when the solution was not X. The line number sequence that the computer follows when X is the solution is 10, 20, 50; and when X is *not* the solution, it follows the line number sequence 10, 20, 30, 40, 10.

The IF . . . THEN statement can be used to compare two strings. Here the symbols greater than (>), less than (<), equal (=), etc., now refer to an alphabetical rather than a numerical order.

PROGRAM 2.2

The following program determines whether A$ is alphabetically before, the same, or after B$.

2.2

```
10 PRINT
20 INPUT "Enter two strings"; A$, B$
30 IF A$ = B$ THEN 70
40 IF A$ > B$ THEN 90
50 PRINT A$; " is before "; B$
60 GOTO 10
70 PRINT A$; " is equivalent to "; B$
80 GOTO 10
90 PRINT A$; " is after "; B$
100 GOTO 10

Ok
RUN

Enter two strings? A,C
A is before C

Enter two strings? MBI,IBM
MBI is after IBM

Enter two strings? CHRIS,CHRIS
CHRIS is equivalent to CHRIS

Enter two strings?
Break in 20
Ok
```

Line 30 directs the computer to line 70 if A$ and B$ are equivalent. Line 40 causes a jump to line 90 if A$ comes after B$ in the alphabet. Line 50 is reached only if both conditions in lines 30 and 40 fail and, therefore, A$ comes before B$ in the alphabet.

Extended Use of the IF . . . THEN Statement, Multiple Statement Lines

In the preceding section the simplest form of the IF . . . THEN statement was given as

IF <condition> THEN <line number>

More flexible usage of IF . . . THEN permits a statement instead of a line number to follow the word THEN. This means that the statement after the condition will be executed only if the condition is true. The form is:

IF <condition> THEN <statement>

The following examples illustrate legal use of the IF . . . THEN statement:

```
IF X<>0 THEN PRINT X
IF Z>1 THEN PRINT "IT IS LARGER THAN ONE"
IF R<=0 THEN R = X + 2
```

The computer allows a series of statements to be entered on a single program line if they are separated from each other by colons (:). Multiple statement lines have special meaning when used with IF . . . THEN. *All* statements following THEN will be executed when the condition following IF is true. *No* statements following THEN will be executed when the condition is false. For example,

$$60 \text{ IF } X = 5 \text{ THEN PRINT ``GOOD'': GOTO } 80$$

has two statements on one line. If the condition X = 5 is true, then "GOOD" will be printed and program control will be passed to line 80. If the condition is false, neither of these actions is taken. Instead, the program will continue on to the line following line 60. This means either the PRINT "GOOD" and the GOTO 80 statements are executed, or neither is executed. Whichever of the two occurs depends upon whether the condition X = 5 be true or false.

PROGRAM 2.3

Program 2.1 can be shortened by using multiple statement techniques.

```
10 INPUT X
20 IF 2*X-18 = 0 THEN PRINT X; "IS THE SOLUTION" : GOTO 10
30 PRINT X; "IS NOT THE SOLUTION" : GOTO 10
Ok
RUN
? 15
 15 IS NOT THE SOLUTION
? 2
 2 IS NOT THE SOLUTION
? 9
 9 IS THE SOLUTION
?
Break in 10
Ok
```

Note that the statement GOTO 10 in line 20 is executed *only* if the condition in the IF . . . THEN statement is true. Otherwise the program proceeds to line 30. The statement GOTO 10 on line 30 will always be executed if line 30 is reached since it is not preceded by an IF . . . THEN statement on the same line.

IF . . . THEN . . . ELSE

The IF . . . THEN statement can be extended by the use of the modifier ELSE to include an alternate statement if the condition of the IF . . . THEN is false. When the IF condition is true, the statement following THEN is executed; otherwise the statement following ELSE is executed. The general form of the IF . . . THEN . . . ELSE is:

IF <condition> THEN <statement> ELSE <statement>

When the following statement is executed, "LARGER" is printed if X>50; otherwise the program will print "SMALLER OR EQUAL"

40 IF X>50 THEN PRINT "LARGER" ELSE PRINT "SMALLER OR EQUAL"

A line number is also valid following ELSE.

40 IF X>50 THEN PRINT "LARGER" ELSE 100

When IF . . . THEN . . . ELSE is used, only one statement may appear between THEN and ELSE. The following line is *not* valid:

70 IF Y = 3 THEN PRINT "DONE": GOTO 200: ELSE 30

More than one statement may appear after the ELSE; and it will only be executed if the condition of the IF is false. When the statement

80 IF Z<>5 THEN 200 ELSE PRINT "RIGHT": GOTO 20

is executed, the program will jump to line 200 if Z<>5; otherwise "RIGHT" is printed and the program jumps to line 20.

REVIEW

1. Allow two numbers, A and B, to be entered in the computer and then print the two numbers in descending order.

2. Allow two names to be entered and then printed in alphabetical order.

```
RUN
ENTER TWO LAST NAMES? PATRICK,GREER
GREER
PATRICK
ENTER TWO LAST NAMES?
Break in 10
Ok
```

AND, OR

The statement modifiers AND and OR can be used in the IF . . . THEN statement when more than one condition is to be considered. The statement

20 IF X>5 AND Y = 3 THEN 50

will cause a transfer to line 50 only if *both* conditions are true. On the other hand, the statement

$$20 \text{ IF } X > 5 \text{ OR } Y = 3 \text{ THEN } 50$$

will cause program control to be transferred to line 50 if *either or both* conditions are true.

PROGRAM 2.4

The following program uses the OR modifier and reviews much of what has been presented.

```
10 INPUT "WHO ARE YOU"; N$
20 IF N$ = "JAMES BOND" OR N$ = "007" THEN 50
30 PRINT "This mission is not meant for you!"
40 PRINT : GOTO 10
50 PRINT "These orders are for your eyes only!"
60 INPUT "ARE YOU ALONE"; A$
70 IF A$ <> "YES" THEN PRINT "Try later." : GOTO 10
80 PRINT : PRINT "  Dr. Goodhead has escaped! Your mission,"
90 PRINT "should you decide to accept it, is to seek"
100 PRINT "out Goodhead and return her to Spandau Prison."
110 PRINT "Contact Agent 004 for further details."
Ok
RUN
WHO ARE YOU? BRAVE SIR ROBIN
This mission is not meant for you!

WHO ARE YOU? JAMES BOND
These orders are for your eyes only!
ARE YOU ALONE? NO
Try later.
WHO ARE YOU? 007
These orders are for your eyes only!
ARE YOU ALONE? YES

   Dr. Goodhead has escaped! Your mission,
should you decide to accept it, is to seek
out Goodhead and return her to Spandau Prison.
Contact Agent 004 for further details.
Ok
```

Line 10 asks the user for a name. The name entered as N$ is compared with the two names at line 20. If N$ is either 'JAMES BOND' or '007', then the program skips to line 50. Otherwise, a message is printed by line 30, and the program returns to line 10. At line 50, a warning message is printed, while line 60 inquires whether Mr. Bond is alone or not. Note that in line 70, any response other than 'YES' will cause the program to print 'TRY LATER' and jump back to line 10. Otherwise, the mission description is printed by lines 80 through 110.

END

The END statement is used to terminate the run of a program. For example,

$$80 \text{ END}$$

will cause the run of a program to stop when line 80 is reached. It is possible to place END statements at more than one location within a program, including insertion in an IF ... THEN statement.

PROGRAM. 2.5

This program uses the END statement to terminate program execution when the name KERMIT is input.

```
10 INPUT "What is your name"; N$
20 IF N$ = "KERMIT" THEN END
30 PRINT "It's good to meet you "; N$
40 PRINT : GOTO 10
Ok
RUN
What is your name? CYNTHIA
It's good to meet you CYNTHIA

What is your name? KERMIT
Ok
```

REVIEW

3. Write a program that will allow a number N to be entered. If the number is between 25 and 112 then the computer should indicate this; otherwise, the computer should say that the number is out of range.

```
RUN
ENTER A NUMBER? 14
  14  is out of range
ENTER A NUMBER? 54
  54  is between 25 and 112
ENTER A NUMBER? 112
  112  is between 25 and 112
ENTER A NUMBER?
Break in 10
Ok
```

4. Write a program in which the user enters a string N$. If it comes alphabetically before Garbage or after Trash, then have the computer print "YES"; otherwise print "NO".

FOR ... TO ... STEP, NEXT

The FOR ... TO ... STEP, NEXT statements provide a simple way of establishing a loop. A loop is a section of a program designed to be executed repeatedly. The FOR ... TO ... STEP, NEXT loops provide a method for generating a large sequence of numbers in a case where each number in the sequence differs from its predecessor by a constant amount. The general form of the FOR ... TO ... STEP, NEXT statement is:

```
┌─ FOR <variable> = <starting value> TO <ending value> STEP <increment>
│      •
│      •
│      •
└─ NEXT <variable>
```

Note that the 'variable' after FOR and NEXT must be the same. A string variable cannot be used in a FOR ... NEXT loop. The STEP portion may be omitted if the increment equals +1.

For example,

```
┌─ 10 FOR X = 2 TO 6
│       •
│       •
│       •
└─ 40 NEXT X
```

```
┌─ 70 FOR H1 = N*2 TO 26 STEP +2
│       •
│       •
│       •
└─ 100 NEXT H1
```

```
┌─ 120 FOR T = 10 TO 0 STEP—1
│        •
│        •
│        •
└─ 180 NEXT T
```

Note that a loop is formed by the FOR ... TO ... STEP and NEXT statements. In the example,

```
┌─ 30 FOR N = 3 to 11 STEP 2
│        •
│        •
│        •
└─ 80 NEXT N
```

the variable N starts at line 30 with a value of 3. N retains the value of 3 until the NEXT N statement is encountered at line 80. At this point, N is increased by the STEP value. In this example N changes from 3 to 5 to 7, etc. All the statements in the lines occurring between lines 30 and 80 are executed in sequence during each consecutive pass through the loop. The program continues to return from line 80 to the line immediately following line 30 until N exceeds the specified limit of 11. At this point, the program exits from the loop and moves on to the line following 80.

PROGRAM 2.6

This program uses READ, DATA, while Program 2.7 uses a FOR . . . TO . . . STEP, NEXT loop to print all integers between 10 and 30, inclusive.

```
10 READ N
20 PRINT N;
30 GOTO 10
40 PRINT " Done"
50 DATA   10,11,12,13,14,15,16,17,18
60 DATA   19,20,21,22,23,24,25,26,27
70 DATA   28,29,30
Ok
RUN
 10   11   12   13   14   15   16   17   18   19
 20   21   22   23   24   25   26   27   28   29
 30
Out of DATA in 10
Ok
```

PROGRAM 2.7

```
10 FOR N = 10 TO 30
20     PRINT N;
30 NEXT N
40 PRINT " Done"
Ok
RUN
 10   11   12   13   14   15   16   17   18   19
 20   21   22   23   24   25   26   27   28   29
 30  Done
Ok
```

Program 2.6 continues to read data until all of it is exhausted. Program 2.7 generates all of the values of N between 10 and 30. Note that the loop in Program 2.7 is completed by a NEXT statement, not a GOTO statement. Unlike Program 2.6, Program 2.7 can therefore proceed to line 40.

PROGRAM 2.8

This program finds solutions to the compound condition $5X + 3 < 100$ and $2X^2 - 1 > 50$ and tests all odd integers from 1 to 25.

```
10 FOR X = 1 TO 25 STEP 2
20      IF 5*X+3 < 100 AND 2*X^2-1 > 50 THEN PRINT X;
30 NEXT X
40 PRINT " Done"
50 END
Ok
RUN
 7   9   11   13   15   17   19   Done
Ok
```

Note that the symbol (^) is used to denote 'raised to the power' (e.g. X^2 means $X*X$). Lines 10 and 30 create a loop for testing the conditions located at line 20. The loop starts at line 10 with X=1. Each time the program reaches the NEXT X statement at line 30, N is incremented by the STEP value which is 2. The program will then return to line 20 unless the value of the loop variable X has exceeded its maximum value of 25, at which point the loop will be exited. Remember that a FOR loop is not completed by a GOTO statement, but by a NEXT statement.

PROGRAM 2.9

The following program illustrates the use of a negative STEP value. The integers from 1 to 10 are printed in descending order.

```
10 FOR X = 10 TO 1 STEP -1
20      PRINT X;
30 NEXT X
40 PRINT
Ok
RUN
 10  9  8  7  6  5  4  3  2  1
Ok
```

REVIEW

5. Write a program that prints the integers between 1 and 25, inclusive.

6. Using a FOR ... TO ... STEP, NEXT loop, have the computer print the following:

```
RUN
 20   18   16   14   12   10
Ok
```

7. Write a program that will allow a number N to be entered. Using N as a STEP value, print numbers between 8 and 20.

```
RUN
STEP VALUE? 2
 8   10   12   14   16   18   20
Ok
```

RESTORE

At times the user might find it desirable to employ a set of data more than once. The RESTORE statement makes it possible to read data again starting at the beginning of the data. For example,

40 RESTORE

causes the next READ statement encountered to read data starting with the first item in the first DATA statement.

PROGRAM 2.10

This program searches DATA statements for a specific student and then prints the student's grades. It employs the RESTORE statement so that each time a student's name is entered, a searching process starts at the beginning of the first DATA statement. How will the program run if line 20 is deleted?

```
10 PRINT : INPUT "NAME"; B$
20 RESTORE
30 FOR P = 1 TO 6
40    READ N$, A, B, C, D
50    IF N$ = B$ THEN 80
60 NEXT P
70 PRINT "Student "; B$; " not found" : GOTO 10
80 PRINT N$; " has the following grades:"
90 PRINT A; B; C; D
100 GOTO 10
110 DATA   WATERS,83,75,52,80,  PARTRIDGE,74,81,92,76
120 DATA   HAYDEN,72,81,63,60,  HAYES,99,84,92,87
130 DATA   GRAHAM,100,93,82,89,  STEHLE,78,93,85,94
140 END
```

```
RUN

NAME? STEHLE
STEHLE has the following grades:
 78  93  85  94

NAME? LYNCH
Student LYNCH not found

NAME? HAYDEN
HAYDEN has the following grades:
 72  81  63  60

NAME?
Break in 10
Ok
```

PART A

1. Write a program to allow two numbers (A and B) to be entered. Have the computer compare them and print a message stating whether A is less than, equal to, or greater than B.

2. Write a program which allows three names to be entered as A$, B$, and C$. Have the computer print the name which is alphabetically last.

3. Allow a string (A$) composed of letters to be entered. Have the computer print A$ if it comes alphabetically after the string "MIDWAY". Use only two line numbers and no colons.

4. Write a program which prints six exclamation marks if BIGWOW is entered for the string X$ but which otherwise prints six question marks. The program is to run until the BREAK key is struck.

5. Use only one line number to enter two strings (A$ and B$) and to print output similar to the following.

```
RUN
? START,FINISH
START          FINISH
FINISH         START
```

6. Allow a number (X) to be entered. Print the message "NOT BETWEEN" if X is either less than –24 or greater than 17. Only one IF . . . THEN statement is permitted.

7. Allow a string (A$) to be entered. Print the message "A$ IS BETWEEN" if A$ comes between "DOWN" and "UP" alphabetically. Only one IF . . . THEN statement is permitted.

8. Allow a number (X) to be entered. Print "IN THE INTERVAL" if X satisfies the inequality $25 < X < 75$, but otherwise print "NOT IN THE INTERVAL". Only one AND and one IF . . . THEN statement are to be used.

9. Rewrite the program of the preceding exercise, using OR instead of AND.

10. Use only one PRINT statement to produce the following rectangle.

```
RUN
************
************
************
```

11. Print the cubes of the odd integers from 11 to –11, inclusive, in that order.

12. Print all the integers which end in 4 from 4 to 84, inclusive.

13. Use a loop to print a line of 40 asterisks.

14. Write a one line IMMEDIATE MODE command for each of the following:
    (A) Find the value of 143 x 74.
    (B) Find the average of 53, 72, 81, and 76.
    (C) Find which is larger, X↑Y or Y↑X, when X = 4 and Y = 5.

PART B
15. Print all of the integers in the set 10, 13, 16, 19, . . ., 94, 97.

16. Using a loop have the computer print a letter I as follows:

```
RUN
*****
 ***
 ***
 ***
 ***
 ***
 ***
*****
```

17. Below is a list of various creatures and the weapon necessary to destroy each.

Creature	Weapon
Lich	Fire Ball
Mummy	Flaming Torch
Werewolf	Silver Bullet
Vampire	Wooden Stake
Medusa	Sharp Sword
Triffid	Fire Hose

Using READ and DATA, have the computer state what weapon is to be used to destroy a given creature. For example:

```
RUN
CREATURE? VAMPIRE
YOU CAN KILL A VAMPIRE WITH A WOODEN STAKE
CREATURE? LICH
YOU CAN KILL A LICH WITH A FIRE BALL
CREATURE? BLOB
CREATURE BLOB NOT FOUND.
CREATURE? MEDUSA
YOU CAN KILL A MEDUSA WITH A SHARP SWORD
CREATURE?
Break in 10
Ok
```

18. Menacing Matilda has written the following program using too many GOTO statements and cannot figure out in what order the lines of the program will be executed. Assist her by listing the line numbers in the sequence in which the computer will execute them.

```
10 READ A,B
20 IF A > 4 OR B > 4 THEN 50
30 IF A < 1 AND B < 1 THEN 60
40 GOTO 70
50 X = A + B : GOTO 80
60 X = A * B : GOTO 80
70 X = A / B
80 IF X > 1 THEN PRINT X : GOTO 10
90 DATA 5,3,-1,-2,0,2
```

19. John Doe's brother Jim has been assigned the following program for homework. Jim is not in shape today, so assist him by stating the exact order in which the lines of the following program are to be executed.

```
10 READ A, B, C
20 S = A + B*C
30 IF S = 10 THEN RESTORE : READ S
40 PRINT S,
50 IF S = 14 THEN END
60 GOTO 10
70 DATA 4,2,3,6,0,2,7
```

20. Write a program which asks for a person's age. If the person is 16 years or older, have the computer print "YOU ARE OLD ENOUGH TO DRIVE A CAR". Otherwise, have the computer indicate how many years the person must wait before being able to drive.

```
RUN
HOW OLD ARE YOU ? 16
YOU ARE OLD ENOUGH TO DRIVE A CAR.
```

21. The Happy Holiday Motel has 10 rooms. Have the computer print a label for each room's door indicating the room number. For example:

```
RUN

---------------------------------
     HAPPY HOLIDAY MOTEL
          ROOM 1
---------------------------------
```

22. As candidate for mayor, you are very busy. Use the computer to print thank you letters to 10 people who have contributed money to your election campaign. Be sure to mention the exact amount each person has contributed.

```
RUN

DEAR RICH BRYBURRY,
    THANK YOU FOR YOUR GENEROUS CONTRIBUTION
OF 25000 DOLLARS TO MY ELECTION CAMPAIGN.  MAYBE
NEXT YEAR WE WILL HAVE BETTER LUCK!
                    SINCERELY,

                    SMILEY R. POLITICO
```

23. Write a program which will produce the following table:

```
RUN
X                   X^2                 X^3

2                   4                   8
4                   16                  64
6                   36                  216
8                   64                  512
10                  100                 1000
```

24. The Bored Auto Company has done it again! Some models of their cars may be difficult to drive because their wheels are not exactly round. Cars with model numbers 102, 780, 119, 220, 189, and 195 have been found to have a defect. Write a computer program that allows 10 of their customers to enter the model number of their car to find out whether or not it is defective.

25. Using only two print statements, write a program to print a triangle that is N lines high and N columns wide. For example:

```
RUN
? 5
*
**
***
****
*****
```

26. Have the computer find all odd integers from 5 to 25 which are simultaneous solutions of the inequalities $X^3 > 500$ and $X^2 + 3X + 2 < 700$. Print only the solutions.

27. The following table contains employee performance data for the Tippecanoe Typing Company.

Employee	Performance
Oakley	69%
Howe	92%
Anderson	96%
Wolley	88%
Goerz	74%

Tippecanoe Typing is suffering from financial difficulties and needs to cut back on its staff. Using READ, DATA and a loop, have the computer print notices of dismissal for any employee whose production performance is below 75%.

```
RUN

DEAR OAKLEY,
   I AM SO SORRY THAT I MUST FIRE YOU.
YOU HAVE BEEN SUCH A FINE EMPLOYEE
WITH A PERFORMANCE RATING OF 69 %
I'M SURE YOU'LL HAVE NO TROUBLE
FINDING ANOTHER JOB.
                    SINCERELY,

                    GEORGE SHWABB


DEAR GOERZ,
   I AM SO SORRY THAT I MUST FIRE YOU.
YOU HAVE BEEN SUCH A FINE EMPLOYEE
WITH A PERFORMANCE RATING OF 74 %
I'M SURE YOU'LL HAVE NO TROUBLE
FINDING ANOTHER JOB.
                    SINCERELY,

                    GEORGE SHWABB
```

28. Wayne Peber bought stock two years ago and wants to use the computer to calculate his profit or loss. He bought 200 shares of Consolidated Technologies at $85.58 per share and 400 shares of American Amalgamated Securities at $35.60 per share. Today C.T. is worth $70.82 a share and A.A.S. is worth $47.32 a share. What is his profit or loss?

29. The Exploitation Oil Company uses the computer to determine the weekly wages of its employees by inputting the hours worked and the hourly wage for each employee. If the employee works over 40 hours, he or she is paid one and a half times the hourly rate for each additional hour.

```
RUN
HOURS WORKED? 45
HOURLY WAGE? 10.00
THE WAGE FOR THE WEEK IS $ 475
```

30. The Last Chance Finance Company is charging a rate of 2% per month on all loans it is making. Write a program that allows Last Chance to calculate the monthly payments charged a customer using the following formula.

$$\text{Monthly Payment} = \frac{L*I}{1-(1+I)^{-m}}$$

where L = Amount Loaned
I = Interest (monthly)
m = Number of months to be loaned

```
RUN
THE AMOUNT OF THE LOAN? 100
LENGTH OF THE LOAN IN YEARS? 5
THE MONTHLY PAYMENT IS $ 2.876801
THE TOTAL AMOUNT PAID WILL BE $ 172.6081
```

31. You have $200.00 to spend on a buying spree. Write a program that, as you buy merchandise, subtracts the cost and the appropriate sales tax (5%) from your remaining money and shows your present total. The program should prevent you from buying items that cost more than you have.

```
RUN
HOW MUCH DOES THE ITEM COST? 10.00
YOUR TOTAL IS NOW $ 189.5

HOW MUCH DOES THE ITEM COST? 250.00
YOU DON'T HAVE ENOUGH
HOW MUCH DOES THE ITEM COST? 25.00
YOUR TOTAL IS NOW $ 163.25

HOW MUCH DOES THE ITEM COST? 0
Ok
```

3

COMPUTER GAMES

This chapter will introduce material which should be interesting, practical, and entertaining. In fact, the emphasis will be placed on techniques to involve the user in computer games, which are often the most enjoyable way to learn computer programming.

RND

In many computer simulations that involve science problems and also in a variety of computer games, the process of generating random numbers becomes essential. The RND function is used to generate random numbers on the computer. The statement

$$X = RND$$

will assign X a random number such that $0 \leq X < 1$.

PROGRAM 3.1

This program will print 5 random numbers. It is run twice. Note that it produces the same set of random numbers each time.

```
10 FOR I = 1 TO 5
20    PRINT RND,
30 NEXT I
Ok
RUN
 .6291626       .1948297       .6305799       .8625749       .736353
Ok
RUN
 .6291626       .1948297       .6305799       .8625749       .736353
Ok
```

RANDOMIZE

In most programs which use RND it is desirable to generate different numbers each time the program is run. This can be accomplished by using the RANDOMIZE statement at the beginning of the program. When the program is run the message

Random Number Seed (−32768 to 32767)?

is printed. Entering a different seed each time will insure that different numbers are generated. For example, if the line

5 RANDOMIZE

was inserted in program 3.1 a possible output would be:

```
5 RANDOMIZE
RUN
Random number seed (-32768 to 32767)? 14
 .2358301       .2419538       .8253283       .4574681       .8517589
Ok
RUN
Random number seed (-32768 to 32767)? 12
 .4230554       .8990278       .1978563       .3086339       .3920117
Ok
```

It is also possible to include the random number seed in the RANDOMIZE statement. If this is done the user is not prompted when the program is run. For example,

5 RANDOMIZE 111

will cause the seed value of 111 to be used. Each time the program is run it will produce the same set of random numbers unless the seed at line 5 is changed.

INT

The statement A = INT(X) sets A to the largest integer that is not greater than X. This function does not round off a positive number but simply truncates its decimals. In the case of a negative number, it takes the next lower negative integer. For example:

INT (3.7640)=3   INT (5.9)=5
INT (−1.7)=−2   INT (−3.01)=−4

At times it is preferable to have the computer pick random integers instead of long random decimals. This can be accomplished by using INT. The following formula can be used to assign X a random integer between A and B inclusive:

$$X = INT ((B-A+1)*RND+A)$$

For example, the statement

$$X = INT (26*RND+75)$$

will assign X a random integer between 75 and 100 inclusive.

PROGRAM 3.2

This game program selects a random number between 1 and 100 and then gives the player an unlimited number of chances to guess it. After each guess the computer informs the player whether the guess is too high, too low, or correct.

```
10 RANDOMIZE
20 PRINT "I'm thinking of a random number between 1 & 100."
30 R = INT(100 * RND + 1)
40 INPUT "What is your guess"; G
50 IF G < R THEN PRINT "Too Low!" : GOTO 40
60 IF G > R THEN PRINT "Too High!" : GOTO 40
70 PRINT "That is correct!!!"
Ok
RUN
Random number seed (-32768 to 32767)? 55
I'm thinking of a random number between 1 & 100.
What is your guess? 50
Too Low!
What is your guess? 75
Too Low!
What is your guess? 86
Too Low!
What is your guess? 90
That is correct!!!
Ok
```

CINT

The CINT function is used to round a number to its nearest integer. The statement Y = CINT (X) will set Y equal to the integer value closest to X. For example,

CINT (3.7640) = 4	CINT (5.9) = 6
CINT (−1.7) = −2	CINT (−3.01) = −3
CINT (8.5) = 9	CINT (9.49) = 9

The value to be rounded must be between −32768 and +32767, inclusive. Values outside this range will generate an error.

The CINT function is also used to round numbers to any desired number of decimal places. For example, CINT (10*X) /10 will round X to one decimal place. If X = 2.57, then CINT (10*X) = CINT (25.7) = 26. If 26 is then divided by 10, the result is 2.6, the correctly rounded value. Furthermore, CINT (100*X) /100 rounds X to two decimal places, CINT (1000*X) /1000 to three places, and so on.

Rounding a number to the nearest tens place (e.g. 257 becomes 260) is accomplished by using CINT (0.1*X) /0.1. A general formula for rounding a number X to N decimal places is:

$$Y = CINT (10{\uparrow}N*X) /10{\uparrow}N$$

For example:

```
PRINT CINT(10 * 14.75) / 10
 14.8
Ok

PRINT CINT(10^(-2) * 2473) / 10^(-2)
 2500
Ok

R = CINT(10^3 * 8.1415) / 10^3
Ok

PRINT R, CINT(100 * R) /100
 8.141          8.14
Ok
```

REVIEW

1. Write a program that will generate 2 random integers between 50 and 150 and find their product.

```
RUN
 116 multiplied by 138 is 16008
Ok
```

2. Write a program similar to Program 3.2 which picks a random number between 1 and 50, inclusive, and gives the player only five attempts to guess it.

```
RUN
Random number seed (-32768 to 32767)? 25
I'm thinking of a random number between 1 & 50.
What is your guess? 25
Too Low!
What is your guess? 37
Too High!
What is your guess? 31
Too Low!
What is your guess? 33
Too Low!
What is your guess? 35
Too Low!
You've had 5 guesses now.
The number was 36
Ok
```

Summation

If the programmer decides to keep score for the number guessing game (Program 3.2), some technique would have to be devised to keep count of the number of guesses taken. One possible technique is to use a summation statement of the form:

$$30 \ A = A + 1$$

The statement $A = A + 1$ makes no sense in mathematics since A can equal A but not $A + 1$. The computer, however, interprets the equal sign to mean "is replaced by" rather than "equal to", and each time it encounters line 30 above, it takes the present value of A, adds 1 to it, and makes that sum the new value of A.

PROGRAM 3.3

This program demonstrates how the summation statement works by printing the values of A until the program is halted with the CTRL-BREAK keys.

```
10 A = A + 1
20 PRINT A;
30 GOTO 10
Ok
RUN
 1  2  3  4  5  6  7  8  9  10  11  12  13  14  15  16  17 ^C
Break in 20
Ok
```

If line 10 is replaced with

$$10 \ A = A + 5$$

then 5 will be added to A each time the statement is encountered.

```
10 A = A + 5
RUN
  5   10   15   20   25   30   35   40   45   50   55   60   65   70 ^C
Break in 20
Ok
```

In this problem the initial value of A is zero for both runs. This is true because the computer sets any undefined numeric variable to zero at the start of a run.

PROGRAM 3.4

Here, Program 3.2 has been modified to record the number of turns required to guess the random number. In this case the variable A acts as a counter, increasing in value by 1 after each guess.

```
10 RANDOMIZE
20 PRINT "I'm thinking of a random number between 1 & 100."
30 R = INT(100 * RND + 1)
40 INPUT "What is your guess";G
50 A = A + 1
60 IF G < R THEN PRINT "Too Low!" : GOTO 40
70 IF G > R THEN PRINT "Too High!" : GOTO 40
80 PRINT "That is correct!!!"
90 PRINT "THAT TOOK YOU"; A; "GUESSES."
Ok
RUN
Random number seed (-32768 to 32767)? 69
I'm thinking of a random number between 1 & 100.
What is your guess? 50
Too Low!
What is your guess? 75
Too High!
What is your guess? 67
Too High!
What is your guess? 59
That is correct!!!
THAT TOOK YOU 4 GUESSES.
Ok
```

Rounding Errors

Because the computer has a finite capacity, any numerical computations involving infinitely repeating decimals cannot be accurate (for example, 1/3 = .3333 . . ., which the computer truncates to a limited number of digits). Since the computer uses binary numbers (0 and 1), any fraction whose denominator is not an integral power of 2 (e.g., 2, 4, 8, 16) will be an infinitely repeating decimal and therefore will be truncated by the computer. In Chapter Nine binary numbers are examined in greater detail.

PROGRAM 3.5

This program illustrates the processes of summation and rounding error.

```
10 FOR X = 1 TO 1500
20    A = A + (1 / 2)
30    B = B + (1 / 3)
40 NEXT X
50 PRINT "A ="; A
60 PRINT "B ="; B
Ok
RUN
A = 750
B = 500.0059
Ok
```

The final value of A is the result of adding 1/2 1500 times which comes out to be exactly 750. B, however, which is the result of adding 1/3 1500 times does not come out to be exactly 500 because of the rounding error. At times the computer does not recognize an equality when one in fact exists. If the line

70 IF B = 500 THEN PRINT "EQUALS" ELSE PRINT "NOT EQUAL"

were added to the above program, then the computer would print "NOT EQUAL".

REVIEW

3. Select 50 random integers between 0 and 9, inclusive, and have the computer tell how many of the numbers were from 0-4 and how many were from 5-9.

```
RUN
There were 31 numbers between 0 and 4.
There were 19 numbers between 5 and 9.
Ok
```

4. Input ten numbers from the keyboard, and have the computer tell how many are odd and how many are even.

```
RUN
ENTER A NUMBER? 42
ENTER A NUMBER? 69
ENTER A NUMBER? 14
ENTER A NUMBER? 111
ENTER A NUMBER? 86
ENTER A NUMBER? 73
ENTER A NUMBER? 164
ENTER A NUMBER? 8218
ENTER A NUMBER? 9
ENTER A NUMBER? 8
 6 EVEN;  4 ODD
Ok
```

FORMATTING OUTPUT

The statements presented in this section allow program output to be formatted. For advanced formatting techniques, which are especially useful in producing tables, refer to Appendix D where the PRINT USING statement is presented.

PRINT TAB

The PRINT TAB statement provides an easy way to format output and allows the programmer to begin portions of the printout at specified locations. The left edge of the screen is TAB (1), and the right edge of the screen is TAB (80). The printing of information at TAB positions 13, 25 and 32 is accomplished by:

```
10 PRINT TAB(13); "This"; TAB(25); "is"; TAB(32); "TAB"
RUN
            This          is     TAB
Ok
```

Here it is important to use semicolons (;) in each instance after the TAB parentheses.

PROGRAM 3.6

The substitution of variables for the numbers in the TAB parentheses is permissible provided these variables have assigned values.

```
10 READ X, Y, Z
20 PRINT TAB(X); "This"; TAB(Y); "is"; TAB(Z); "TAB"
30 DATA 13, 25, 32
Ok
RUN
            This          is     TAB
Ok
```

PROGRAM 3.7

This program draws a triangle on the display screen.

```
10 PRINT TAB(10); "*******"
20 FOR X = 1 TO 5
30     PRINT TAB(X + 10); "*"; TAB(16); "*"
40 NEXT X
50 PRINT TAB(16); "*"
Ok
RUN
        *******
         *     *
          *    *
           *   *
            *  *
             **
              *
Ok
```

The PRINT TAB statement does not move the cursor to the left, but only to the right. If a TAB position is specified which is to the left of the current TAB position, then it will be printed on the next line.

```
10 PRINT TAB(10); "##"; TAB(15); "##"
20 PRINT TAB(15); "##"; TAB(10); "##"
Ok
RUN
        ##    ##
              ##
        ##
Ok
```

CLS

The CLS statement is used to clear the entire display screen. CLS may also be used in the immediate mode.

POS

The POS function is used to find the current horizontal position of the cursor. The statement

$$X = POS (0)$$

will assign X a value corresponding to the horizontal position (the current TAB position) of the cursor on the screen. X = 1 for the left edge and 80 for the right edge.

PROGRAM 3.8

The following program demonstrates TAB and POS.

```
10 PRINT TAB(32); "ROCK";
20 PRINT POS(0)
30 PRINT TAB(21); POS(0)
Ok
RUN
                                              ROCK 36
                                21
Ok
```

LOCATE

The video display can hold 25 lines, each consisting of 80 characters. The LOCATE statement allows output to begin at any of these positions. The simplest form of LOCATE is:

LOCATE <row> , <column>

where 'row' can have values from 1 to 25, and 'column' from 1 to 80. For example,

10 LOCATE 1,1
20 PRINT "HERE"

will print "HERE" in the upper left hand corner, while

10 LOCATE 12,40
20 PRINT A$

will print the contents of the string variable A$ in the middle of the screen.

The 'row' and 'column' can be numeric variables. For instance, if X = 25 and Y = 10 then

10 LOCATE X,Y
20 PRINT "CARROTS";

will place the word CARROTS at row 25, column 10. The trailing semicolon leaves the cursor positioned immediately after CARROTS. A subsequent PRINT statement will begin output at that point on the screen.

PROGRAM 3.9

The following program will print "M*A*S*H" and "4077" fifteen times in diagonals on the screen using the LOCATE statement.

```
10 CLS
20 FOR I = 0 TO 14
30     LOCATE I+1,4 * I + 1 : PRINT "M*A*S*H"
40     LOCATE I+1,57 - 4*I : PRINT " 4 O 7 7"
50 NEXT I
RUN
```

```
M*A*S*H                                                        4 0 7 7
    M*A*S*H                                                 4 0 7 7
        M*A*S*H                                         4 0 7 7
            M*A*S*H                                  4 0 7 7
                M*A*S*H                           4 0 7 7
                    M*A*S*H                    4 0 7 7
                        M*A*S*H  4 0 7 7
                            4 0 7 7
                        4 0 7 7M*A*S*H
                    4 0 7 7            M*A*S*H
                4 0 7 7                    M*A*S*H
            4 0 7 7                           M*A*S*H
        4 0 7 7                                  M*A*S*H
    4 0 7 7                                         M*A*S*H
 4 0 7 7                                               M*A*S*H
Ok
```

ADDING SOUND TO GAMES

BEEP

The BEEP command causes the computer to produce a short beeping sound which will attract the users attention. For example,

20 BEEP

will cause the computer to BEEP when line 20 is encountered in a program.

SOUND

Some game programs can be made more interesting with the use of sound. This can be done on the computer with the SOUND statement. The general form of this statement is,

SOUND <frequency> , <duration>

where the frequency is in Hertz (cycles per second). The allowable frequency range is 37 to 32767 Hz. Duration is in clock ticks (18.2 clock ticks = 1 second). For example,

$$SOUND\ 523,18.2$$

will play a middle C for 1 second.

The following table shows notes and their corresponding frequencies.

Note	Frequency	Note	Frequency
C	130.810	C	523.250
D	146.830	D	587.330
E	164.810	E	659.260
F	174.610	F	698.460
G	196.000	G	783.990
A	220.000	A	880.000
B	246.940	B	987.770
C	261.630	C	1046.500
D	293.660	D	1174.700
E	329.630	E	1318.500
F	349.230	F	1396.900
G	392.000	G	1568.000
A	440.000	A	1760.000
B	493.880	B	1975.500

Substituting 0 for the duration in the SOUND statement will terminate the note created by any previous SOUND statement.

PROGRAM 3.10

This program will play a simple scale starting at middle C.

```
1 REM    D = DURATION OF SOUND
2 REM    F = FREQUENCY OF SOUND
10 D = 4
20 FOR I = 1 TO 8
30    READ F
40    SOUND F,D
50 NEXT I
60 DATA 523,587,659,698,784,880,988,1047
```

GAME PROGRAMS

Three game programs are presented here with a minimal explanation of how they work. The programmer should study them carefully, and then attempt to modify them to write other game programs.

PROGRAM 3.11

This program simulates a slot machine with three windows; each window can display either the word CHERRY, PLUM, LEMON, BAR, or ORANGE. The words will flash by and stop in a random sequence. If two of the windows display the same word, the player wins $1.00. If all three windows display the same words, the player wins $10.00. It costs $1.00 to play.

```
1 REM     M = AMOUNT OF MONEY
2 REM     C,P,L,B,O = NUMBER OF CHERRIES, PLUMS,
                       LEMONS, BARS, ORANGES
10 RANDOMIZE
20 CLS
30 REM     SHOW THE SPIN
40 FOR I = 1 TO 10
50     FOR J = 1 TO 3
60         LOCATE 10, J*10
70         R = INT(5 .* RND + 1)
80         IF R = 1 THEN PRINT "CHERRY" : C = C + F
90         IF R = 2 THEN PRINT " PLUM " : P = P + F
100        IF R = 3 THEN PRINT "LEMON " : L = L + F
110        IF R = 4 THEN PRINT " BAR  " : B = B + F
120        IF R = 5 THEN PRINT "ORANGE" : O = O + F
130    NEXT J
140     IF I = 9 THEN F = 1
150 NEXT I
160 LOCATE 15,16 : PRINT "YOU LOST $1.00."
170 REM
180 REM
200 REM     CHECK FOR A WINNING COMBINATION
210 LOCATE 15,16
220 IF C=2 OR P=2 OR L=2 OR B=2 OR O=2
        THEN PRINT "YOU WIN $1.00. "
230 IF C=3 OR P=3 OR L=3 OR B=3 OR O=3
        THEN PRINT "YOU WIN $10.00. "
```

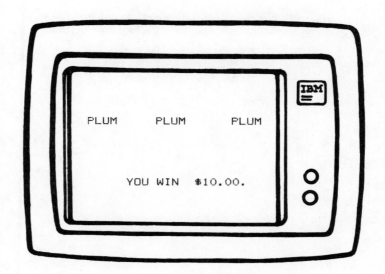

PROGRAM 3.12

This program simulates a roulette wheel which has two colors (red and black) and thirty numbers. The player is asked to make a bet and pick a color and number. Picking the correct color returns the bet, picking the correct number but wrong color wins thirty times the bet, and picking the correct number and color wins the player sixty times the bet.

```
1 REM     N = NUMBER GUESSED BY PLAYER
2 REM     C = COLOR GUESSED BY PLAYER
3 REM     NC = NUMBER PICKED BY COMPUTER
4 REM     CC = COLOR PICKED BY COMPUTER
5 REM     B = AMOUNT BET BY PLAYER
6 REM     M = MONEY MADE OR LOST BY THE PLAYER
10 REM    GET PLAYERS GUESS AND BET
20 RANDOMIZE : CLS
30 INPUT "WHAT NUMBER";N
40 INPUT "WHAT COLOR (1=RED 2=BLACK)";C
50 INPUT "WHAT IS YOUR BET";B
60 M = -B
70 REM
80 REM
100 REM    SPIN WHEEL
110 NC = INT(30*RND + 1)
120 CC = INT(2*RND +1)
130 PRINT "THE WHEEL STOPPED ON:";
140 PRINT NC;
150 IF CC = 1 THEN PRINT "RED"
            ELSE PRINT "BLACK"
160 REM
170 REM
200 REM    CHECK FOR CORRECT COLOR AND/OR NUMBER
210 IF NC = N THEN M = M + 31*B : PRINT "YOU GOT THE NUMBER ";
220 IF CC = C THEN M = M + 2*B : PRINT "YOU GOT THE COLOR."
230 PRINT
240 IF NC = N AND CC = C THEN M = M + 28*B
250 REM
260 REM
300 REM    PRINT THE PERSONS WINNINGS OR LOSS
310 IF M < 0 THEN PRINT "YOU LOST $";-M
            ELSE PRINT "YOU WON $";M
Ok
RUN
Random number seed (-32768 to 32767)? 111
WHAT NUMBER? 42
WHAT COLOR (1=RED 2=BLACK)? 2
WHAT IS YOUR BET? 14
THE WHEEL STOPPED ON: 20 BLACK
YOU GOT THE COLOR.

YOU WON $ 14
Ok
```

PROGRAM 3.13

This game starts by playing a short song and then plots a target at a random location. The player's mission is to destroy the target by guessing its correct coordinates. Each guess causes the coordinates struck to flash and the sound of a shot to be heard. Note that delay loops are needed to keep the display on the screen long enough to be seen.

```
1 REM    A,B = COORDINATES FIRED AT BY PLAYER
2 REM    X,Y = RANDOM COORDINATE FOR TARGET
3 REM    F   = FREQ OF NOTE
4 REM    D   = DURATION OF NOTE
10 RANDOMIZE
20 REM    PLAY AN ATTACK SONG
30 FOR I = 1 TO 7
40    READ F,D
50    SOUND F,D
60 NEXT I
70 REM
80 REM
100 REM PLOT THE RANDOM TARGET ON THE SCREEN
110 CLS
120 X = INT(79 * RND + 1) : Y = INT(22 * RND + 2)
130 LOCATE Y,X : PRINT "*"
140 REM
150 REM
200 REM     GET COORDINATES TO SHOOT AT FROM PLAYER
210 LOCATE 1,1
220 INPUT "COORDINATES TO FIRE AT (2-23,1-79)";A,B
230 LOCATE 1,37 : PRINT "        "
240 REM
250 REM
300 REM     FLASH COORDINATE STRUCK
310 LOCATE A,B : PRINT "#"
320 SOUND 1000,3 : SOUND 500,3 : REM  HEAR THE SHOT
330 FOR I = 1 TO 300: NEXT I : REM DELAY LOOP
340 LOCATE A,B : PRINT " " : REM A SPACE TO BLANK OUT THE SHOT
350 REM
360 REM
400 REM     CHECK FOR A HIT
410 LOCATE 1,1
420 IF A = Y AND B = X THEN 510
430 PRINT "MISSED...                                 "
440 FOR K = 1 TO 700 : NEXT K : REM DELAY
450 GOTO 210
460 REM
500 REM     A HIT HAS BEEN MADE SO MAKE THE DESTRUCTION SOUND
510 FOR J = 65 TO 37 STEP -4
520    SOUND J,1
530 NEXT J
540 PRINT "A HIT!!! GOOD WORK.                "
600 REM     DATA FOR THE SONG
610 DATA 294,3,330,3,349,3,440,5,349,2,440,9,698,13
```

3 EXERCISES

PART A

1. Generate ten random numbers between 0 and 1, but print only those which are greater than 0.5.

2. Generate three random numbers between 0 and 1, and print their sum.

3. Input a number (N). Print it only if it is an integer. (Hint: compare N and INT(N)).

4. Allow a user to guess a random integer between –3 and 4, inclusive. Print whether the guess was correct or not. If the guess was wrong, the correct value is also to be printed.

```
RUN
Random number seed (-32768 to 32767)? -1701
Guess a number between -3 and 4, inclusive? 4
Incorrect. The number was -1
Ok
RUN
Random number seed (-32768 to 32767)? 16003
Guess a number between -3 and 4, inclusive? 0
Incorrect. The number was  4
Ok
RUN
Random number seed (-32768 to 32767)? 1
Guess a number between -3 and 4, inclusive? 4
Correct!
Ok
```

5. Determine randomly how many coins you find on the street. You are to find from 2 to 5 nickels, 1 to 4 dimes, and 0 to 3 quarters. Lunch costs 99 cents. The program is to report the amount that you found and whether you are able to buy lunch with it.

```
RUN
Random number seed (-32768 to 32767)? 14
YOU FOUND $ .95
SORRY, YOU CAN'T BUY LUNCH.
Ok
RUN
Random number seed (-32768 to 32767)? 8
YOU FOUND $ 1.1
YOU CAN BUY LUNCH.
Ok
```

6. Input an integer (N), and print the sum of N random numbers between 0 and 1. Also print N/2 for comparison with the sum.

7. A child puts pennies into a piggy bank once each week for four weeks. The bank already contains 11 pennies in it when the child first receives it. Write a program to allow pennies to be added each week and to print the dollar value of the bank's contents after each addition.

8. Have the computer produce the following output.

```
RUN
1234567890123456789012345678901234567890

*        9    ?    -         !    )         *
Ok
```

9. Use LOCATE to draw a straight diagonal line (composed of asterisks) starting at the upper left hand corner and moving 2 spaces over for each space down until the line hits the bottom of the screen.

10. Put a flashing notice on the screen which advertises Uncle Bill's Whamburgers for $0.59.

```
-------------------------------------
!                                   !
!  TODAY ONLY!                      !
!       UNCLE BILL'S                !
!       WHAMBURGERS                 !
!              ONLY $0.59 !         !
!                                   !
-------------------------------------
```

PART B

11. Les Brains wrote both of the following programs but has forgotten what their output is. Determine the output, and check your answer by running the program.

(a)
```
10 FOR Z = 1 TO 4
20    PRINT TAB(Z);Z
30 NEXT Z
40 FOR Y = 1 TO 4
50    PRINT TAB(Y),Y
60 NEXT Y
```

(b)
```
10 G = 123.456
20 PRINT INT(10 * G)/10, INT(10 * G + .5) / 10
30 PRINT INT(100 * G)/100, INT(100 * G + .5) / 100
```

12. Write a program that generates 10 random integers between 8 and 25, inclusive, and prints them on the same line. The output should be similar to the following:

17 12 22 25   8 17 19 11 21 23

13. Make a chart showing in their correct order the values taken by the variables X and Y. Circle those values that are printed by the computer. Check by running the program.

```
10 FOR X = 1 TO 3
15    READ Y
20    IF Y > 0 THEN 35
25    Y = Y + X
30    IF X = 2 THEN Y = Y - 1 : GOTO 40
35    PRINT X,Y
40 NEXT X
45 DATA 5,0,-1
```

14. (a) Determine a possible output for the program below.
(b) Rewrite the program so that the message LEARN THE MULTIPLICATION TABLE is printed if three wrong answers are given.
(c) Rewrite the program so that five different questions are asked and the message NICE GOING, HOTSHOT is printed if all five questions are answered correctly.

```
10 CLS
20 A = INT(10 * RND + 1)
30 B = INT(10 * RND + 1)
40 PRINT TAB(12);A;"*";B;"=";
50 INPUT C
60 IF C = A * B THEN 90
70 PRINT "YOU ARE WRONG.   TRY AGAIN."
80 GOTO 40
90 PRINT TAB(12);"CORRECT"
```

15. Write a program that contains one FOR . . . NEXT loop which finds the sum of all the odd integers from 13 to 147, inclusive. The output should be as follows:

THE SUM = 5440

16. Suzy Fowlup, one of the slower members of the computing class, wrote the following program. It allows the user to enter at the keyboard any integer greater than 1 and to have the computer tell the user whether or not the integer is prime. A prime number is an integer that contains only itself and 1 as factors. The computer tests the integer by repeatedly dividing it by integers smaller than itself but larger than 1 and checking whether the quotient is whole. If so, the integer entered by the user is not prime. The program contains three errors. Find them, rewrite the program, and run it. The output should look like this:

```
RUN
INTEGER > 1 PLEASE? 12
THAT INTEGER IS NOT PRIME.
Ok
RUN
INTEGER > 1 PLEASE? 17
THAT INTEGER IS PRIME.
```

— — — — — — — — — — — — — — — — — — — —

```
20 READ "INTEGER > 1 PLEASE";N
30 FOR X = 2 TO N-1
40    IF N / X = INT(N/X) THEN 70
50 NEXT N
60 PRINT "THAT INTEGER IS PRIME."
70 PRINT "THAT INTEGER IS NOT PRIME."
```

17. Generate 1000 random integers between 1 and 9, inclusive, and print how many were even and how many were odd. The output should be similar to the following:

```
RUN
THERE WERE 530 ODD INTEGERS.
THERE WERE 470 EVEN INTEGERS.
```

18. Write a program that allows the user and computer to alternately select integers between 3 and 12, inclusive, keep a sum of all the integers selected, and declare the winner to be the one who selects that integer which makes the sum greater than 100. Have the program ask the user if he or she would like to proceed first or second.

19. A bank pays interest once a year at a yearly rate of 5%. A man deposits $1000 on January 1, 1983 and wishes to leave it there to accrue interest until the balance is at least $2000. Compute the balance on Jan. 1 of each year, starting with 1984 and ending in the year when the balance exceeds $2000. The output should resemble the following:

```
DATE              BALANCE
JAN 1, 1984       $ 1050
JAN 1, 1985       $ 1102.5
. . .             . . .
. . .             . . .
. . .             $ 1979.93
. . .             $ 2078.93
```

20. Input a positive integer N, and print all positive integers that are factors of N. The output should resemble the following:

```
RUN
A POSITIVE INTEGER, PLEASE? 1.4
YOUR NUMBER WAS NOT AN INTEGER
A POSITIVE INTEGER, PLEASE? 12
 1   2   3   4   6   12
Ok
```

21. Print the radius (cm.) of a sphere, given its volume (cm.³). Round off the results to the nearest hundredth.

DATA: 690, 720, 460, 620
Note: Volume = $(4/3)$ (π) R^3, where π = 3.14159

22. (a) Print twenty random integers between 0 and 100, inclusive.
   (b) Change the program so that sixty percent of the twenty integers printed will be less than 25.

23. Write a program that will produce the following triangle. The figure is centered on TAB(15).

RUN

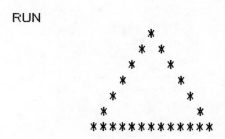

24. Using LOCATE, write a program that will draw a football made of asterisks. (Hint: use the equation of a circle.)

25. (a) Have the computer print the dart board pictured below, and have it fire ten random shots, using an asterisk to indicate the spot hit. The top of the outer square is on line 3 and its two vertical sides are at TAB(10) and TAB(30).

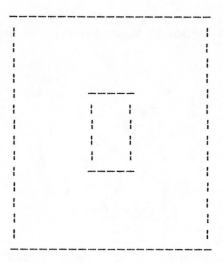

(b) Rewrite program (a) to give the score at the end of a game. A hit in the center square is worth 10 points, the outer square 4 points, and the region outside both -1 points.

26. Have the computer randomly select a number of quarters (from 0 to 7), dimes (from 0 to 4), and pennies (from 0 to 9) and print the exact number of coins and their total value. The user has ten chances to determine how many quarters, dimes and pennies were selected.

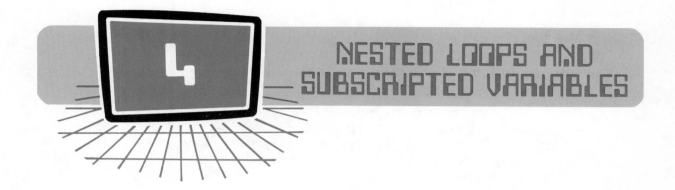

We have previously observed that the FOR . . . TO . . . STEP, NEXT statements set up loops. This chapter proceeds further by showing how to combine two or more loops in such a way as to place one loop inside another.

The second part of this chapter deals with subscripted variables which use a fixed variable name in conjunction with a variable subscript (e.g. A(N)), where A is fixed and N varies. This technique enables a program to deal conveniently with a large amount of data. Subscripted variables usually employ FOR . . . NEXT loops to generate the values for the subscripts.

Nested FOR . . . NEXT Loops

The concept of a FOR . . . NEXT loop was presented in Chapter Two. In this chapter, the concept of nested FOR . . . NEXT loops (that is, one loop placed or 'nested' within another) is introduced. For example:

```
10 FOR P = 1 TO 20
20      FOR Q = 3 TO 10
30      NEXT Q
40 NEXT P
```

By definition, nested loops must never cross. One loop must be contained entirely within another, or entirely separate from another. For example, the following arrangement is not permissible because the loops cross each other:

```
10 FOR P = 1 TO 20
20 FOR Q = 3 TO 10
30 NEXT P
40 NEXT Q
```

When this program is run, the following error message will result:

NEXT WITHOUT FOR IN 40

PROGRAM 4.1

This program uses nested loops to print a portion of the multiplication table.

```
10 FOR X = 1 TO 5
20     FOR Y = 1 TO 3
30         PRINT X; "*"; Y; "="; X*Y,
40     NEXT Y
50 PRINT
60 NEXT X
Ok
RUN
 1 * 1 = 1      1 * 2 = 2      1 * 3 = 3
 2 * 1 = 2      2 * 2 = 4      2 * 3 = 6
 3 * 1 = 3      3 * 2 = 6      3 * 3 = 9
 4 * 1 = 4      4 * 2 = 8      4 * 3 = 12
 5 * 1 = 5      5 * 2 = 10     5 * 3 = 15
Ok
```

Line 10 establishes the outer X loop and starts X with the value 1. X retains this value until it is incremented by the execution of line 60. Line 60 is not executed, however, until the inner Y loop, lines 20-40, has run its entire course. X therefore retains the value 1 while Y changes from 1 to 2 to 3. When the Y loop has finished its cycle of three passes, line 60 is executed, incrementing X to 2. The program returns to line 20 and starts the Y loop over again at its initial value of 1. Whenever a program encounters the FOR . . . TO statement of a loop, the loop variable is reset to its initial value. Since this program does not return to line 10, the X loop is never reset back to 1. Notice that Y will take on its values of 1, 2 and 3 five times. Indentation is used in the above program in order to clarify the program's structure, and the contents of each loop are indented to clarify the boundaries of the loop.

PROGRAM 4.2

This program calculates and prints all possible combinations of coins that add up to fifty cents, using quarters, dimes, and nickels.

```
LIST
10 PRINT "Quarters", "Dimes", "Nickels"
20 FOR Q = 0 TO 2 : REM Quarters
30     FOR D = 0 TO 5 : REM Dimes
40         FOR N = 0 TO 10 : REM Nickels
50             IF Q*25 + D*10 + N*5 = 50 THEN PRINT Q, D, N
60         NEXT N
70     NEXT D
80 NEXT Q
Ok
```

```
RUN
Quarters        Dimes           Nickels
   0              0               10
   0              1                8
   0              2                6
   0              3                4
   0              4                2
   0              5                0
   1              0                5
   1              1                3
   1              2                1
   2              0                0
Ok
```

Q represents the number of quarters, D the number of dimes, and N the number of nickels. There may be anywhere from 0 to 2 quarters in a combination. Similarly, there may be anywhere from 0 to 5 dimes and from 0 to 10 nickels. Using three nested loops, *every* possible combination that *might* work is checked at line 50.

REVIEW

1. Use nested loops to produce the following output. The outer loop runs from 20 to 24, and the inner loop runs from 1 to 3.

```
Ok
RUN
Outer Loop: 20
Inner: 1        Inner: 2        Inner: 3
Outer Loop: 21
Inner: 1        Inner: 2        Inner: 3
Outer Loop: 22
Inner: 1        Inner: 2        Inner: 3
Outer Loop: 23
Inner: 1        Inner: 2        Inner: 3
Outer Loop: 24
Inner: 1        Inner: 2        Inner: 3
Ok
```

WHILE. . .WEND

The FOR. . .NEXT statements allow a loop to be established so that every statement within the loop is executed a predetermined number of times. Sometimes it may be desirable to execute one or more statements only so long as a given condition is true. This may be done by using the WHILE. . .WEND statements.

The general form of WHILE. . .WEND is:

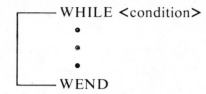

WHILE <condition>
•
•
•
WEND

When the WHILE statement is encountered, the 'condition' is evaluated. If the condition is true, the statements between WHILE and WEND are executed. The computer then returns to the WHILE statement and evaluates the 'condition' again. If the condition is still true, the process is repeated, otherwise execution resumes with the statement immediately following WEND.

PROGRAM 4.3

This program reads and prints data until the word "DONE" is encountered.

```
10 WHILE B$ <> "DONE"
20      READ B$
30      PRINT B$
40 WEND
50 PRINT "Finished the loop"
60 DATA IBM, CHEER, TIRE, DONE, MORE, HAPPY
Ok
RUN
IBM
CHEER
TIRE
DONE
Finished the loop
Ok
```

It is good programming practice to indent the contents of a WHILE. . .WEND loop to indicate clearly which statements are contained within the loop. Note that each WHILE statement must have a corresponding WEND.

WHILE. . .WEND loops may be nested in the same manner as FOR. . .NEXT loops being careful to insure that none of the loops cross one another. For example, the following structure is *invalid:*

WHILE T = 5
    FOR N = 8 TO 24 STEP +2
        •
        •
    WEND
NEXT N

4.4

The following structure is *valid:*

```
┌──────WHILE T = 5
│       ┌──────FOR N = 8 TO 24 STEP +2
│       │              •
│       │              •
│       └──────NEXT N
└──────WEND
```

The Need for Subscripted Variables

The following section demonstrates the usefulness of subscripted variables.

PROGRAM 4.4

```
10 RANDOMIZE 7721
20 FOR X = 1 TO 10
30     Y = INT(RND*20)+1
40        PRINT Y;
50 NEXT X
Ok
RUN
 6   15   16   10   20   8   11   7   10   19
Ok
```

Every time a new value is assigned to Y, it replaces the previous value for Y. Since the previous values of Y are not remembered, it is impossible to prevent repetition by comparing the old values of Y with the new value of Y. If a box analogy is used here, the first two cycles of Program 4.3 would appear as:

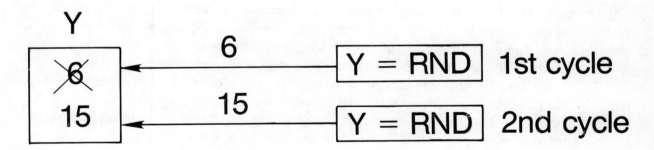

This program prints four random numbers between 1 and 20 without any repetition. The technique can be expanded to have the program choose 10 numbers if the user is willing to type the program lines required.

```
5 RANDOMIZE 3347
10 Y1 = INT(RND*20)+1
20 PRINT Y1;
30 Y2 = INT(RND*20)+1
40 IF Y2 = Y1 THEN 30
50 PRINT Y2;
60 Y3 = INT(RND*20)+1
70 IF Y3 = Y2 OR Y3 = Y1 THEN 60
80 PRINT Y3;
90 Y4 = INT(RND*20)+1
100 IF Y4 = Y3 OR Y4 = Y2 OR Y4 = Y1 THEN 90
110 PRINT Y4
Ok
RUN
 15   11   20   14
Ok
```

The similarity between the three sets of lines 30-50, 60-80, and 90-110 is obvious. In each set the first line selects a random number between 1 and 20, while the second line checks to see if the number is a repetition of a number previously chosen. If this is the case, then execution goes back to the first line in the set so that another number may be chosen. Finally, the third line of the set prints the random number selected. The use of subscripted variables will eliminate the need for the repetition of these sets.

Single Subscripted Variables

In mathematics, a set of single subscripted numeric variables (e.g. X_1, X_2, X_3, . . .) is symbolized by a letter and a subscript which is written below the line of the letter. On the computer, the same set of subscripted variables would be referred to as X(1), X(2), X(3), and so on, where the integer enclosed in parentheses is the subscript.

The name for a set of single subscripted numeric variables consists of one of the usual numeric variable names, followed by the parenthesized subscript. For example, A(1), B2(17), and X(8) are all legal subscripted variable names. Similarly, single subscripted string variable names such as Z$(5), Y1$(20), and M$(14) are acceptable.

The subscript variable L(2) is *not* the same as the variable L2. Furthermore, the subscript is a part of the variable name and must not be confused with the value of the variable. For example, in the statement L(5) = 32 the subscript is 5 and the value of L(5) is 32.

PROGRAM 4.6

This program illustrates the difference between the subscript and the value of a subscripted variable.

```
10 L(1) = 7
20 L(2) = 5
30 L(3) = 4
40 PRINT "L(1) ="; L(1),  "L(2) ="; L(2),  "L(3) ="; L(3)
50 PRINT "L(1 + 2) ="; L(1+2)
60 PRINT "L(1) + L(2) ="; L(1)+L(2)
70 X = 2
80 PRINT "L(X) ="; L(X)
Ok
RUN
L(1) = 7        L(2) = 5        L(3) = 4
L(1 + 2) = 4
L(1) + L(2) = 12
L(X) = 5
Ok
```

Lines 10 through 30 set the value of L(1) through L(3) as follows:

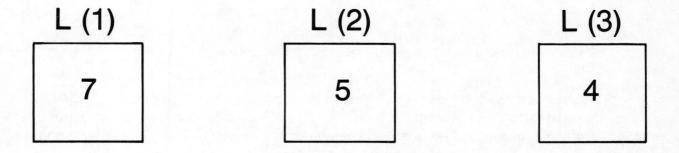

Lines 50 and 60 point out the difference between adding two subscripts and adding the values of two variables. L(1 + 2) is identical to L(3) and has a value of 4. L(1) + L(2) calls for the values 7 and 5 to be added, thus producing a total of 12. Since the subscript X equals 2 in line 80, a value of 5 is printed. Thus, as can be seen, it is permissible to use a numeric variable as the subscript of a subscripted variable.

PROGRAM 4.7

Like Program 4.3, this program selects 10 random numbers between 1 and 20 and makes no attempt to prevent repetition. Yet unlike Program 4.3, it stores the numbers chosen in a subscripted variable.

```
5 RANDOMIZE 7123
10 FOR X = 1 TO 10
20     R(X) = INT(RND*20)+1
30 NEXT X
40 PRINT "Ten random numbers have been stored in R()."
50 PRINT
60 FOR N = 1 TO 10
70     PRINT "R("; N; ") has a"; R(N); "stored in it."
80 NEXT N

Ok
RUN
Ten random numbers have been stored in R().

R( 1 ) has a 5 stored in it.
R( 2 ) has a 4 stored in it.
R( 3 ) has a 4 stored in it.
R( 4 ) has a 20 stored in it.
R( 5 ) has a 11 stored in it.
R( 6 ) has a 14 stored in it.
R( 7 ) has a 19 stored in it.
R( 8 ) has a 8 stored in it.
R( 9 ) has a 20 stored in it.
R( 10 ) has a 17 stored in it.
Ok
```

This program has two loops which are not nested but which follow one another. Each loop is executed 10 times. In the first loop, line 20 chooses a random number and stores it in one of the subscripted R() variables. The first time through this loop (X = 1), a random number is stored in R(1); the second time (X = 2), a new number is stored in R(2), and so on 10 times. After the above run of this program, the R() boxes had contents as follows:

R (1)	R (2)	R (3)	R (4)	R (5)
5	4	4	20	11

R (6)	R (7)	R (8)	R (9)	R (10)
14	19	8	20	17

4.8

The second loop (lines 60 through 80) prints the contents stored in the boxes.

The ability to store numbers in this way will allow the writing of a new program to choose 10 random numbers *without* repetition. By checking whether a chosen random number equals any of those previously selected, a program can determine whether to accept the random number chosen or to make another selection.

PROGRAM 4.8

This program uses nested loops and subscripted variables to pick 10 random numbers between 1 and 20 without repetition.

```
5 RANDOMIZE 7123
10 FOR X = 1 TO 10
20      Y(X) = INT(RND*20)+1
30      IF X = 1 THEN 70
35      REM Check for repeats
40      FOR Q = 1 TO X-1
50          IF Y(X) = Y(Q) THEN 20
60      NEXT Q
70      PRINT Y(X);
80 NEXT X
Ok
RUN
 5   4   20   11   14   19   8   17   2   9
Ok
```

Line 20 selects a random number between 1 and 20 and stores it in one of the subscripts of Y(). Since Y(1) is the first random number, line 30 is included to ensure Y(1) will be printed immediately since it is obviously not a repeat of another number. Lines 40 to 60 constitute a nested loop which determines if a number just chosen, Y(X), is equal to any of the previously chosen numbers, Y(1) through Y(X-1). The X-1 in line 40 ensures that Y(X) is not rejected by being checked against itself. If X rather than X-1 were used, then Q would eventually equal X. Line 50 would determine that Y(X) was a repeated number when Q equalled X and would then mistakenly return to line 20.

There is an additional reason for including line 30. When X and Q are equal to 1, Y(X) will equal Y(Q) and without line 30 program flow would continuously jump back to line 20.

PROGRAM 4.9

The following program will randomly read a list of 5 names into a subscripted string variable N$(), without repeating any of the names.

```
5 RANDOMIZE
10 FOR X = 1 TO 5
20      Y = INT(RND*5)+1
30      IF N$(Y) <> "" THEN 20
40      READ N$(Y)
50 NEXT X
60 FOR Z = 1 TO 5
70      PRINT N$(Z)
80 NEXT Z
90 DATA TED, JOHN, MARY, KEITH, ANN
```

```
Ok
RUN
Random number seed (-32768 to 32767)? 5421
MARY
JOHN
TED
KEITH
ANN
Ok
RUN
Random number seed (-32768 to 32767)? 7736
MARY
TED
JOHN
ANN
KEITH
Ok
```

This program reads the names in the DATA statement in the order of occurrence, but randomly places them in N$(1) to N$(5). Repetition is avoided by checking each new box as it is selected to discover whether it contains a name. If it is full, a new box is tried by selecting a new random number. At line 30 the consecutive double quotes ("") refer to the box being empty. Unassigned subscripted string variables contain an empty space, which is represented on the compuer by ("").

REVIEW

2. Using subscripted variables, write a program in which 3 numbers are input. Then have the computer type them back in reverse order.

```
RUN
? 4
? 6
? 1
  1
  6
  4
Ok
```

3. Six words are to be entered from the keyboard. Have the computer randomly select and print four of the words as a "sentence" (which may not make sense). Repetition of words is allowed.

```
RUN
? JACK
? AND
? JILL
? RAN
? AWAY
? SCREAMING
SCREAMING RAN JILL JILL .
Ok
```

4. Modify the program of the previous exercise so that words are not repeated.

```
RUN
? JACK
? AND
? JILL
? RAN
? AWAY
? HAPPILY
HAPPILY RAN JILL JACK .
Ok
```

DIM

Whenever the highest subscript of a subscripted variable exceeds 10, the computer must be informed. The DIM (dimension) statement is used to direct the computer to open enough boxes in its memory to accommodate the anticipated input. Program 4.8 could store 100 names by making the appropriate changes in several lines and by adding the line

5 DIM N$(100)

If the ages of the people were also to be stored, a numeric subscripted variable would have to be added and the DIM statement modified.

5 DIM N$(100), A(100)

It is possible to request more space (i.e. boxes) in memory than the computer can supply. This results in the error message:

OUT OF MEMORY

It is a good idea to place DIM statements at the beginning of a program since the DIM statement must be executed before using more than 10 subscripts of a subscripted variable. Though it is possible to have several DIM statements in a program, each subscripted variable may only be dimensioned once. If there are two DIM statements for the same variable or if a DIM statement is executed more than once, the error message

DUPLICATE DEFINITION

will result.

Double Subscripted Variables

The computer can also use double subscripts to name a variable. This is similar to single subscripting except that there are two numbers within the parentheses instead of one. For example,

$$A(1,5) \quad B3(7,3) \quad C\$(4,9)$$

are all double subscripted variables. The computer reserves space in memory for a double subscripted variable by placing them in rows and columns, rather than in a single column (as is the case with a single subscripted variable). This procedure provides a convenient technique for dealing with problems in which the data is two-dimensional in nature, such as the location of seats in a theater.

To understand more clearly how the double subscripted variable operates, the box analogy is again helpful. The first integer in the subscript identifies the row and the second the column in which the variable is located. For example, A(2,3) is located at the second row, third column.

	Col. 1	Col. 2	Col. 3	Col. 4
Row 1	A (1, 1)	A (1, 2)	A (1, 3)	A (1, 4)
Row 2	A (2, 1)	A (2, 2)	A (2, 3)	A (2, 4)
Row 3	A (3, 1)	A (3, 2)	A (3, 3)	A (3, 4)

PROGRAM 4.10

A classroom has 5 rows of seats with 3 seats to a row. The following program randomly assigns a class of 14 students to seats, leaving one seat empty.

```
10 RANDOMIZE 1234
20 DIM N$(5,3)
30 FOR X = 1 TO 14
40      READ S$ : REM Get a student
50      R = INT(RND*5)+1 : REM row #
60      C = INT(RND*3)+1 : REM column #
70      IF N$(R,C) <> "" THEN 50 : REM Seat occupied?
80      N$(R,C) = S$ : REM Put student in seat
90 NEXT X
100 REM Print seating arrangement
110 FOR R1 = 1 TO 5
120     FOR C1 = 1 TO 3
130         IF N$(R1,C1) = "" THEN PRINT "Empty",
                            ELSE PRINT N$(R1,C1),
140         NEXT C1
150     PRINT
160 NEXT R1
170 DATA  ANNE, DON, SHERRY, CINDY, ERIC, LESTER, KIM
180 DATA  BILL, MARY, MARK, SUSAN, KEVIN, WENDELL, ROB

Ok
RUN
BILL            ANNE            MARK
LESTER          Empty           SHERRY
DON             MARY            KIM
CINDY           WENDELL         KEVIN
ERIC            ROB             SUSAN
Ok
```

The computer also allows 3, 4, etc., all the way up to 255 dimensions in a subscripted variable (e.g. DIM X(5,5,8,2,3,19)). However, the more dimensions that a subscripted variable has, the smaller each dimension must be. This is due to the limited amount of space available in the computer's memory.

5. Six numbers are to be input from the keyboard as X(K). These are subsequently to be printed in a vertical column, and then a second time, closely spaced on a single line.

```
RUN
?  23
?  67
?  128
?  37
?  42
?  143
 23
 67
 128
 37
 42
 143

 23   67   128   37   42   143
Ok
```

6. Use the double subscripted variable X$(I,J) for which the row variable I runs from 1 to 5 and the column variable J from 1 to 3. Enter the letters A, B, C as the first row, D, E, F as the second, up to M, N, O as the fifth. Have the program print the following (making the rows become columns). (Hint: Use READ, DATA)

```
RUN
A D G J M
B E H K N
C F I L O
Ok
```

Some Final Notes on Subscripted Variables

Subscripted string and numeric variables greatly enhance the programmer's ability to store and deal with large quantities of data within any one program run. It must be remembered, however, that if the program is run again, all of the stored data in the computer's memory is erased. This means that all of the boxes become either null ("") or zero at the start of the next run. A method for permanently storing data is presented in chapters 9 and 10.

ERASE

Large arrays use up much of the computer's memory. If an array is no longer needed by a program it can be erased in order to free space in memory. The statement

100 ERASE B

will remove the subscripted variable B and its contents from the computer's memory.

OPTION BASE

The lowest numbered element in a single or double subscripted variable is numbered 0 (for example, A (0), B$ (0), A$ (0, 0)). If the 0 element is not wanted, it is possible to start the numbering at 1 rather than 0. This can be done by using the statement

5 OPTION BASE 1

which must appear in a program before any reference is made to a subscripted variable or any DIM statement is executed.

Extended Variable Names

Previously, variable names have consisted of a single letter, possibly followed by a digit. As was pointed out in this chapter, these names may also be subscripted. Actually, they may be of any length up to forty characters.

PART A

1. Using a nested loop have the computer print a rectangle consisting of eight lines of thirty asterisks each.

2. Show the output of the following program and check by running it. Rerun the program after removing line 50.

```
10 FOR I = 1 TO 5
20    FOR J = 1 TO 2 * I - 1
30       PRINT ".";
40    NEXT J
50    PRINT
60 NEXT I
```

3. Enter values of X(I) for I=1 to 6. Print the values of I and X(I) in two columns with I proceeding in the order 1, 3, 5, 2, 4, 6.

4. Enter 15 letters of the alphabet (not necessarily different), and print them in reverse order as a single block of letters.

5. Have the computer compute the values of A(I,J), where A(I,J)=3*I+J*J, I varies from 1 to 4, and J varies from 1 to 12. The user is to input a number N from 1 to 4 so that all values of A(N,J) can be printed.

6. Using a DATA statement have the computer enter one letter of the alphabet for each member of A$(I,J), where I runs from 1 to 11 and J from 1 to 3. The letters are first to be printed in the form of an 11 word sentence, with each word consisting of 3 letters. Then, the letters are to be printed again as a 3 word sentence, with each word consisting of 11 letters. The words may or may not make sense.

PART B

7. (a) Les Brains, who has forgotten where the computer is, needs to know the output for the following programs. Predict the output in each case, and check by running the program.

(a)
```
10 FOR L1 = 1 TO 3
20     FOR L2 = 5 TO 6
30         PRINT L1,L2
40     NEXT L2
50 NEXT L1
```

(b)
```
10 FOR X = 10 TO 15 STEP 2
20     FOR Y = 15 TO 10 STEP -2
30         IF Y = X THEN 99
40         IF X < Y THEN PRINT X : GOTO 60
50         PRINT Y
60     NEXT Y
70 NEXT X
99 END
```

(c)
```
10 FOR S = 1 TO 10
20     READ A(S)
30 NEXT S
40 PRINT A(3),A(7),A(10)
50 DATA 23,12,45,2,87,34,89,17,2,35,70
```

8. Suzy Fowlup has done it again and has written another program that will not run properly. Assist her by correcting the program. The output should look like this:

```
RUN
 3          4
 4          3
 4          4
 5          3
 5          4
```

— — — — — — — — — — — — —

```
10 FOR A = 3,5
20     FOR B = 1 ,4
30         IF A * B < = 10 GOTO 50
40         PRINYAB
50     NEXT A
60 NEXT B
```

9. The following program is designed to print the numbers in the DATA statement in decreasing order. However, there are some errors in the program. Correct and run the program to produce this output:

```
RUN
 40  37  27  27  16  9  8  5  2  1
Ok
```

— — — — — — — — — — — — — — — — — —

```
10 FOR X = 40 TO 1
20     FOR Y = 1 TO 10
30         READ N
40          IF N = X THEN PRINT N;
50     NEXT X
60 NEXT Y
70 DATA 5,27,37,16,27,8,2,40,1,9
```

10. What is the exact output for the following program?

```
10 READ B1,B2,B3,B4,B5,B6
20 FOR X = 1 TO 6
30     READ B(X)
40 NEXT X
50 PRINT "B4=";B4;" BUT B(4)=";B(4)
60 PRINT B1 + B2 + B3 , B(1) + B(2) + B(3) , B(1+2+3)
70 DATA 3,7,4,1,8,12
80 DATA 14,42,69,86,12,111
```

11. The following program is designed to find random integers between 1 and 99, inclusive, until it encounters a duplicate. At that point it should print how many numbers it has found and then print all of them. However, there are a number of errors in the program. Correct them to produce output similar to:

```
RUN
Random number seed (-32768 to 32767)? -42
DUPLICATE AFTER 14 NUMBERS
 48  64  26  29  97  23  47  95  31  54  88  90  19  97
Ok
```

— — — — — — — — — — — — — — — — — — —

```
5 RANDOMIZE
20 FOR X = 1 TO 100
30     N(X) = INT(99*RND + 1)
40     FOR Y = 1 TO 100
50         IF N(X) <> N(Y) THEN 70
60         PRINT "DUPLICATE AFTER";X;"NUMBERS"
70         FOR Z = 1 TO X : PRINT N(X); : NEXT Z
80     NEXT Y
90 NEXT X
Ok
```

12. Write a program that reads the names, street addresses, towns, and zip codes of five people into subscripted variables N$(X), A$(X), T$(X), and Z$(X). The user enters a name, and the program prints the full name and address of that person. If the name is not there, have the program print PERSON NOT FOUND.

13. A Pythagorean Triple is a set of three integers which are the lengths of the sides of a right triangle ($C^2 = A^2 + B^2$). Find all sets of three integers up to C = 50 which are Pythagorean triples. For example, A = 3, B = 4, C = 5 is a solution. (Note that due to rounding errors, it is better to use A*A + B*B = C*C rather than A ↑ 2 + B ↑ 2 = C ↑ 2 to check for equalities.)

14. Stan's Grocery Store has 3 aisles and in each aisle there are five items. Write a program that will read 15 items into the subscripted variable I$(X,Y), dimensioned 3x5. Let his customers type in the item they want to buy, and be informed by the computer of the aisle and the item's number.

```
RUN
WHAT ARE YOU LOOKING FOR ? CHERRIES
YOU WILL FIND CHERRIES IN AISLE # 1   ITEM # 4
WHAT ARE YOU LOOKING FOR ? BREAD
YOU WILL FIND BREAD IN AISLE # 2   ITEM # 1
WHAT ARE YOU LOOKING FOR ? PEPPER
I'M SORRY, WE DON'T HAVE PEPPER
WHAT ARE YOU LOOKING FOR ?
Break in 70
Ok
```

15. Pick 20 random integers between 10 and 99, inclusive. Print the odd integers on one line and the even integers on the next line. The output should look like this:

```
RUN
ODD INTEGERS: 11   47   73   85   79   43   77   23   13
EVEN INTEGERS: 64   16   92   14   14   78   44   68   48   34   60
Ok
```

16. Find the average of four grades for each of five students. The output should give in columns on consecutive lines each student's name, four grades, and average. Each column should have a heading. The last student's average should be underlined and the class average printed below it in the same column.

```
RUN
STUDENT # 1 ? DON
ENTER FOUR GRADES: ? 42,86,99,99
STUDENT # 2 ? LESTER
ENTER FOUR GRADES: ? 100,99,98,97
STUDENT # 3 ? LIZ
ENTER FOUR GRADES: ? 99,98,99,99
STUDENT # 4 ? MARY
ENTER FOUR GRADES: ? 67,72,71,68
STUDENT # 5 ? SUE
ENTER FOUR GRADES: ? 89,91,93,90

NAME            1       2       3       4       AVE.
DON             42      86      99      99      81.5
LESTER          100     99      98      97      98.5
LIZ             99      98      99      99      98.75
MARY            67      72      71      68      69.5
SUE             89      91      93      90      90.75
                                                -----
                                                87.8
Ok
```

17. Marcus Welby wants you to program the computer to keep track of his busy schedule. (a) Write a program to allow a patient to choose the day and time he or she wants to see the doctor. There are 5 days and 6 time slots for each day. If the desired slot is empty, the patient enters his or her name. If it is full, the program asks for another slot. (b) Add the steps needed to allow Dr. Welby to print his schedule for any particular day.

18. Susie Gossip has 3 skirts—red, green, and purple; 2 pairs of jeans—white and electric purple; 4 blouses—blue, pink, orange, and black; and 2 slightly tight sweaters—yellow and green. Have the computer print a list of all possible combinations of the articles she can wear (e.g., red skirt and blue blouse, or white jeans and yellow sweater).

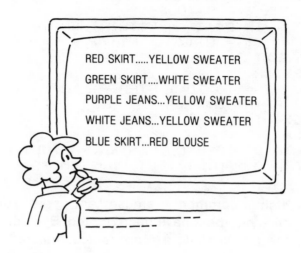

```
RED SKIRT.....YELLOW SWEATER
GREEN SKIRT....WHITE SWEATER
PURPLE JEANS...YELLOW SWEATER
WHITE JEANS...YELLOW SWEATER
BLUE SKIRT...RED BLOUSE
```

19. Write an extended version of the game high-low. In this game, the computer picks a secret random number between 1 and 100 and gives the player an unlimited number of chances to guess it. For each wrong guess the computer tells whether to guess higher or lower and stores the guess in a subscripted variable. If the player guesses the same number twice, the computer should produce the message WAKE UP! YOU GUESSED THAT NUMBER BEFORE.

20. Betty Bright has written the following two programs to sort data. Read the programs carefully and predict the output.

```
(a)   10  DIM A(10)
      20  FOR B = 1 TO 10
      30     READ A(B)
      40  NEXT B
      50  FOR C = 2 TO 10
      60     FOR D = 1 TO C-1
      70        IF A(D) < A(C) THEN 90
      80        E = A(D) : A(D) = A(C) : A(C) = E
      90     NEXT D
     100  NEXT C
     110  FOR F = 1 TO 10
     120     PRINT A(F)
     130  NEXT F
     200  REM
     210  DATA 1,3,7,2,4,9,0,2,5,8
```

(b)

```
(b)    10 DIM Q$(10)
       20 FOR M = 1 TO 10
       30    READ Q$(M)
       40 NEXT M
       50 FOR R = 5 TO 10
       60    FOR Z = 5 TO R-1
       70       IF Q$(Z) < Q$(R) THEN 90
       80       T$ = Q$(Z) : Q$(Z) = Q$(R) : Q$(R) = T$
       90    NEXT Z
      100 NEXT R
      110 FOR I = 10 TO 1 STEP -1
      120    PRINT Q$(I)
      130 NEXT I
      200 REM
      210 DATA DON,FRENCH,LESTER,FAZIOLI,MARY
      220 DATA SUSAN,LIZ,ELI,ROB,KIM
```

21. The game Penny Pitch is common in amusement parks. Pennies are tossed onto a checkerboard on which numbers have been printed. By adding up the numbers in the squares on which the pennies fall, a score is accumulated. Write a program which simulates such a game in which ten pennies are to be randomly pitched onto the board shown below.

Have the computer print the board with an X indicating where each penny has landed and then the score. Below is a sample run. Note that more than one penny can land in one square.

```
RUN
 X  X  X  1  1  X
 1  2  2  2  2  1
 1  2  3  3  2  1
 X  2  X  3  2  X
 1  2  2  2  2  1
 1  X  X  1  1  1

SCORE IS 12
Ok
```

22. Write a program that rolls two dice 1000 times and prints the number of times each different point total (2, 3, 4, 5, ..., 12) appeared. The output should resemble the following:

```
RUN
POINT TOTAL    TIMES APPEARING
   2               34
   3               56
   4               83
  ...             ...
  12               32
```

23. Write a program which makes up 15 "words" (i.e. groups of letters, whether pronounceable or not) composed of from one to seven randomly chosen letters, and print them. (Hint: use addition of strings. For example if A$(2)="B" and A$(12)="L" then A$(2)+A$(12)="BL".)

24. Use the computer to play a modified game of Othello. Have it randomly fill an 8x8 subscripted string variable with X's and O's and print the array by row (horizontal) and column (vertical). Examples are below. The X's are for player 1, the O's for player 2. Have the program alternately ask the players for the row and column of the opponent's piece that should be flipped (changed from an X to an O or vice versa). All of the opponent's pieces along the horizontal or vertical line passing through the flipped piece are also flipped. For example, if player 1 flipped the 0 at 1,8, board A would be changed to board B.

```
A   1 2 3 4 5 6 7 8        B   1 2 3 4 5 6 7 8
 1  O O O X O O X O         1  X X X X X X X X
 2  X O O O X O O O         2  X O O O X O O X
 3  X X X O X X O X         3  X X X O X X O X
 4  X O X O O X O O         4  X O X O O X O X
 5  X X O X O O O X         5  X X O X O O O X
 6  O O X O O X X O         6  O O X O O X X X
 7  O O X X X X O O         7  O O X X X X O X
 8  O X X O X O X O         8  O X X O X O X X
```

25. Mr. and Mrs. Charles Windsor want to start a bank account for their newborn son, William. They open the account with $500. At the beginning of each successive year they deposit $60 more. When William is 21, how much money will be in the account? (Assume the interest rate to be 6% compounded quarterly).

5 PROGRAMMING TECHNIQUES

In a well written program the purpose and sequence of each line should be obvious. As a whole, the lines should serve as a clear indication of what the program does and the sequence it must follow.

The term 'code' is used to define the instructions which comprise a program. Each line of a program contains statements referred to as code. If presented in a clear and logical style, the code is less likely to contain errors. Furthermore, a well written program is easily read and understood by another programmer with a minimum of effort.

The first step in writing a program is to understand precisely the problem to be solved. Next, a plan should be developed to break the problem down into a series of smaller units; each can then be programmed as a unit. A common mistake made by many inexperienced programmers is to start writing the code before the problem or its solution is understood. From this, there results a program which is frequently modified by adding or deleting lines of code until the desired output is achieved. The resulting program is usually a "mish-mash" of statements which do not flow logically from one to another. When GOTO and IF . . . THEN statements have to be added to a program to make it work, the sequential top to bottom flow from line-to-line—a sign of good programming—is often destroyed. Therefore, one should plan a program as thoroughly as possible before approaching the computer. As the computer pioneer, R.W. Hamming has declared; "Typing is no substitute for thinking."

Structuring a Program

The structure of a program determines the ease with which it can be read and understood. Several techniques which follow help to achieve such a structure.

1. REM statements strategically placed throughout a program can be helpful in explaining how the program works. It is a good practice to use REM statements at the beginning

of a program to indicate what the program does and to list and define the variables used within the program.

2. Indent the lines within FOR . . . NEXT and WHILE . . . WEND loops to clarify where the loops begin and end and what portions of the program are contained within each loop.

3. Break a program down into separate units in which each unit performs a specific task. It is a good practice to separate each unit from the others by choosing appropriate line numbers. For example, if a program contains three units and each is about 15 lines long, number the lines of the first unit from 100 to 250, the second unit from 300 to 450, and the third from 500 to 650. Separate each unit from the next using blank REM statements and begin each unit with a REM statement which explains the function of that unit.

4. The IF . . . THEN . . . ELSE statement is extremely powerful, and if used properly, it can substantially reduce the amount of code required within a program. Although its structure can be confusing, it may be clarified by being segmented. For example, Program 5.1 will use an IF . . . THEN . . . ELSE statement to cause the program to jump to line 230 if A = X*Y. It will print ANSWER TOO HIGH if A>X*Y, or print ANSWER TOO LOW if A <X*Y.

```
190 IF A = X*Y THEN 230 ELSE IF A>X*Y THEN PRINT "ANSWER TOO HIGH"
ELSE PRINT "ANSWER TOO LOW"
```

With so much of the code all on a single line, it is difficult to determine exactly its function. If this line is structured

```
190 IF A = X*Y THEN 230
            ELSE IF A > X*Y THEN PRINT "ANSWER TOO HIGH"
                       ELSE PRINT "ANSWER TOO LOW"
```

then it is obviously much easier to read. Notice that the line is broken and indented where the ELSE occurs. To split a line of code strike the ENTER key while depressing the CTRL key. The ENTER key is struck alone only after the complete line of code has been entered.

PROGRAM 5.1

The four programming techniques presented above are used here to produce a clear, easy-to-read program. This program tests a student on multiplication and division by giving ten problems of each type, and he or she has five chances to answer each one correctly. If a wrong answer is given, the computer will inform the student whether his or her answer is too high or too low. The student's score is based on receiving five points for a correct answer on the first try, four for a correct answer on the second try, and so on. No points are received if the problem is not answered correctly after five responses.

Read the program carefully, note its structure, and try to predict its output. Many of the programming details are left for the reader to analyze.

```
1 REM      This program tests a student on multiplication and
              division.   There are ten problems of each type.
2 REM      N = Number of the question (1-10)
3 REM      T = Number of points awarded
4 REM      X,Y = Two random numbers used in question
5 REM      A = Student's answer
6 REM      S = Student's score
7 REM
8 REM
100 REM      Multiplication Problems
110 PRINT "You will be asked ten multiplication problems"
120 PRINT "and be given five chances to get each correct."
130 FOR N = 1 TO 10
140      X = INT(10*RND+1)
150      Y = INT(10*RND+1)
160      FOR T = 5 TO 1 STEP -1
170          PRINT "What does ";X;" * ";Y;" = ";
180          INPUT A
190          IF A = X * Y THEN 230
                         ELSE IF A > X*Y THEN PRINT "Answer too high"
                                         ELSE PRINT "Answer too low"
200      NEXT T
210      PRINT "You got the answer wrong five times, it is";X*Y
220      GOTO 240
230      S = S + T
240 NEXT N
250 REM
260 REM
300 REM      Division problems
310 PRINT "You will be asked ten division problems"
320 PRINT "and be given five chances to get each correct."
330 FOR N = 1 TO 10
340      X = INT(10*RND+1)
350      Y = INT(10*RND+1)
360      FOR T = 5 TO 1 STEP -1
370          PRINT "What does ";X;" / ";Y;" = ";
380          INPUT A
390          IF A = X/Y THEN 430
                         ELSE IF A > X/Y THEN PRINT "Answer too high"
                                         ELSE PRINT "Answer too low"
400      NEXT T
410      PRINT "You got the answer wrong five times, it is";X/Y
420      GOTO 440
430      S = S + T
440 NEXT N
450 REM
460 REM
500 REM      Print score
510 PRINT "Your score is =";  S
520 END
```

REVIEW

1. Using the techniques discussed in this chapter structure both of the following programs.

```
a). 10 INPUT "Are you COMING or GOING";A$
    20 IF A$="COMING" THEN PRINT "HELLO" ELSE PRINT "GOOD-BYE"
    30 END
```

```
b). 1 REM    Shellsort of the list of club members
    2 INPUT "How many names in the list";N
    3 FOR X = 1 TO N
    4 INPUT "Member";M$(X)
    5 NEXT X
    6 S=N
    7 S=INT(S/1.5) : Q=S
    8 F=0
    9 FOR X=1 TO N
    10 Q=X+S
    11 IF Q > N THEN 14
    12 IF M$(X) > M$(Q)  THEN T$=M$(X):M$(X)=M$(Q):M$(Q)=T$:F=1
    13 NEXT X
    14 IF S > 1 THEN 7
    15 IF F = 1 THEN 8
    16 FOR X=1 TO N
    17 PRINT M$(X)
    18 NEXT X
    19 END
```

DEBUGGING

Debugging is the process of locating errors or "bugs" in a program and then correcting them. Obviously, the best approach is to avoid bugs by carefully planning a program, but even the most carefully written program often contains errors.

There are three types of errors which will cause a program to fail in producing proper output.

Syntax Errors

Syntax errors are caused by typing an improper statement. For example,

10 REED X, Y

should be

10 READ X, Y

Happily, the computer detects this type of error and informs the programmer by printing an error message.

Runtime Errors

Runtime errors are detected when a program is run. For example,

    10 READ A$, B
    20 DATA 35, SMITH

is a format violation since the computer attempts to assign the string "SMITH" to the numerical variable B. Another common runtime error is caused by using two different variables to define a FOR . . . NEXT loop.

    10 FOR X = 1 TO 10
    20   PRINT X, X ^ 2, X ^3
    30 NEXT Y

The computer detects a runtime error and prints an appropriate error message.

Logic Errors

Although the computer accepts and runs a program, the output may not reflect the programmer's true intent. Yet if the program does not violate any of the syntax rules of BASIC it is not rejected. The errors in the program may stem instead from the programmer's incorrect analysis of how to develop a logical sequence of statements to achieve the intended goal. These forms of errors—referred to as logic errors—are the most difficult to detect and correct.

PROGRAM 5.2

This program is supposed to print the areas of circles whose radii are integers varying from 1 to 100 except for those whose computed areas are integers (note line 30). The equation $A = \pi R^2$ is used with the value of π taken as 3.1.

```
10 FOR X = 1 TO 10
20        A = 3.1 * X^2
30        IF A = INT(A) THEN 10
40        PRINT A,
50 NEXT X
60 END
RUN
3.1            12.4         27.9         49.6         77.5         111.6
     151.9         198.4        251.1        3.1          12.4         27.9
      49.6          77.5         111.6        151.9        198.4        251.1
      3.1           12.4         27.9         49.6         77.5         111.6
     151.9         198.4        251.1        3.1          12.4         27.9
      49.6          ^C
Break in 40
Ok
```

Note that the printed areas go as high as 251.1 and then start to repeat. The program actually goes into an infinite loop, which means that it keeps running until the BREAK key is struck.

A useful technique used for detecting the logic error in Program 5.2 is the placing of an extra PRINT statement in the program in order to print the loop variable X. This extra statement can later be removed when the error has been corrected.

25 PRINT "X ="; X,

```
RUN
X = 1          3.1        X = 2        12.4        X = 3          27.9
    X = 4      49.6        X = 5        77.5        X = 6          111.6
    X = 7      151.9       X = 8        198.4       X = 9          251.1
        X = 10    X = 1     3.1        X = 2        12.4        X = 3
        27.9      X = 4     49.6        X = 5        77.5        X = 6
        111.6     X = 7     151.9       X = 8        198.4       X = 9
        251.1     X = 10    X = 1       3.1        X = 2        12.4
        X = 3      27.9     X = 4       49.6        X = 5        77.5
        ^C
Break in 20
Ok
```

The output indicates that X only reaches 10 and then starts repeating rather than continuing on to 100 as it should. The problem results from the fact that line 30 should send the program to line 50 rather than to line 10, where it restarts the X loop at one.

In longer programs it is often useful to place additional print statements at a number of locations to check the value of variables and then remove them when the program is operating properly.

Another technique is to place a line in the program to indicate whether it is getting to a certain point as anticipated.

50 PRINT "I'M AT LINE 50 NOW"

The line can later be removed when no longer needed.

Hand Tracing

It is almost impossible to guarantee that a program will run properly for all possible situations that it may encounter, but one technique that creates confidence in the validity of a program is called hand tracing. By using test data, calculations are solved by hand and the results are checked with those produced by the program. If the computer program produces identical answers for the same data, the programmer is then confident that the program at least works for the data that is being tested.

TRON—TROFF

To follow the sequence in which the lines of a program are executed, type the command TRON before typing RUN. Each line number will then be printed as the line is processed by the computer, thus allowing the programmer to easily trace program flow. To stop the line tracing, the command TROFF is typed after the computer completes its run.

PROGRAM 5.3

This program prints the combinations of quarters and dimes which add up to $1.00.

```
1 REM     Q = Quarters
2 REM     D = Dimes
3 REM
10 FOR Q = 0 TO 4
20      FOR D = 0 TO 10
30          IF 25*Q + 10*D = 100 THEN PRINT "Q=";Q, "D=";D
40      NEXT D
50 NEXT Q
60 END
Ok
RUN
Q= 0            D= 10
Q= 2            D= 5
Q= 4            D= 0
Ok
TRON
Ok
RUN
[1][2][3][10][20][30][40][30][40][30][40
][30][40][30][40][30][40][30][40][30][40
][30][40][30][40][30]Q= 0    D= 10
[40][50][20][30][40][30][40][30][40][30]
[40][30][40][30][40][30][40][30][40][30]
[40][30][40][30][40][50][20][30][40][30]
[40][30][40][30][40][30][40][30]Q= 2
   D= 5
[40][30][40][30][40][30][40][30][40][30]
[40][50][20][30][40][30][40][30][40][30]
[40][30][40][30][40][30][40][30][40][30]
[40][30][40][30][40][50][20][30]Q= 4
   D= 0
[40][30][40][30][40][30][40][30][40][30]
[40][30][40][30][40][30][40][30][40][30]
[40][50][60]
Ok
TROFF
Ok
```

Follow the program flow carefully for both loops. Notice that each time a NEXT statement is executed, it returns the program to the statement following the corresponding FOR . . . TO statement.

STOP and CONT

A useful debugging technique is the halting of a program at certain points by using one or more STOP statements. Upon interruption the values of the program's variables may be examined. Typing CONT will continue program execution from the point at which it was interrupted.

PROGRAM 5.4

```
10 FOR X = 1 TO 100
20      A = 3*X^3 + 2*X^2 + 5
30      B = 7*X^2 + 2*X + 5
40      IF B > A THEN PRINT B;">";A
50 NEXT X
60 END
Ok
RUN
 14 > 10
Ok
```

When Program 5.4 is run, the computer prints one solution to the condition at line 40 and then gives the appearance of being at rest, until it finally prints READY. Is there only one solution or is there a bug in the program? The values of A and B can be checked when X = 50 by adding the line:

$$45 \text{ IF } X = 50 \text{ THEN STOP}$$

The values of A and B can then be examined when the program is halted by typing PRINT A,B. Typing CONT allows this program to continue on to completion. Since A is much larger than B when X = 50, it is obvious that there will be no other solutions than the first one. Hence there is no bug in the program.

```
Ok
RUN
 14 > 10
Break in 45
Ok
PRINT A,B
 380005          17605
Ok
CONT
Ok
```

REVIEW

2. Each of the following programs contains a 'bug'. Find it and correct it.

a).
```
10  INPUT A
20  FOR X=10 TO 1
30      C = A/X
40        PRINT INT(C)
50  NEXT X
```

b).
```
10  INPUT N
20  IF N < 0 THEN 10 : REM Prevents negative input
30  P=N*5
40  IF P < 0 THEN PRINT "The product is negative"
            ELSE PRINT "The product is positive"
50  END
```

1. Each of the following programs contains an error. In each case identify and correct the error(s).

(a)
```
10 READ A,B,C,D
20 E = A*B+C+D
30 PRINT E
40 DATA 2,3,4
50 END
```

(b)
```
10 READ A,B
20 DATA 1,2,3,4
30 PRINT A/B
40 GOTO 20
50 END
```

(c)
```
10 READ A,B,C
20 PRINT A*/B+C
30 PRINT D/F=;D/F
40 DATA 5,6,10
50 END
```

(d)
```
10 READ F,G
20 IF F > 5 OR < 10 THEN 40
30 GOTO 10
40 PRINT F G
50 DATA 1,10,6,9,11,4
60 END
```

(e)
```
10 FOR X = 1 TO 8
20    FOR Y = 1 TO 3
30        X = X + Y
40    NEXT X
50 NEXT Y
60 PRINT X
70 END
```

(f)
```
10 READ C,D,F
20 DATA 3,6,9,4,7,10
30 PRINT C+D+E
40 GOTO 20
50 END
```

2. Trace the following program by hand and determine its output. Use the TRON command to check your results.

```
10 READ N,A,B
20 FOR I = 1 TO N
30     FOR J = 2 TO N+1
40         A = 2 * A + B
50         B = 2 * B + A
60     NEXT J
70     PRINT A;B
80 NEXT I
90 DATA 3,-1,2
100 END
```

3. What output is produced by the following program? (Do not run the program.)

```
10 FOR X = 1 TO 5 STEP 2
20     READ K1,K2
30     A = A + K1 - K2
40     B = B - K1 + K2
50 NEXT X
60 PRINT A,B
70 DATA 1,3,2,4,3,5
80 END
```

4. The following simple programs have errors in logic (i.e., the program runs, but the output is illogical). Find and correct the errors.

(a)
```
10 READ A,B,C
20 PRINT A + B + C
30 GOTO 20
40 DATA 1,2,3,4,5,6
50 END
```

(b)
```
10 FOR X = 1 TO 10
20     IF X > 5 THEN 50
30     PRINT X;"IS GREATER THAN 5"
40     GOTO 60
50     PRINT "X;"IS LESS THAN 5"
60 NEXT X
70 END
```

(c)
```
10 READ A,B,C
20 FOR X = 1 TO 10
30     Y = (A*B)/(C-X)
40     IF Y < 1 THEN 50
50     PRINT "Y<1";Y
60 NEXT X
70 DATA 20,10,5,5,10,20
80 END
```

5. Each of the following programs contains errors which will result in error messages being printed by the computer when the program is run. Find and correct the errors.

(a)
```
10 PRINT "WHAT IS THE FORMULA WEIGHT OF THE ELEMENTS";
20 INPUT FORMULA WIGHT
30 IF X > 20 THEN 50
40 X = X/2
50 PRINT X
999 END
```

(b)
```
15 FOR X = 1 TO 2
25    FOR Y = 1 TO 3
35       IF Y = X THEN A = A + 1 : GOTO 50
45    NEXT Y
55    PRINT "X AND Y ARE EQUAL";A;"TIMES"
65 NEXT X
75 END
```

(c)
```
5 READ B,A,C
10 X1 = (B + (SQR(B^2 - 4*A*C) / 2 * A)
20 X2 = (B - (SQR(B^2 - 4*A*C) / 2 * A)
30 IF X1 > X2 THEN 50
40 GOTO 5
50 PRINT "X1=";X1; "X2=";X2
60 GOTO 5
70 DATA 1,2,3,4,5,6
80 END
```

(d)
```
10 READ A,B,C
20 X = A * B + C
30 IF X > 200 THEN LINE 10
40 PRINT X
50 DATA 25,26,27,28,29,30
60 END
```

(e)
```
10 FOR X = 1 TO 26
20    A$ = A$ + X
30 NEXT X
40 PRINT A$
50 END
```

(f)
```
10 FOR X = 1 TO 260
20   A$ = A$ + "X"
30 NEXT X
40 PRINT A$
50 END
```

6. The following program is designed to arrange sets of numbers in descending order. If the second number is larger than the first, the computer interchanges the two values. (This occurs in lines 30 and 40.) Explain the output and correct the program to give the desired output.

```
10 READ A,B
20 IF A > B THEN 50
30 A = B
40 B = A
50 PRINT A,B
60 GOTO 10
70 DATA 10,20,20,10
80 END

RUN
  20              20
  20              10
Out of DATA in 10
Ok
```

7. The area of a square that measures one inch on a side is equal to one square inch. If the computer takes various slices of this same square and sums the areas of the slices, the answer should be one square inch. In the following program 100, 1000, and 1024 slices are used and the output printed below. Explain the results.

```
10 READ N
20 FOR X = 1 TO N
30    Y = Y + 1/N
40 NEXT X
50 PRINT Y;"SQUARE INCHES FOR";N;"SLICES"
60 Y = 0
70 GOTO 10
80 DATA 100,1000,1024
Ok
RUN
 .9999994 SQUARE INCHES FOR 100 SLICES
 .9999907 SQUARE INCHES FOR 1000 SLICES
 1 SQUARE INCHES FOR 1024 SLICES
Out of DATA in 10
Ok
```

8. Structure the following programs by adding spaces and REM statements and by indenting where appropriate and necessary.

(a)
```
1 REM THIS PROGRAM DECIDES WHICH MOVIE WE WILL SEE
2 RANDOMIZE
3 N=INT(20*RND+6)
4 X=1
5 FORK=1TON
6 X=X*-1
7 IFK=NTHENPRINT"WEWILLSEE";ELSEPRINT
8 IFX>0THENPRINT"ANNIE"ELSEPRINT"POLTERGEIST"
9 NEXTK
10 END
```

(b)
```
1 DIMJ(10,10)
2 FORX=0TO9
3 PRINTTAB(X*4+6);X+1;
4 NEXTX
5 PRINT
6 FORX=0TO8
7 PRINTTAB(X*4+7);"--";
8 NEXTX
9 PRINTTAB(43);"--";
10 FORX=1TO10
11 FORY=1TO10
12 J(X,Y)=X+Y
13 IFF=0THENPRINTX;":";
14 PRINTTAB(F*4+6);J(X,Y);
15 F=F+1
16 IFF=10THENPRINT:F=0
17 NEXTY
18 NEXTX
19 END
```

6 MATHEMATICAL FUNCTIONS

This chapter covers the various mathematical functions that the computer can perform. The extent to which they can be useful to any individual depends on his or her mathematical background. Generally speaking, the functions presented here are primarily employed by mathematicians, scientists, and engineers.

Order of Operations

What is the value of 2+20/4? Should the 2 be added first to the 20 and then the division performed afterward, or should the 20 first be divided by 4 and then be increased by 2? The latter procedure is correct because division is carried out before addition. When parentheses are used, the operations in the innermost parentheses are completed first. For example, (2+20)/4 = 22/4 = 5.5.

The computer performs arithmetic operations in the same order as that employed by mathematicians. Quantities in parentheses are evaluated first (starting from the innermost), followed by raising to a power, then by multiplication and division, and finally by addition and subtraction. Operations of equal priority are carried out from left to right. For example:

6/3*2   The result is 4. Although the answer might seem to be 6/6=1, the computer starts at the left and performs the division first, then the result of the division is multiplied by 2.

3*(5 + 6)   The result is 33. The computer first adds 5 and 6 and then multiplies the sum by 3.

5 + (3*(6/2))   The result is 14. The computer first divides 6 by 2, the operation within the innermost parentheses. Next it multiplies that result by 3 and finally adds 5.

12 + 4/0	The result is an error message. The computer does not divide by zero.
2 ∧ 3 ∧ 2	The result is 64 just as it would be for (2 ∧ 3) ∧ 2. Again, the left-to-right rule is in operation. Remember that (∧) is used to raise to a power.

SQR

The SQR function calculates the positive square root of a number.

$$10 \text{ PRINT SQR}(14)$$

The square root of a number N is defined as that value which, when multiplied by itself, gives N. For instance, the square root of 36 is 6 because 6x6=36.

PROGRAM 6.1

This program illustrates the square root function.

```
10 FOR X = 1 TO 4
20      PRINT "The square root of"; X; "is"; SQR(X)
30 NEXT X
Ok
RUN
The square root of 1 is 1
The square root of 2 is 1.414214
The square root of 3 is 1.732051
The square root of 4 is 2
Ok
```

In the expression SQR(X), SQR is the function name and X is called the argument. With the SQR function, the argument may be any mathematical expression with a non-negative value. For example, SQR(3*X+5) is perfectly acceptable provided that the expression 3*X+5 produces a non-negative value.

Note that the argument of a function must be enclosed in parentheses. In its evaluation of a mathematical function, the computer first evaluates the argument and then the function, using the value previously obtained for the argument. Some functions have a limitation on the value of the argument. Such limitations will be indicated as the functions are introduced.

SGN and ABS

In some situations it may be necessary to know if a variable is positive or negative. The SGN function has only three possible values: 1, 0, and −1.

$$\text{SGN}(X) = 1 \qquad \text{if } X > 0$$
$$\text{SGN}(X) = 0 \qquad \text{if } X = 0$$
$$\text{SGN}(X) = -1 \qquad \text{if } X < 0$$

PROGRAM 6.2

This program finds the SGN (signum) of the numbers from 6 to −6, incrementing by −1.2.

```
10 FOR X = 6 TO -6 STEP -1.2
20       A = SGN(X)
30         PRINT "SGN("; X; ") =";A
40 NEXT X
Ok
RUN
SGN( 6 ) = 1
SGN( 4.8 ) = 1
SGN( 3.6 ) = 1
SGN( 2.4 ) = 1
SGN( 1.2 ) = 1
SGN( 0 ) = 0
SGN(-1.2 ) =-1
SGN(-2.4 ) =-1
SGN(-3.6 ) =-1
SGN(-4.8 ) =-1
SGN(-6 ) =-1
Ok
```

The ABS function can be used to find the absolute value of a number. The ABS function yields values according to the rule:

$$\text{ABS}(X) = X \qquad\qquad \text{if } X >= 0$$
$$\text{ABS}(X) = -1*X \qquad\qquad \text{if } X < 0$$

PROGRAM 6.3

This program illustrates the use of the ABS function.

```
10 FOR X = 6 TO -6 STEP -1.2
20      A = ABS(X)
30      PRINT A;
40 NEXT X
Ok
RUN
 6  4.8  3.6  2.4  1.2  0  1.2  2.4  3.6  4.8  6
Ok
```

FIX

The FIX function returns the integer portion of a number, that is, it truncates all digits to the right of a decimal point. The statement

$$N = FIX(2.41)$$

will assign N the value 2, truncating the decimal portion .41. Unlike the INT function, the FIX function does not return the next lower value of a number when the number is negative.

INT(5.01) = 5	FIX(5.01) = 5
INT(4.7) = 4	FIX(4.7) = 4
INT(−8.7) = −9	FIX(−8.7) = −8
INT(−6.2) = −7	FIX(−6.2) = −6

The FIX function is useful in determining the fractional portion of a number. The statement

$$N = ABS (X - FIX(X))$$

will assign N the fractional portion of X. For example, if X = 4.237, then N = ABS (4.237 − FIX(4.237)) = 0.237.

REVIEW

1. What is X when X = FIX(ABS(−12 + 6*SGN(−9 +9/3) + 1.8)−18.2)?

2. Write a program that will take a number N and print the fractional portion of N rounded to two decimal places.

```
Ok
RUN
? 18.648
INPUT: 18.648                    OUTPUT: .65
Ok
```

Trigonometric Functions: SIN, COS, TAN

The computer is able to find the values of several trigonometric functions. The functions SIN(X), COS(X) or TAN(X) will produce the value of the sine, cosine, or tangent of the angle X, where X is measured in radians. To convert an angle from degrees to radians, multiply it by 3.14159265 and then divide the result by 180 (180 degrees equals π radians).

PROGRAM 6.4

The following program illustrates these functions.

```
10 INPUT "Value"; A
20 X = A * 3.14159 / 180
30 PRINT A; "Degrees equals"; X; "Radians."
40 PRINT "SIN("; A; ") ="; SIN(X)
50 PRINT "COS("; A; ") ="; COS(X)
60 PRINT "TAN("; A; ") ="; TAN(X)
70 PRINT
80 GOTO 10

Ok
RUN
Value? 30
  30 Degrees equals .5235983 Radians.
SIN( 30 ) = .4999997
COS( 30 ) = .8660257
TAN( 30 ) = .5773496

Value? 45
  45 Degrees equals .7853975 Radians.
SIN( 45 ) = .7071064
COS( 45 ) = .7071072
TAN( 45 ) = .9999988

Value?
Break in 10
Ok
```

Note the rounding error that occurs in the output.

ATN

The only inverse trigonometric function supplied by the computer is the principal arctangent function ATN. The function ATN(X) is used to find the angle whose tangent is X. The value produced by the ATN function is in radians. Thus, the arctangent of 1 is $\pi/4$ radians = .785398163. To convert an angle from radians to degrees, multiply it by 180 and then divide the result by 3.14159265. The ATN function, just like the principal arctangent function in mathematics, gives values only between $-\pi/2$ and $\pi/2$ radians. There is no limitation on the value that the argument may assume.

PROGRAM 6.5

This program finds the angle whose tangent is entered and prints the result in degrees.

```
10 INPUT "Enter a tangent value"; T
20 R = ATN(T)
30 D = R * 180 / 3.14159
40 PRINT "The angle whose Tangent is"; T; "is"; D; "Degrees."
50 PRINT : GOTO 10
Ok
RUN
Enter a tangent value? 1
The angle whose Tangent is 1 is 45.00005 Degrees.

Enter a tangent value? 0
The angle whose Tangent is 0 is 0 Degrees.

Enter a tangent value? 0.57735
The angle whose Tangent is .57735 is 30.00002 Degrees.

Enter a tangent value?
Break in 10
Ok
```

To find the principal arcsine of a number, it is necessary to use the trigonometric identity:

$$\text{ARCSINE } (X) = \text{ARCTAN} \frac{X}{\sqrt{1-X^2}}$$

Therefore, to find the principal angle whose sine is X, the expression ATN(X/SQR(1−X↑2)) is used. This angle will be measured in radians and will be between $-\pi/2$ and $\pi/2$. The value of X, however, must be between −1 and 1, not inclusive.

To find the arccosine of X, use the expression ATN(SQR(1−X↑2)/X). This gives the angle which is between $-\pi/2$ and $\pi/2$ (whose cosine is X). In this expression, X must be between −1 and 1, inclusive, but not equal to 0.

PROGRAM 6.6

   This program finds the arcsine and arccosine of X in both radians and degrees.

```
10 INPUT "Value"; X
20 S = ATN(X / SQR(1-X^2))
30 S1 = S * 180 / 3.14159
40 C = ATN(SQR(1-X^2) / X)
50 C1 = C * 180 / 3.14159
60 PRINT "The angle whose Sine is"; X; "is"; S; "Radians."
70 PRINT "The angle whose Cosine is"; X; "is"; C; "Radians."
80 PRINT "The angle whose Sine is"; X; "is"; S1; "Degrees."
90 PRINT "The angle whose Cosine is"; X; "is"; C1; "Degrees."
100 PRINT : GOTO 10
Ok
RUN
Value? 0.5
The angle whose Sine is .5 is .5235988 Radians.
The angle whose Cosine is .5 is 1.047198 Radians.
The angle whose Sine is .5 is 30.00003 Degrees.
The angle whose Cosine is .5 is 60.00006 Degrees.

Value? 0.8777
The angle whose Sine is .8777 is 1.071041 Radians.
The angle whose Cosine is .8777 is .499755 Radians.
The angle whose Sine is .8777 is 61.36621 Degrees.
The angle whose Cosine is .8777 is 28.63388 Degrees.

Value?
Break in 10
Ok
```

Logarithms and the Exponential Function: LOG, EXP

   The LOG function can be used to find natural logarithms, that is, logarithms to the base e. To find the natural logarithm of X, LOG(X) is used. Do not confuse the natural logarithm with the common logarithm usually studied in a second year algebra course. The common logarithm, that is, logarithm to base 10, can be found from the natural logarithm by using the formula:

$$\log_{10} (X) = \frac{\ln(X)}{\ln(10)}$$

where ln(x) designates the natural logarithm of X. Therefore, to find $\log_{10}$ (X) simply use LOG(X)/LOG(10). The argument in the LOG function must always be positive.

   The function EXP(X) is used to find values of the exponential function, e^X, where e = 2.71828. This number is the same as the base of the natural logarithm function.

PROGRAM 6.7

This program illustrates the use of the above functions.

```
10 INPUT "Enter X"; X
20 PRINT "LN(X) ="; LOG(X)
30 IF X < 87 THEN PRINT "e raised to X =";EXP(X)
40 T = LOG(X) / LOG(10)
50 PRINT "The common logarithm of"; X; "is"; T
60 PRINT : GOTO 10

RUN
Enter X? 1
LN(X) = 0
e raised to X = 2.718282
The common logarithm of 1 is 0

Enter X? 0.01
LN(X) =-4.60517
e raised to X = 1.01005
The common logarithm of .01 is-2

Enter X? 10000
LN(X) = 9.210341
The common logarithm of 10000 is 4

Enter X? 0.525
LN(X) =-.644357
e raised to X = 1.690459
The common logarithm of .525 is-.2798407

Enter X?
Break in 10
Ok
```

DEF

Several standard functions, such as SQR, ABS, and LOG, have already been introduced in this chapter. In addition, the programmer can define other functions by using a DEF statement. The major advantage of DEF lies in the fact that the expression for the function need only be written once, even though the function can be evaluated at more than one location within the program. The form of a DEF statement is:

DEF FN <function name> (<variable name>) = <expression>

The function name may be any acceptable numeric variable name (e.g., FNA, FNF, FNG3). The variable name (i.e, the argument) following the function name must always appear within parentheses and may be any appropriate numeric variable.

In the following example,

$$10 \text{ DEF FNP}(X) = X \wedge 2 - 2*X - 1$$

P is the function name, X is the variable name, and X^2-2X-1 is the expression used to compute the function's value. For instance, when X = 5, FNP(X) = 14 because $5 \uparrow 2 - 2*5 - 1 = 14$.

PROGRAM 6.8

The following program evaluates the polynomial function FNP(X) several times.

```
Ok
LIST
10 DEF FNP(X) = X^2 - 2*X - 1
20 PRINT "X", "FNP(X)"
30 FOR A = 1 TO 5
40     PRINT A, FNP(A)
50 NEXT A
60 INPUT X
70 PRINT "The result of FNP("; X; ") IS "; FNP(X)
Ok
RUN
X                FNP(X)
 1               -2
 2               -1
 3                2
 4                7
 5               14
? -10
The result of FNP(-10 ) IS   119
Ok
```

When the function is evaluated at line 40, the variable in parentheses is A. When it is evaluated on line 70, the variable is X. The name of the variable in parentheses may be the same as or different from the variable name used in the DEF statement. Note also that if the DEF statement were not used, the formula on line 10 would have to appear twice (lines 40 and 70). Economy results from the fact that though the function is defined only once, it may be evaluated at any place within the program.

Another advantage obtained by the use of the DEF statement is that it can be easily retyped to define a different function. This is illustrated by re-running Program 6.8 with line 10 changed to:

```
10 DEF FNP(X) = X^3 - 5*X^2 + 1
Ok
RUN
X                  FNP(X)
 1                  -3
 2                  -11
 3                  -17
 4                  -15
 5                   1
? -10
The result of FNP(-10 ) IS -1499
Ok
```

String functions may also be defined using DEF. This technique is handy for simplifying certain string operations such as the addition of strings.

PROGRAM 6.9

This program illustrates how a user defined string function can be implemented.

```
Ok
LIST
10 DEF FNG$(A$) = A$ + " is yellow"
20 B$ = "The Sun"
30 PRINT FNG$(B$); " and "; FNG$("BIG Mellow"); "."
Ok
RUN
The Sun is yellow and BIG Mellow is yellow.
Ok
```

Note the output produced by line 30. FNG$() is evaluated twice, first with "The Sun" and then with "BIG Mellow".

User defined functions may have more than one variable within the parentheses. For example, the statement

$$DEF\ FNR(A,B) = RND(B-A+1) + A - 1$$

defines the function FNR(A,B) which returns a random integer between A and B, inclusive. The statement

$$DEF\ FNC\$ (X\$,Y\$,Z\$) = X\$ + "," + Y\$ + "," + Z\$$$

defines a function which combines three string variables, and inserts commas between each item.

PROGRAM 6.10

This program illustrates several multivariable user defined functions.

```
10 RANDOMIZE
20 DEF FNR(A,B) = INT(RND*(B-A)+A)
30 DEF FNW$(X$,Y$,Z$) = X$ +", " + Y$ + ", or " + Z$
100 REM
110 REM    Print a few random numbers using FNR()
120 FOR K = 1 TO 4
130      S = INT(25*RND+1)-12 : T = INT(75*RND+1) + S
140      PRINT "A random number between "; S; "and"; T;
150      PRINT TAB(38); "is"; FNR(S,T)
160 NEXT K
170 X = 18 : Y = 25
180 PRINT FNR(X,Y), FNR(10,11), FNR(X,X*2), FNR(-5,-2)
200 REM
210 REM Use a string function now...
220 PRINT : PRINT FNW$("This", "That", "The Other Thing")
230 R$ = "KAHN" : V$ = "Mr. Spock"
240 PRINT "Who will defeat: "; FNW$(R$,V$,"a Klingon!")
250 J$ = FNW$("Crystal","Alexis","Blake") + " will move."
260 PRINT J$

Ok
RUN
Random number seed (-32768 to 32767)? 234
A random number between  5 and 78    is 66
A random number between  9 and 41    is 31
A random number between  4 and 70    is 44
A random number between  0 and 57    is 33
 19              10              30              -3

This, That, or The Other Thing
Who will defeat: KAHN, Mr. Spock, or a Klingon!
Crystal, Alexis, or Blake will move.
Ok
```

REVIEW

3. Write a program that will produce the following output. Two user defined functions should be used: one to convert degrees to radians; the other to convert radians to degrees.

```
RUN
DEGREES? 30
That is .5235983 radians.

RADIANS? .785375
That is 44.99871 degrees.
Ok
```

EXERCISES

PART A

1. When a number is input have the computer generate the following output. Be sure to prevent a negative input.

        RUN
        ? 4
        N = 4   SQUARE ROOTS = + OR − 2

2. Write a program which prints the integers from 121 to 144, inclusive, and their respective square roots. Label each column of the output.

3. Perform each of the following computations on paper. Check your results by using immediate mode on the computer.

    (A) 3↑2↑3   (B) 5 - 4↑2
    (C) 3*(5 + 16)   (D) 5 + 3 * 6/2
    (E) 640/10/2 * 5   (F) 5 + 3 * 4 - 1
    (G) 2↑3↑2   (H) 2↑(3↑2)
    (I) 64/4 * 0.5 + ((1 + 5) * 2↑3) * 1/(2 * 4)

4. Input a number N. If N is zero, print 0. Otherwise, print ABS(N)/N. What does the program do?

5. Input a number N, and print the product of SGN(N) and N. What does this program do?

6. Input a number N, square it, and print the square root of the result. What should the program produce?

7. Print a table consisting of 2 columns with headings showing each angle in radians and degrees. The angles in radians are to be 0, .25, .5, .75, . . ., 3.0. Remember that 180° = 3.14159 radians.

8. Input an angle in degrees and convert it to a fraction of a revolution (1 rev. = 360°) and to radians.

9. Input an angle in degrees. Of the three functions sine, cosine, and tangent, print the value of the one which has the greatest value.

10. For angles from 0° to 180° (at intervals of 10°) print the angle in degrees, the sine, the cosine, and the sum of their squares in columns with headings. What patterns emerge?

11. Input two numbers (A, B). Print the quantity F(B)-F(A), given that $F(X) = 9X^3 - 7X^2 + 4X - 1$.

12. Input a number N. Print the values of F(N) and F(F(N)), where F(X) = 20 * SQR (ABS(X))—10 * SGN (X) + 5 * INT (X).

13. Print a table (with headings) of X, the natural logarithm of X, and the exponential function of X for X = 1 to 15.

14. Print a table (with headings) of X, the logarithm of X to the base 10, and 10 raised to the power X for X = 1 to 15.

PART B
15. What is the exact output for the following program? Check by running the program.

```
10 READ A,B,C,D
20 PRINT SQR(A),INT(B),SQR(INT(C)),INT(SQR(D))
30 DATA 25,-3.4,9.7,24
```

16. Print the square roots of the integers from 50 to 60, inclusive.

17. What is the exact output for the following program? Check by running the program.

```
10 DEF FNF(N) = 3 * N - 6
20 FOR X = -4 TO 6 STEP 2
30    IF FNF(X) > 0 THEN PRINT "FNF(";X;") IS POSITIVE"
40    IF FNF(X) = 0 THEN PRINT "FNF(";X;") IS ZERO"
50    IF FNF(X) < 0 THEN PRINT "FNF(";X;") IS NEGATIVE"
60 NEXT X
```

18. Input a number, and print the square root, sign, log, and sine of the number. For example:

```
RUN
? 16
SQR( 16 ) = 4
SGN( 16 ) = 1
LOG( 16 ) = 2.772589
SIN( 16 ) =-.2879034
```

19. What is the exact output for the following program? Check by running the program.

```
10 FOR X = -3 TO 4
20    READ A
30    PRINT SGN(X) * ABS(X)
40 NEXT X
50 DATA 3,-5,1,6,-2,4,-9,5
```

20. Using three user-defined functions, have the computer evaluate the following for the integers from -10 to 10.

$$X^2 + 3X + 2$$

$$LOG(X^2 + 1) - X$$

$$ATN(SIN(X))$$

21. Write a program to convert from polar to rectangular coordinates (i.e., from (r,θ) to (X,Y)).

6.14

22. If two functions, f and g, are inverse to each other, the following relations hold: f(g(x)) = x and g(f(x)) = x.

(a) Tabulate the values of the following quantities for X = -5 to 10: X, EXP(X), LOG(EXP(X)).
(b) Print a table for X = 1 to 151 of X, LOG(X), EXP(LOG(X)), using STEP 10.
(c) Do EXP and LOG appear to be inverse to each other?

23. Produce your own sequence of random numbers without using the RND command. To do this let X vary from 1 to 100 in steps of 1. Obtain SIN(X) and multiply this by 1000, calling the absolute value of the product Y. Divide INT(Y) by 16, and let the remainder R serve as your random number. Hint: the remainder of A ÷ B is A/B—INT (A/B).

24. Six year old Dennis the Menace has decided to invest 50¢ in the Last Chew Bubble Gum Company. Starting with the 11th year, he withdraws 5¢ at the beginning of each year. His money earns 8% interest compounded continually. The formula for interest compounded continually is $P = P_0 e^{it}$, where t is the elapsed time in years, P_0 is the initial deposit, P is the amount at time t, and i is the interest rate. In this case the formula would be $P = P_0 e^{.08t}$. How much is Dennis's deposit worth after 50 years?

25. Use the SIN function to generate the following:

```
RUN
                                        SHAZAM!
                                          SHAZAM!
                                            SHAZAM!
                                             SHAZAM!
                                              SHAZAM!
                                               SHAZAM!
                                                SHAZAM!
                                                SHAZAM!
                                                SHAZAM!
                                                SHAZAM!
                                               SHAZAM!
                                              SHAZAM!
                                             SHAZAM!
                                           SHAZAM!
                                          SHAZAM!
                                        SHAZAM!
                                      SHAZAM!
                                    SHAZAM!
                                  SHAZAM!
                                SHAZAM!
                              SHAZAM!
                            SHAZAM!
                           SHAZAM!
                          SHAZAM!
                          SHAZAM!
                          SHAZAM!
                           SHAZAM!
                            SHAZAM!
                              SHAZAM!
                                SHAZAM!
                                  SHAZAM!
```

26. (a) Write a program which will solve a triangle (compute the unknown sides and angles) if two sides and the included angle are input. Modify the program to solve for the unknown sides and angles for the following situations:
   (b) input two angles and any side,
   (c) input three sides.

SUBROUTINES AND ERROR HANDLING

Writing long, complex programs may require special programming techniques. It is often helpful to divide these programs into sections, called subroutines. Subroutines are useful because they perform a specified task and may be accessed from anywhere in the program. A long program may be divided into a main section and a series of subroutines. The main section directs the order in which the subroutines do their specialized jobs. This type of organization usually reduces the size of a program because the lines needed to perform a certain task have only to be placed once in a program, even though the task may be performed several times.

GOSUB—RETURN

In the case of programs whose various portions are repeated at different places, it may be efficient to use a subroutine. A subroutine is entered by the statement GOSUB <line number> and exited by the statement RETURN. For example:

```
10 ........
20   GOSUB 200
30 ........
40 ........
200 ........┐
210 ........│
220 ........│
230   RETURN┘
999   END
```

The skeleton program illustrates the use of a subroutine. At line 20 the program jumps to the subroutine which begins at line 200, executes the subroutine, and then returns from line 230 to the body of the program at line 30. It is legal to use more than one RETURN statement within a subroutine. You should remember that the computer always returns to the first statement after the GOSUB statement which caused the subroutine to be executed. The only difference between GOSUB and the GOTO statement is that GOSUB permits the use of RETURN whereas GOTO does not. Subroutines are usually placed towards the bottom of a program. They may be written so that one subroutine can access another.

PROGRAM 7.1

Given the numbers of pennies, nickels, dimes, and quarters as input, this program will output the total amount of money represented by these coins. One subroutine processes and reports the amount of money involved for each of the four types of coins.

```
10 A$ = "PENNIES" : V = 1 : REM Descripton & Value
20 GOSUB 200
30 A$ = "NICKELS" : V = 5
40 GOSUB 200
50 A$ = "DIMES" : V = 10
60 GOSUB 200
70 A$ = "QUARTERS" : V = 25
80 GOSUB 200
90 PRINT "The Total value of the coins is $"; T/100
100 END
200 REM   Subroutine
210 PRINT "Number of "; A$;
220 INPUT N
230 PRINT N; A$; " ="; N*V; "Cents"
240 T = T + N*V
250 RETURN
Ok
RUN
Number of PENNIES? 4
 4 PENNIES = 4 Cents
Number of NICKELS? 9
 9 NICKELS = 45 Cents
Number of DIMES? 3
 3 DIMES = 30 Cents
Number of QUARTERS? 6
 6 QUARTERS = 150 Cents
The Total value of the coins is $ 2.29
Ok
```

Line 10 assigns the type (A$) and value (V) of the first coin. Line 20 causes a jump to the subroutine, which begins at line 200 where the number of coins is input. Line 210 prints information about the particular coin being considered, and line 240 adds its contribution to the previous total value of all coins up to this point. Line 250 returns the program back to the line following the most recently used GOSUB statement. This entire process, beginning at line 200, repeats itself three more times, and then the dollar total is printed. What would happen if line 100 were deleted?

REVIEW

1. Write a program where names are input and then printed. If DONALD is input use a subroutine to underline the name.

```
RUN
Name? MARY
MARY
Name? SHERRY
SHERRY
Name? DONALD
DONALD
------
Name?
Break in 10
Ok
```

ON—GOTO

The GOTO statement allows a program to jump to a single specified line. The ON—GOTO statement allows jumps to one of several lines, depending on the value of a numeric variable at the time the statement is encountered. This statement takes the form:

ON <variable> GOTO <list of line numbers>

For example:

50 ON X GOTO 100, 120, 140, 160

If X = 1, the program jumps to line 100; if X = 2, it jumps to line 120, and so on. Note that X should not be less than one or greater than the number of line numbers in the list.

PROGRAM 7.2

This program simulates the random path taken by a mouse through the following maze:

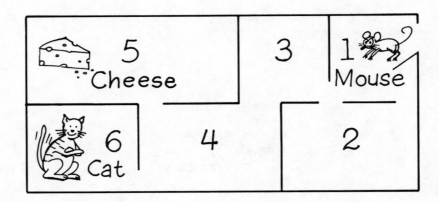

Once the mouse enters the maze, the door is shut. The mouse wanders about until it either finds the cheese or stumbles upon the cat.

```
90 RANDOMIZE
100 PRINT 1;
110 X = INT(RND*2) + 1
120 ON X GOTO 200,300
200 PRINT 2;
210 X = INT(RND*2) + 1
220 ON X GOTO 100,300
300 PRINT 3;
310 X = INT(RND*3) + 1
320 ON X GOTO 100,200,400
400 PRINT 4;
410 X = INT(RND*3) + 1
420 ON X GOTO 300,500,600
500 PRINT 5
510 PRINT "The mouse is gorging itself!"
520 END
600 PRINT 6
610 PRINT "The cat has been awakened by its lunch."
Ok
RUN
Random number seed (-32768 to 32767)? 17034
 1  3  2  3  1  2  3  2  3  4  6
The cat has been awakened by its lunch.
Ok
```

At line 100, the program prints a 1 to indicate that the mouse is in room #1. Line 110 randomly picks either the number 1 or the number 2. The ON GOTO statement at line 120 sends program execution to line 200 if X = 1, and to 300 if X = 2; lines 200 and 300 correspond to rooms 2 and 3, respectively. Once in one of the other rooms, the program prints the room number and decides where the mouse will go from there. Execution continues until the mouse finds itself either in room 5 or room 6.

REVIEW

2. Write a program to draw five cards from a deck. The computer picks two random numbers, the first is between 1 and 4 inclusive, and the second between 1 and 13 inclusive. An ON GOTO statement should use the first number to pick each suit. The second represents the card's value within the suit.

```
RUN
Random number seed (-32768 to 32767)? -32613
Card 1 is the 4 of Diamonds
Card 2 is the 11 of Spades
Card 3 is the 6 of Spades
Card 4 is the 13 of Hearts
Card 5 is the 8 of Clubs
Ok
```

ON—GOSUB

The ON—GOSUB statement operates in much the same way as the ON—GOTO statement. If there are a number of subroutines in a program, they can be called using the ON—GOSUB statement.

50 ON X GOSUB 300, 400, 500

If X = 1, the program jumps to the first subroutine at line 300; if X = 2, to the second subroutine at line 400; and if X = 3, to the third subroutine at line 500. When the subroutine is completed, the RETURN statement directs the program back to the first statement after line 50.

Using Subroutines to Structure Programs

Subroutines are useful both in reducing the amount of code required to write a program and in breaking a program down into its separate functions to help clarify its structure.

PROGRAM 7.3

This program tests a student on addition, subtraction, multiplication and division. Without the use of subroutines much of the code would have to be repeated four times.

```
10 PRINT "   You will be asked 2 questions on Addition (1),"
11 PRINT "Subtraction (2), Multiplication (3), or Division (4),"
12 PRINT "and be given 2 tries to answer each one correctly. You"
13 PRINT "can choose which type of question you want by"
14 PRINT "responding with the appropriate number."
15 PRINT
18 RANDOMIZE
20 INPUT "WHAT TYPE DO YOU WANT"; N
30 FOR X = 1 TO 2
40     A = INT(RND*10) + 1
50     B = INT(RND*10) + 1
60     ON N GOSUB 200,300,400,500
70     FOR Y = 1 TO 2
80         INPUT "What is your answer"; D
90         IF D = C THEN PRINT "Correct!" : GOTO 130
100        PRINT "Your answer is WRONG!"
110    NEXT Y
120    PRINT "You are WRONG a SECOND time! The answer is"; C
130    PRINT
140 NEXT X
150 GOTO 20
160 REM
170 REM
200 REM Addition
210 PRINT "WHAT IS"; A; "+"; B
220 C = A + B
230 RETURN
240 REM
250 REM
300 REM Subtraction
310 PRINT "WHAT IS"; A; "-"; B
320 C = A - B
330 RETURN
340 REM
350 REM
400 REM Multiplication
410 PRINT "WHAT IS"; A; "*"; B
420 C = A * B
430 RETURN
440 REM
450 REM
500 REM Division
510 PRINT "WHAT IS"; A; "/"; B
520 C = A / B
530 RETURN
```

```
RUN
     You will be asked 2 questions on Addition (1),
Subtraction (2), Multiplication (3), or Division (4),
and be given 2 tries to answer each one correctly. You
can choose which type of question you want by
responding with the appropriate number.

Random number seed (-32768 to 32767)? 42
WHAT TYPE DO YOU WANT? 3
WHAT IS 10 * 5
What is your answer? 50
Correct!

WHAT IS 3 * 5
What is your answer? 8
Your answer is WRONG!
What is your answer? 16
Your answer is WRONG!
You are WRONG a SECOND time! The answer is 15

WHAT TYPE DO YOU WANT? 2
WHAT IS 2 - 10
What is your answer? -8
Correct!

WHAT IS 5 - 8
What is your answer? -2
Your answer is WRONG!
What is your answer? -3
Correct!

WHAT TYPE DO YOU WANT? 1
WHAT IS 8 + 5
What is your answer? 13
Correct!

WHAT IS 1 + 8
What is your answer? 9
Correct!

WHAT TYPE DO YOU WANT?
Break in 20
Ok
```

ON ERROR GOTO and RESUME

If an error can be anticipated before a program is run, it is possible to "trap" the error
by using the ON ERROR GOTO statement which allows the program to continue execution.
When an error is encountered, this statement suppresses the printing of an error message

and causes the program to jump to the specified line. For example,

30 ON ERROR GOTO 60

sends the program to line 60 *when* an error occurs.

Examples of two frequently encountered errors are that of dividing a number by zero or of taking the square root of a negative number. To trap these errors the ON ERROR GOTO statement must be placed in the program before the error occurs. Then, if there is an error, the program will jump to the specified line.

The RESUME statement performs two functions after an error has been trapped. It returns the program to the point where the error occurred and resets the error trap so that new errors may be trapped. If the RESUME statement is not used, the program will continue from the point where it was sent by the ON ERROR GOTO statement and will therefore be unable to trap any future errors. It is important to correct an error, before executing the RESUME statement; otherwise, the error may occur again and may put the program into an infinite loop.

PROGRAM 7.4

This program finds the square roots of a number supplied by the user.

```
10 REM    Find the square roots of X,
20 REM    where X is entered by the user
30 REM
40 ON ERROR GOTO 100
50 INPUT "What is X"; X
60 R = SQR(X)
70 PRINT "The square roots of"; X; "are  +";R; " and  -";R
80 PRINT : GOTO 50
100 PRINT "The square root of "; X; "is an Imaginary Root!"
110 X = ABS(X)
120 RESUME
130 END

Ok
RUN
What is X? 4
The square roots of 4 are  + 2   and  - 2

What is X? -25
The square root of -25 is an Imaginary Root!
The square roots of 25 are  + 5   and  - 5

What is X? 2
The square roots of 2 are  + 1.414214   and  - 1.414214

What is X?
Break in 50
Ok
```

Note that if an error occurs, the program will assign a value of one to N and D and then resume.

$$RESUME <line\ number>$$

instructs the computer to continue execution at the specified line. Changing line 120 to

$$120\ RESUME\ 20$$

and deleting line 110 eliminates the need of reassigning N and D values before resuming.

$$RESUME\ NEXT$$

instructs the computer to continue execution at the statement immediately following the one where the error occurred. In Program 7.4, the line

$$120\ RESUME\ NEXT$$

will send the program to line 40 when executed.

ERR and ERL

Program 7.4 has the drawback of handling all errors alike whether they are anticipated or not. The ERR and ERL functions allow the program to be more discriminating in handling errors.

```
RUN
Range? -2,4
Printer is out of paper!
Press <return> when Ready?
VALUE          ROOT
-2             Imaginary
-1             Imaginary
 0             0
 1             1
 2             1.414214
 3             1.732051
 4             2
```

ERR returns a number that identifies the specific error that has occurred.

20 PRINT ERR

will return a number corresponding to an error listed below.

Code	Explanation	Code	Explanation
1	NEXT without FOR	26	For without NEXT
2	Syntax error	27	Out of paper
3	RETURN without GOSUB	29	WHILE without WEND
4	Out of data	30	WEND without WHILE
5	Illegal function call	50	FIELD overflow
6	Overflow	51	Internal error
7	Out of memory	52	Bad file number
8	Undefined line number	53	File not found
9	Subcript out of range	54	Bad file mode
10	Duplicate Definition	55	File already open
11	Division by zero	57	Device I/O Error
12	Illegal direct	58	File already exists
13	Type mismatch	61	Disk full
14	Out of string space	62	Input past end
15	String too long	63	Bad record number
16	String formula too complex	64	Bad file name
17	Can't continue	66	Direct statement to file
18	Undefined user definition	67	Too many files
19	No RESUME	68	Device Unavailable
20	RESUME without error	69	Communication buffer overflow
21	Unprintable error	70	Disk Write Protect
22	Missing operand	71	Disk not Ready
23	Line buffer overflow	72	Disk Media Error
24	Device Timeout	73	Advanced Feature
25	Device Fault	—	Unprintable error

ERL returns a number equal to the line number where the most recent error occurred. For example,

30 PRINT ERL

PROGRAM 7.5

This program can respond correctly to two different types of errors—out of paper and the square root of a negative number.

```
10 REM   Print on the printer the positive square roots
20 REM   of the integers between A and B,
30 REM   where A and B are supplied by the user.
40 REM
50 ON ERROR GOTO 200
60 INPUT "Range"; A, B
70 LPRINT "VALUE", "ROOT"
80 FOR W = A TO B
90     D = SQR(W)
100    LPRINT W,D
110 NEXT W
120 END
200 IF ERR = 5 THEN LPRINT W, "Imaginary" : RESUME 110
210 IF ERR = 27 THEN PRINT "Printer is out of paper!" :
                    INPUT "Press <return> when Ready"; Z$ :
                    RESUME
220 PRINT "?Error number"; ERR; "occurred at Line"; ERL : RESUME NEXT
Ok
RUN
Range? -2,4
Printer is out of paper!
Press <return> when Ready?
VALUE           ROOT
-2              Imaginary
-1              Imaginary
 0               0
 1               1
 2               1.414214
 3               1.732051
 4               2
```

The statement

55 ON ERROR GOTO 0

nullifies any previous ON ERROR GOTO statement. If this line were included in Program 7.5 the errors would no longer be trapped.

PART A

1. Have the computer produce the printout below. Use a subroutine to print out "PART" and the appropriate number.

```
RUN

PART 1
************************************************
PART 2
!            !            !
PART 3
ABABABABABABABABABABABABABABABABABABABABABABAB
Ok
```

2. Have the computer pick a random integer from 1 to 4 which will determine whether the prize to be awarded will be a ball, balloon, toy car, or candy bar.

3. Input an integer from 1 to 4. The integer should cause one of the following four suggestions to be printed.

DON'T LET YOUR COMPUTER TURN TO TRASH.
DON'T LET BUGS GET IN YOUR TRASH.
STUDY HARD AND YOU WON'T NEED A TRUSS.
NEVER PLAY WITH TRASH.

4. What is the exact output for the following program?

```
10 READ X
20 ON X GOTO 30,40,50,60,70,80,100
30 PRINT "MERRILY, "; : GOTO 10
40 PRINT "ROW, "; : GOTO 10
50 PRINT "YOUR BOAT" : GOTO 10
60 PRINT "GENTLY DOWN THE STREAM" : GOTO 10
70 PRINT "LIFE IS BUT A DREAM" : GOTO 10
80 PRINT : GOTO 10
90 DATA 2,2,2,3,4,1,1,1,1,6,5,7
100 END
```

5. (a) Give the exact order in which the lines of the following program are executed.
   (b) If line 80 is changed to:

$$80 \ \text{DATA} \ 3,0,4,-5,-1,-8,1,5,999$$

what will be the output?

```
10 READ X
20 IF X = 999 THEN 90
30 ON SGN(X) + 2 GOSUB 50,60,70
40 GOTO 10
50 N = N + 1 : RETURN
60 Z = Z + 1 : RETURN
70 P = P + 1 : RETURN
80 DATA 6,-1,0,999
90 PRINT "N =";N, "Z =";Z, "P =";P
100 END
```

6. (a) Give the exact order in which the lines of the following program are executed.
   (b) If line 90 were changed to:

$$90 \ DATA \ 1,8,-2,5,-3,-6,2,4,-7,0$$

what would the output be?

```
10 READ X
20 IF X = 0 THEN 95
30 GOSUB 60
40 T = T + X
50 GOTO 10
60 IF X < 0 THEN 80
70 P = P + X
80 RETURN
90 DATA 5,2,-9,0,3,5
95 PRINT "T =";T,"P =";P
100 END
```

7. Write a program which reads the dimensions of a triangle from a DATA statement and prints its area and perimeter if it is a right triangle. The program should call a subroutine to check whether the triangle is a right triangle or not.

8. Let X and Y be the coordinates of a point in a plane. Write a program which randomly picks X and Y, each as an integer from -5 and 5, inclusive. The user of the program is to guess X and Y, with the guesses being called X1 and Y1. A subroutine must be used to print the distance between the guessed point and the actual point after each guess. The user is to be given 3 guesses and, if unsuccessful, is then to be given the value of X as well as 2 more tries to guess Y.

9. Isolated in his ski-lodge in the Swiss Alps, Bjorn Rich oftens gets his mail late. As a result the statements from his Swiss bank account rarely arrive on time. To solve this problem, write a program to assist Bjorn in keeping his account up to date. Have three subroutines which take care of deposits, withdrawals, and the interest (5¾% compounded quarterly).

```
RUN
WITHDRAWAL(1),DEPOSIT(2), OR CALCULATE INTEREST(3)? 2
HOW MUCH WOULD YOU LIKE TO DEPOSIT? 500.00
YOUR BALANCE STANDS AT 500 DOLLARS.
WITHDRAWAL(1),DEPOSIT(2), OR CALCULATE INTEREST(3)? 3
HOW MANY MONTHS SINCE LAST CALCULATION? 5
YOUR BALANCE STANDS AT 507.1875 DOLLARS.
WITHDRAWAL(1),DEPOSIT(2), OR CALCULATE INTEREST(3)? 1
HOW MUCH WOULD YOU LIKE TO WITHDRAW? 175.50
YOUR BALANCE STANDS AT 331.6875 DOLLARS.
WITHDRAWAL(1),DEPOSIT(2), OR CALCULATE INTEREST(3)? 3
HOW MANY MONTHS SINCE LAST CALCULATION? 1
TOO SOON
YOUR BALANCE STANDS AT 331.6875 DOLLARS.
WITHDRAWAL(1),DEPOSIT(2), OR CALCULATE INTEREST(3)?
Break in 10
Ok
```

10. The area of any triangle may be found from Hero's formula;

$$AREA = \sqrt{S(S-A)(S-B)(S-C)}$$

where A, B, and C are the length of each side of the triangle and S is the semiperimeter. S = (A+B+C)/2. Write a program that uses Hero's formula in a subroutine to calculate the area of a triangle.

11. Write a program that prints all the results of 10 divided by the log of all even integers between 20 and 0 inclusive. Your program should trap the error that occurs when you try calculating log(0).

12. Write a program that uses the Quadratic Formula: $\dfrac{-b \pm \sqrt{b^2 - 4ac}}{2a}$

to find the roots of an equation. Input a,b,c and have the computer print the two roots. Your program should have an error trap for the error that might occur when the computer attempts to take the square root of a negative number. When this situation arises have the computer print "roots are imaginary."

COLOR GRAPHICS

Graphics are useful for simplifying the presentation and analysis of large bodies of data. Relationships hidden in a mass of information are often uncovered when the information is presented in graphical form. This chapter introduces the statements needed for producing graphics and shows how graphics programs utilize them.

The IBM Color/Graphics Monitor Adapter provides three modes for displaying data: text mode, medium resolution mode, and high resolution mode. The text mode allows character data (letters, digits, etc.) to be displayed in a variety of colors and backgrounds. The medium resolution mode provides a graphing area which is divided into 200 rows. Each row is further subdivided into 320 points which may be individually referenced. The high resolution mode divides the graphing area into 200 rows, but each row is subdivided into 640 points. Unfortunately, only black and white points may be plotted in the high resolution mode.

On the IBM Personal Computer, output is normally directed to the Monochrome Display. It is possible to direct output to the Color/Graphics Monitor, but no single command is provided for this.

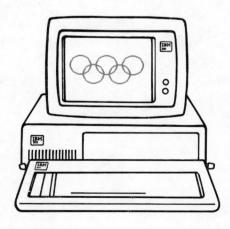

PROGRAM 8.1

The following program must be used to switch from the Monochrome Display to the Color/Graphics Monitor.

```
10 REM SWITCH TO COLOR DISPLAY
20 DEF SEG = 0
30 POKE &H410, (PEEK(&H410) AND &HCF) OR &H10
40 SCREEN 1,0,0,0 : SCREEN 0 : WIDTH 40
50 LOCATE ,,1,6,7 : DEF SEG : END
```

PROGRAM 8.2

This program is used to switch output from the Color/Graphics Monitor back to the Monochrome Display.

```
10 REM SWITCH TO MONOCHROME DISPLAY
20 DEF SEG = 0
30 POKE &H410, (PEEK(&H410) OR &H30)
40 SCREEN 0 : WIDTH 40 : WIDTH 80
50 LOCATE ,,1,12,13 : DEF SEG : END
```

Once a display unit has been selected by calling one of the previous programs, all output will be directed to that display.

SCREEN

When the Color/Graphics Monitor is being used, it is necessary to select the display mode: text mode, medium resolution graphics, or high resolution graphics. The statement,

SCREEN <mode>, <burst>

will set the screen attributes of the Color/Graphics Monitor as follows:

mode	meaning	burst
0	Text Mode	0 = disable color 1 = enable color
1	Medium Resolution Graphics Mode	0 = enable color 1 = disable color
2	High Resolution Graphics Mode	no effect

For example, the statement

$$50 \text{ SCREEN } 1,0$$

will select medium resolution graphics with color enabled on the Color/Graphics Monitor. The statement

$$70 \text{ SCREEN } 2$$

will switch the Color/Grahpics Monitor to the high resolution mode. The 'burst' is not needed since high resolution mode allows only black and white images.

COLOR

The COLOR statement is used to set the color characteristics of the Color/Graphics Monitor after the SCREEN statement has been used. The syntax of the COLOR statement depends upon whether text mode or graphics mode is in effect, as set by the SCREEN statement.

COLOR TABLE

0	Black	8	Gray
1	Blue	9	Light Blue
2	Green	10	Light Green
3	Cyan	11	Light Cyan
4	Red	12	Light Red
5	Magenta	13	Light Magenta
6	Brown	14	Yellow
7	White	15	Bright White

COLOR (Text Mode)

The text mode is used for displaying letters, numbers, and all the special characters in the regular character set. It is not used for displaying graphics.

In this mode, the COLOR statement is used to select 1 of 16 foreground colors, 1 of 8 background colors, and 1 of 16 border colors. The general form of the COLOR statement in the text mode is:

COLOR <foreground>,<background>,<border>

The 'foreground' selects the color from the Color Table in which the text will be displayed. Characters can be made to blink by adding 16 to this value. For example, selecting a foreground color of 4 will display the text in red. A foreground color of 20 will display text in flashing red.

The 'background' color may be 1 of 8 values (0-7) from the Color Table. The 'border' color selects the color of the edges of the display screen. Any one of the 16 available colors may be selected for the border. For example, the statement

60 COLOR 4, 9, 6

will select a light blue background with a brown border. Characters will appear in red.

COLOR (Graphics Mode)

The COLOR statement is used to select 1 of 16 background colors from the COLOR TABLE and 1 of 2 color palettes in the medium resolution graphics mode. It may not be used in the high resolution mode. There is no separate border color. The general form of the COLOR statement in graphics mode is:

COLOR <background>, <palette>

Each palette has 3 colors which may be selected from plotting points and lines. The programmer may select 1 of 2 palettes as follows:

	Palette 0	Palette 1
(1)	Green	Cyan
(2)	Red	Magenta
(3)	Brown	White

For example, the statement

110 COLOR 1, 0

will select the background color blue. When plotting points and lines on the Color/Graphics Monitor, 1 of 4 colors may be used: three from the preselected palette, plus the background color. If the preselected palette is 0, then lines and points may be plotted in green, red, brown, or the background color. The statement

145 COLOR 8, 1

will select a gray background and color palette 1. Data may then be plotted in cyan, magenta, white, or gray.

PSET

The PSET statement is used to plot a single point on the Color/Graphics Monitor. The monitor must be placed in Graphics mode using the SCREEN statement prior to using PSET. The general form of the PSET statement is:

$$PSET \ (X,Y),<color>$$

The coordinates (X,Y) specify the location on the screen to be used for plotting the point, where X is the horizontal position and Y is the vertical position. In medium resolution mode, X may have values between 0 and 319, and Y may have values between 0 and 199, inclusive.

The 'color' value specifies which color will be plotted based on the palette previously selected with the COLOR statement.

Color	Palette 0	Palette 1
0	(Use background color)	
1	Green	Cyan
2	Red	Magenta
3	Brown	White

For example,

```
200 SCREEN 1, 0
210 COLOR 9, 0
220 PSET (250, 125), 2
```

will plot a red point at coordinates (250, 125) on the medium resolution screen. Remember that only four colors are available for plotting as determined by the preselected palette.

PROGRAM 8.3

This program draws a vertical line from (30, 10) to (30, 120) and then erases it by setting each point to the background color.

```
10 SCREEN 1,0
20 COLOR 2,0 : REM Green background, Palette 0
30 FOR Y = 10 TO 120
40     PSET (30,Y),2 : REM Plot a point
50 NEXT Y
60 REM Now erase line just plotted
70 FOR Y = 10 TO 120
80     PSET (30,Y),0 : REM Erase a point
90 NEXT Y
100 SCREEN 0,1 : COLOR 7,0,0
```

When using PSET in the high resolution mode, X may have values between 0 and 639; Y may have values between 0 and 199. The 'color' may either be 0 to indicate black or 1 to indicate white. For example,

```
40 SCREEN 2
50 PSET (450, 100), 1
```

will plot a single white point at coordinates (450, 100) on the high resolution screen.

LINE

The LINE statement is used to plot a single line on the Color/Graphic Monitor. The general form of the LINE statement is:

LINE (X1, Y1) - (X2, Y2), <color>

This statement will draw a line from coordinates (X1, Y1) to (X2, Y2) using the 'color' chosen from the previously selected palette of colors. For example,

```
300 COLOR 9, 1
310 LINE (10, 40) - (120, 165), 2
```

will plot a magenta line from coordinates (10, 40) to (120, 165) on the medium resolution screen.

In high resolution mode, a 'color' of 0 indicates a black line while a 'color' of 1 indicates a white line.

If the first coordinates are omitted in either medium or high resolution mode, the line produced is drawn from the last point references (i.e. by LINE, PSET, etc.). For example,

```
230 COLOR 0, 0
240 PSET (40, 75), 1
250 LINE - (280, 112), 1
```

will plot a green line from coordinates (40, 75) to (280, 112).

The LINE statement can also be used to draw a rectangular box on the Color/Graphics Monitor. The statement

LINE (X1, Y1) - (X2, Y2), <color>, B

will draw a box where (X1, Y1) and (X2, Y2) are the coordinates for two opposite corners of the box.

Rather than just drawing the outline of the box, the box may be filled in with the selected color by using the statement:

LINE (X1, Y1) - (X2, Y2), <color>, BF

PROGRAM 8.4

This program illustrates the various features of the LINE statement.

```
10 REM Print a figure using LINE
20 SCREEN 1,0 : COLOR 8,0
30 LINE (40,10) - (90,10),2 : LINE - (70,50),1
40 LINE - (10,50),2 : LINE - (40,10),1
50 LINE (70,50) - (40,10),2
60 REM Plot a rectangle
70 LINE (30,80) - (140,110),1,B
80 REM Plot a filled-in box
90 LINE (70,100) - (110,135),2,BF
100 REM Draw another box, overlapping the 1st two
110 LINE (90,115) - (10,85),2,B
Ok
RUN
```

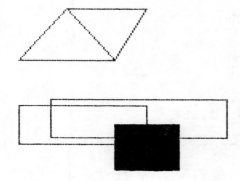

REVIEW

1. Write a program that will allow a single word to be entered. The computer should then clear the screen and print the word in the center of the Color/Graphics Monitor. The word should appear flashing blue. The background should be light red with a brown border.

2. Have the computer produce the following figure in brown with a blue background.

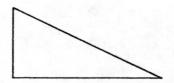

POINT

The POINT function returns the value of the color currently displayed at a specified point on the Color/Graphics Monitor. The statement

$$70 \ N = POINT \ (X,Y)$$

will assign N a value between 0 and 3 when using medium resolution mode. A value of 0 indicates that the color of the selected point is the same as the background color. A value of 1, 2, or 3 corresponds to a color from the color palette as selected by the COLOR statement. If -1 is returned by the POINT function, then the coordinates given are not on the screen. Remember that in medium resolution mode, $0 \leq X \leq 319$, and $0 \leq Y \leq 199$.

In high resolution mode, the POINT function will return either 0 for a black point or 1 for a white point. A value of -1 is returned if the specified coordinates are not on the screen.

PROGRAM 8.5

This program illustrates the POINT function.

```
10 SCREEN 1,0
20 COLOR 8,0 : LOCATE 9,1
30 PSET (18,12),1
40 LINE (10,20) - (85,20),2
50 LINE (15,25) - (62,45),3,BF
60 FOR T = 1 TO 4
70    READ X,Y : REM Coordinates
80    R = POINT(X,Y)
90    PRINT "Point at ("; X; ","; Y; ") is "; R
100 NEXT T
110 DATA 20,30, 18,12, 45,11, 47,20
Ok
RUN
```

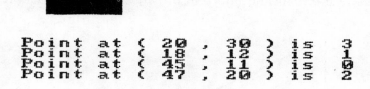

```
Point at ( 20 , 30 ) is  3
Point at ( 18 , 12 ) is  1
Point at ( 45 , 11 ) is  0
Point at ( 47 , 20 ) is  2
```

CIRCLE

The CIRCLE statement is used to draw a circle or an ellipse on the Color/Graphics Monitor. The general form of the CIRCLE statement is:

CIRCLE (X,Y), <radius>, <color>

The coordinates (X,Y) specify the center of the circle. The 'radius' specifies the distance from the center of the circle to its perimeter. In medium resolution mode, the 'color' selects a color from the current palette previously defined by the COLOR statement.

PROGRAM 8.6

Using the CIRCLE statement, this program will produce the Olympic rings.

```
10 SCREEN 1,0 : COLOR 8,0
20 FOR R = 20 TO 22
30      CIRCLE (50,50),R,2
40      CIRCLE (99,50),R,2
50      CIRCLE (146,50),R,2
60      CIRCLE (74,70),R,2
70      CIRCLE (122,70),R,2
80 NEXT R
Ok
RUN
```

The CIRCLE statement can be expanded to print just an arc of a circle by specifying the starting and ending angles in radians.

CIRCLE (X,Y), <radius>, <color>, <start>, <end>

The 'start' and 'end' angles specify where drawing is to begin and end as follows:

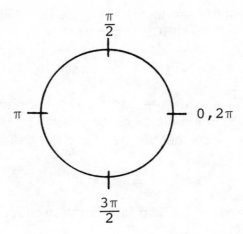

Any value between 0 and 2π may be specified. If the 'start' or 'end' angle is negative, the arc will be connected to the center (X,Y) with a line. The angles are then treated as if they were positive.

PROGRAM 8.7

This program illustrates the arc feature of the CIRCLE statement.

```
10 PI = 3.14159
20 SCREEN 1,0 : COLOR 0,1 : LOCATE 1,1
30 PRINT "Some Simple Arcs:"
40 CIRCLE (20,40),20,2,PI/2,PI
50 CIRCLE (60,20),20,1,PI,2*PI
60 CIRCLE (115,40),15,3,5*PI/16,2*PI
70 CIRCLE (175,40),25,1,0,PI : CIRCLE (225,40),25,1,PI,2*PI
100 LOCATE 11,1 : PRINT "Arcs with negative angles:"
110 CIRCLE (21,120),20,1,-PI/2,-PI
120 CIRCLE (60,120),20,2,-3*PI/2,PI/2
130 CIRCLE (122,120),22,3,-5*PI/4,-3*PI/4
140 CIRCLE (175,135),38,2,-3*PI/8,-5*PI/8
150 CIRCLE (240,122),35,1,PI/2,-2*PI
Ok
RUN
```

Some Simple Arcs:

Arcs with negative angles:

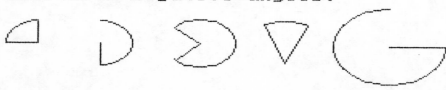

The CIRCLE statement can be expanded to draw ellipses by including the ratio of the X-radius to the Y-radius.

CIRCLE (X,Y), <radius>, <color>, <start>, <end>, <ratio>

If the 'ratio' is *less* than 1, then the 'radius' will be the X-radius, that is, the horizontal distance from the center (X,Y) of the ellipse to its perimeter. The Y-radius will then be equal to 'ratio' * 'radius'.

If the 'ratio' is *greater* than 1, then the 'radius' will refer to the Y-radius, the vertical distance from the center (X,Y) to the perimeter of the ellipse. The X-radius will be equal to 'radius' / 'ratio'. For example, the statement

70 CIRCLE (100,85), 60,1,,,0.5

will produce:

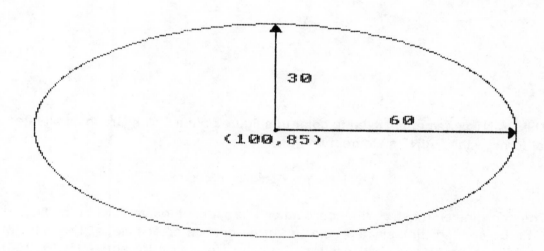

PROGRAM 8.8

This program will draw several ellipses using the CIRCLE statement. Note that the 'start' and 'end' angles may be omitted, causing a complete ellipse to be plotted.

```
10 SCREEN 1,0 : COLOR 0,1 : PI = 3.14159
20 CIRCLE (70,40),60,1,,,.278 : REM Horizontal Ellipse
30 CIRCLE (160,70),60,3,,,3.6 : REM Vertical Ellipse
40 CIRCLE (65,90),50,2,-PI,-2*PI,.4 : REM Boat
50 CIRCLE (220,70),45,2,0,PI,1.5 : REM Arch
Ok
RUN
```

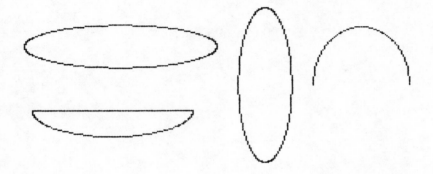

PAINT

The PAINT statement is used to color in a figure on the Color/Graphics Monitor. The general form of the PAINT statement is:

PAINT (X,Y), <color>, <edge>

The coordinates must be the coordinates of any point located within the figure. The figure will be shaded the selected color from the current color palette. The color of the figure's outline must be specified in 'edge'. For example, if a circle centered at (60,150) has a red perimeter and is to be filled in with the color green, the statement

100 PAINT (60,150), 1,2

may be used.

PROGRAM 8.9

This program illustrates the PAINT statement by drawing a pie chart of sales for Southern Engineering & Metal Products Corp. The user is asked for 4 sales figures: mail order, retail, wholesale and foreign. The program then totals the sales, computes the percentage of the total represented by each, and then draws a pie chart in color showing each sales figure as a slice of the pie. Note that the output on the Color/Graphics Monitor will show each pie slice in a different color.

```
10 REM Piechart Program
20 FOR I = 1 TO 4
30      READ D$ : REM Prompt
40      PRINT D$;
50      INPUT P(I) : REM Amount
60      T = T + P(I) : REM Total
70 NEXT I
100 PI = 3.14159 : A(0) = 0
110 SCREEN 1,0 : COLOR 8,0
120 FOR C = 1 TO 4
130     A(C) = -(2*PI * (P(C) / T) + ABS(A(C-1))) :REM Wedge Size
140     CIRCLE (160,75),45,2,A(C-1),A(C)
150 NEXT C
160 LOCATE 1,11 : PRINT "Southern Engineering"
170 LOCATE 2,11 : PRINT " & Metal Products"
200 RESTORE
210 FOR F = 0 TO 3
220     AO = ABS(A(F)) + PI/8
230     X = CINT(20 * COS(AO)) + 160
240     Y = 75 - CINT(20 * SIN(AO))
250     PAINT (X,Y),F,2
260     LINE (58,152+8*F) - (66,157+8*F),F,BF
270     READ D$
280     LOCATE 20+F,10
285     PRINT "- "; D$; TAB(29); CINT(P(F+1)/T*1000)/10; "%"
290 NEXT F
300 LINE (58,152) - (66,157),3,B
1000 DATA Mail Order Sales, Retail Sales
1010 DATA Wholesale Sales, Foreign Sales
Ok
RUN
Mail Order Sales? 175
Retail Sales? 325
Wholesale Sales? 250
Direct Sales? 190
```

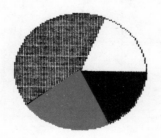

Southern Engineering
& Metal Products

☐ - Mail Order Sales   18.6 %
▦ - Retail Sales   34.6 %
▨ - Wholesale Sales   26.6 %
■ - Foreign Sales   20.2 %

3. Have the computer plot a square green box with a red background. The box should be 50 dots on each side and centered at (160, 100).
4. Allow the user to enter 3 numbers: A, B, and R. Have the computer plot a circle of radius R with its center at (A,B) on the high resolution screen.

SHIFTING AND SCALING A GRAPH

A hand-drawn graph usually includes an X-axis drawn horizontally, a Y-axis drawn vertically, and a continuous curve drawn through a number of plotted points. There are some obvious limitations to graphs produced by the computer, (for example, the lack of connection between plotted points). The graphing area on the display screen contains a limited number of points available for plotting. Thus, certain adjustments of the X and Y-axes may be necessary to accommodate functions which produce values that exceed the number of graphing points available. This problem is solved by determining the domain (smallest and largest X values) and the range (smallest and largest Y values) for a function where Y = f(X) and then scaling the axes accordingly. These processes are referred to as shifting and scaling.

Shifting is achieved by subtracting the minimum value of Y from each Y value. For example, if a function has values between -10 and +15, Y minus the minimum value (Y-(-10)) shifts the graph to points between 0 and 25 on the Y-axis. This does not affect the shape of the graph.

Scaling, on the other hand, takes the difference between the largest and smallest values and divides this difference by one less than the number of points available for a particular axis. The one extra space allows the axis to start with the smallest plotted value. For example, if the interval between the largest and smallest Y values for a particular graph is 400 units and the display screen has only 200 vertical points for plotting, the 400 is divided by (200-1) or 199 to produce the proper scale. Approximately every 2 points on the graph's Y-axis corresponds to 1 point on the screen.

PROGRAM 8.10

The following program illustrates how the function Y = 150*SIN(X) is shifted and scaled to fit on the Color/Graphics Monitor.

```
10 SCREEN 1,0 : COLOR 0,0 : PI = 3.14159
20 FOR X = -3*PI TO 3*PI STEP .05
30      Y = 150 * SIN(X) : REM The Function...
40      YO = Y / (300/199) : REM Scale Y-axis
50      YO = YO + 100 : REM Shift Y-axis
60      XO = X / (6*PI/319) : REM Scale X-axis
70      XO = XO + 160 : REM Shift X-axis
80      PSET (XO,YO),2
90 NEXT X
Ok
RUN
```

The function is evaluated at line 30 with a domain of -3π to 3π in increments of 0.05. The result (Y) is scaled by dividing Y by the ratio 300/199. The 300 represents the absolute range of the function. The 199 represents the vertical width of the screen minus 1. X is scaled in a similar fashion by line 60. Both X and Y are shifted by lines 70 and 50 respectively.

PROGRAM 8.11

This program plots the function Y = 1/X on the display screen. Note how the graph has been shifted and scaled.

```
10 SCREEN 1,0 : COLOR 8,1
20 REM Draw axes
30 LINE (159,9) - (161,199),1,BF
40 LINE (0,99) - (319,101),1,BF
50 LOCATE 1,18 : PRINT "Y-axis";
60 FOR A = 10 TO 310 STEP 50
70     LINE (A-1,97) - (A+1,103),1,BF
80 NEXT A
90 FOR A = 10 TO 190 STEP 45
100       LINE (157,A-1) - (163,A+1),1,BF
110 NEXT A
120 LINE (159,9) - (161,199),1,BF
130 LINE (9,99) - (319,101),1,BF
140 REM Label axes
150 FOR A = 1 TO 11
160     READ V,H,D$
170     LOCATE V,H : PRINT D$;
180 NEXT A
200 REM Plot function Y = 1/X
210 FOR X = -12 TO 12 STEP .1
220     IF X<>0 THEN Y = 1/X ELSE 280
225     IF ABS(Y) > 1.5 THEN 280
230     X1 = X / (24/299) : REM Scale X range
240     X1 = X1 + 160 : REM Shift X range to center
250     Y1 = Y / (2/179) : REM Scale Y range
260     Y1 = 100 - Y1 : REM Shift Y range
270     PSET (X1,Y1),3
280 NEXT X
1000 DATA 12,1,-12,   12,7,-8,    12,14,-4,   12,20,0
1010 DATA 14,26,4,    14,33,8,    14,39,12,   2,19,1
1020 DATA 7,18,.5,    18,22,-.5,  24,22,-1
Ok
RUN
```

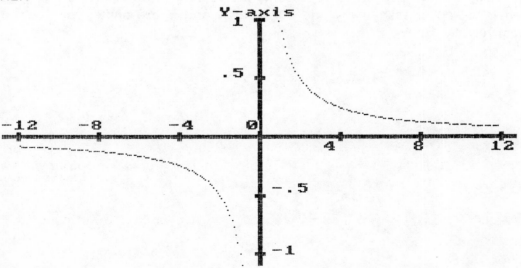

The analysis of this program is left as an exercise for the reader.

EXERCISES

1. Have the computer draw a solid red rectangle with its upper left corner at (38, 18), a length of 70 columns, and a height of 30 rows.

2. Have the computer draw a green letter L about two inches high in the upper left corner of the screen.

3. Using medium resolution graphics, draw a cyan vertical line and a white horizontal line which intersect at (140, 80).

4. Have the computer construct a brown right triangle with the altitude from (250, 20) to (250, 110) and the base from (250, 110) to (130, 110). Use only one LINE statement.

5. Place a flashing red notice on the text screen which advertises Uncle Bill's Whamburgers for 79¢. The screen should have a gray background and a green border.

6. In high resolution mode draw the letter A with the top at (350, 30) and the lowest point of the left side at (200, 160).

7. Have the computer generate 200 random integers between 1 and 10, inclusive. Using medium resolution graphics, plot a properly labeled bar graph showing the number of occurrences of each random number.

8. Modify Program 8.9 so that the piechart can be divided into N pieces.

9. Produce the following Hatman in yellow with a green hat. The Hatman should be surrounded by the color red.

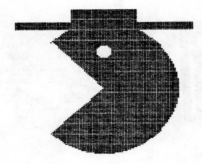

10. The following table shows production output per day for each employee of Papa's Pizza Parlor. Plot a bar graph showing the average output per week for each of Papa's employees.

Employee	Pizza Production
Dellacona	18, 12, 9, 10, 16, 22, 14
Munyan	12, 21, 19, 16, 28, 20, 22
Ricardo	18, 20, 14, 19, 11, 16, 23
Fazioli	23, 27, 18, 16, 21, 14, 24

11. Using only a single CIRCLE statement and a single FOR ... NEXT loop, have the computer produce the following sphere:

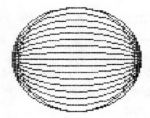

12. Using high resolution graphics, have the computer produce the following figure:

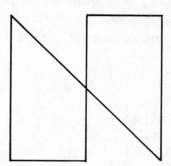

13. Using medium resolution graphics have the computer generate a 90 x 90 circular dart board using the colors 1 through 3, where brown (color 3, palette 0) occupies the center of the board. The colors red and green should form a border around the colors inside it. Have the computer take 10 random shots at points on the board. Use the POINT function to tabulate the computer's score (i.e. if the point of impact is within the brown area, the computer scores 3 points; if within the red area, 2 points are scored; etc.). Show where each dart hits by plotting a smallblack circle at the point of impact.

14. Have the computer fill the first 160 columns of the medium resolution screen with randomly colored points.

    A. Using the POINT function, duplicate the left portion of the screen on the right side of the screen in columns 161 through 320.

    B. Rewrite part A such that the right portion of the screen is a mirror image of the left portion.

15. Using a single loop and one CIRCLE statement, produce the following wagon wheel in red:

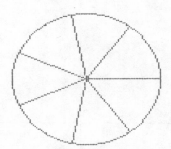

16. Using Program 8.11 as a guide, write a general purpose graphing program. The user is to enter the function (FNF (X)) to be graphed as the first line of the program before the program is run. The program should ask for the domain (range of X-values to plot) and the range (range of Y-values produced by the function). For example,

```
10 DEF FNF(X) = 2 * X * COS(X)
RUN
Domain (Min,Max)? -10,22
Range (Min,Max)? -40,40
```

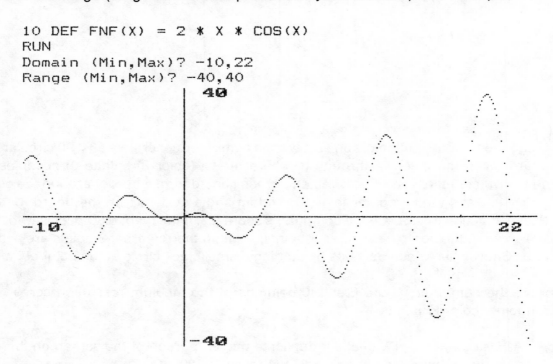

```
10 DEF FNF(X) = X^2 - 3 * LOG(ABS(X)) - 5
RUN
Domain (Min,Max)? -5,5
Range (Min,Max)? -10,10
```

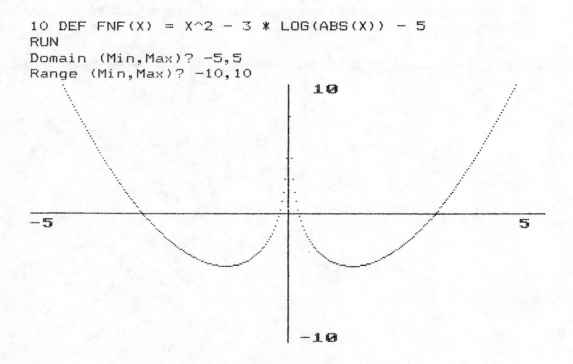

8.20

17. The ancient puzzle 'Towers of Hanoi' uses 5 different sized disks and 3 pegs. The 5 disks are initially stacked on the left peg in order of decreasing size. The object of the game is to move all of the disks to the right peg. Only 1 disk can be moved at a time and a larger disk cannot be placed on top of a smaller disk.

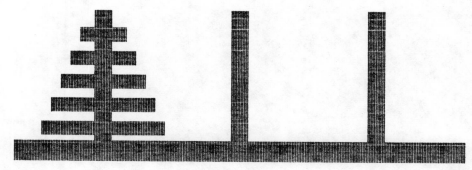

Initial Configuration for Towers of Hanoi

A. Write a program using medium resolution graphics that will draw a green base with green pegs and plot the initial configuration of 5 red disks on the left tower.

B. Expand the program from part A to allow movement of the disks. The user should be able to enter two values (P and Q). This should cause the top disk on tower P to be moved to the top of the stack on tower Q. (Hint: Set up a subscripted variable A(X,Y) with maximum values X=3, Y=5). There are 15 possible slots for disks; 3 towers, 5 slots per tower. When a slot is occupied, the subscripted variable A(X,Y) should contain the disk number occupying that slot (1-5). If the slot is free, the appropriate position in A(X,Y) should contain a zero).

9 STRING FUNCTIONS AND DATA TYPES

Modern computers have resulted from the union of the binary number system with the principles of electricity. The binary number system uses only two digits, 0 and 1, and can therefore be represented by the two states of an electric circuit, off or on. This concept has made digital computers possible, since they operate by reducing all data to a binary code. How different types of data can be reduced to a binary system is explained in this chapter.

Binary Code

The most familiar number system, the decimal system, uses ten digits: 0,1,2,3, 4,5,6,7,8,9 and is therefore considered to be base ten. In contrast, the binary system, which uses only the digits 0 and 1, is base two.

In the base ten system, columns are used to represent powers of ten with the first column left of the decimal point representing 10^0, the second 10^1, the third 10^2, and so on. For example, in the numeral 458, 8 represents 8×10^0, 5 represents 5×10^1 and 4 represents 4×10^2. The numeral itself represents the sum: $4 \times 10^2 + 5 \times 10^1 + 8 \times 10^0$.

The base two system works identically *except the columns represent powers of two* instead of ten. For example, in the numeral 101, the 1 on the right represents 1×2^0, the 0 represents 0×2^1, and the 1 on the left represents 1×2^2. The numeral itself represents the sum $1 \times 2^2 + 0 \times 2^1 + 1 \times 2^0$, which is known as five in the base ten system.

Base Two	Base Ten
$11 = 1 \times 2^1 + 1 \times 2^0$	$= 3$
$1011 = 1 \times 2^3 + 0 \times 2^2 + 1 \times 2^1 + 1 \times 2^0$	$= 11$
$11001 = 1 \times 2^4 + 1 \times 2^3 + 0 \times 2^2 + 0 \times 2^1 + 1 \times 2^0$	$= 25$

To convert a number from base ten to base two, we must find which powers of two add up to the number. Since $13 = 8 + 4 + 1$, the base two representation for 13 is 1101 ($1x8 + 1x4 + 0x2 + 1x1$).

Base Ten		Base Two
$6 = 4 + 2 = 1x2^2 + 1x2^1 + 0x2^0$		$= \quad 110$
$29 = 16 + 8 + 4 + 1 \ 1x2^4 + 1x2^3 + 1x2^2 + 0x2^1 + 1x2^0$		$= 11101$
$52 = 32 + 16 + 4 = 1x2^5 + 1x2^4 + 0x2^3 + 1x2^2 + 0x2^1 + 0x2^0$		$= 110100$

Computer Memory and Processing

The computer is composed of a solid-state electronic memory which stores information and a central processing unit (CPU) which performs calculations, makes decisions, and moves information.

Because electricity has two basic states, ON and OFF, it is ideal for expressing binary numbers. A circuit (called a "flip-flop") when on stands for a "1", and when off stands for a "0". By designing computers to contain millions of simple flip-flop circuits, huge quantities of information can thus be stored.

A single binary digit (0 or 1) is called a "bit", and eight of these bits constitute a "byte". Single characters require one byte and integers two bytes of memory for storage. The memory stores both instructions for the CPU and data as binary digits.

The power of a computer is vastly increased when it is capable of storing letters and special characters as well as numbers. In order to do this, a code has been established to translate letters and special characters into numbers which can then be stored in binary form. This code has been standardized by the computer industry as the American Standard Code for Information Interchange (ASCII). In this code, each letter of the alphabet, both upper case and lower case, each symbol, and each control function used by the computer is represented by a number. For example, the name JIM is translated by the computer into ASCII numbers 74,73,77. In turn these numbers are then stored by the computer in binary form.

$$J = 74 = 01001010$$
$$I = 73 = 01001001$$
$$M = 77 = 01001101$$

In order for the computer to store a name such as JIM, or any piece of non-numeric information, it must be entered in the form of a string, converted character by character into ASCII numbers, and then stored in memory as binary numbers. The following is a table of the ASCII character codes available on the computer.

The following is a table of the ASCII character codes.

ASCII value	Character	ASCII value	Character	ASCII value	Character	ASCII value	Character	ASCII value	Character
0	(null)	52	4	104	h	156	£	208	╨
1	☺	53	5	105	i	157	¥	209	╤
2	☻	54	6	106	j	158	Pt	210	╥
3	♥	55	7	107	k	159	ƒ	211	╙
4	♦	56	8	108	l	160	á	212	╘
5	♣	57	9	109	m	161	í	213	╒
6	♠	58	:	110	n	162	ó	214	╓
7	(beep)	59	;	111	o	163	ú	215	╫
8	◘	60	<	112	p	164	ñ	216	╪
9	(tab)	61	=	113	q	165	Ñ	217	┘
10	(line feed)	62	>	114	r	166	ª	218	┌
11	(home)	63	?	115	s	167	º	219	█
12	(form feed)	64	@	116	t	168	¿	220	▄
13	(carriage return)	65	A	117	u	169	⌐	221	▌
14	♫	66	B	118	v	170	¬	222	▐
15	☼	67	C	119	w	171	½	223	▀
16	►	68	D	120	x	172	¼	224	α
17	◄	69	E	121	y	173	¡	225	β
18	↕	70	F	122	z	174	«	226	Γ
19	‼	71	G	123	{	175	»	227	π
20	¶	72	H	124	¦	176	░	228	Σ
21	§	73	I	125	}	177	▒	229	σ
22	▬	74	J	126	~	178	▓	230	μ
23	↨	75	K	127	⌂	179	│	231	τ
24	↑	76	L	128	Ç	180	┤	232	Φ
25	↓	77	M	129	ü	181	╡	233	Θ
26	→	78	N	130	é	182	╢	234	Ω
27	←	79	O	131	â	183	╖	235	δ
28	(cursor right)	80	P	132	ä	184	╕	236	∞
29	(cursor left)	81	Q	133	à	185	╣	237	Ø
30	(cursor up)	82	R	134	å	186	║	238	ε
31	(cursor down)	83	S	135	ç	187	╗	239	∩
32	(space)	84	T	136	ê	188	╝	240	≡
33	!	85	U	137	ë	189	╜	241	±
34	"	86	V	138	è	190	╛	242	≥
35	#	87	W	139	ï	191	┐	243	≤
36	$	88	X	140	î	192	└	244	⌠
37	%	89	Y	141	ì	193	┴	245	⌡
38	&	90	Z	142	Ä	194	┬	246	÷
39	'	91	[	143	Å	195	├	247	≈
40	(	92	\	144	É	196	─	248	°
41	)	93	]	145	æ	197	┼	249	•
42	*	94	∧	146	Æ	198	╞	250	·
43	+	95	—	147	ô	199	╟	251	√
44	,	96	`	148	ö	200	╚	252	^{n}
45	-	97	a	149	ò	201	╔	253	^{2}
46	.	98	b	150	û	202	╩	254	■
47	/	99	c	151	ù	203	╦	255	(blank 'FF')
48	0	100	d	152	ÿ	204	╠		
49	1	101	e	153	Ö	205	═		
50	2	102	f	154	Ü	206	╬		
51	3	103	g	155	¢	207	╧		

Data Types

When information is entered into the computer, it can take one of three forms: ASCII characters, integers, or floating point numbers. An integer is a number without decimal places, while a floating point number has either a decimal point or an implied decimal point and decimal places. For example, the number 29 could be either integer or floating point, but 29.73 is definitely floating point.

Floating point numbers on the computer can be specified to be either single precision or double precision. A single precision floating point number is stored internally with seven significant figures, and up to seven are printed, but only six are accurate. A double precision floating point number is internally accurate to seventeen significant figures but rounded to sixteen when printed.

Storage of an integer requires 16 bits, a floating point number either 32 or 64 bits, depending on whether it is single or double precision, and an ASCII character 8 bits. Because of storage requirements it is important to distinguish between the several forms. When files are presented in Chapters 9 and 10, the significance of this factor in planning efficient storage of data will become apparent.

The four data types employ different symbols to inform the computer which is being used. Strings of ASCII characters employ the familiar symbol ($) for string variable names; (e.g., G$, B3$). Integers, which have the disadvantage of being restricted to the range −32768 to 32767 are denoted by a percent sign (%). For example, B% and Z% are variable names for integers. While integers have a severe range limitation, they are processed fastest by the computer. Single precision floating point variables are denoted by an exclamation mark (!); (e.g., C!, HI!). Double precision floating point variables are denoted by a number sign (#); (e.g., G7#, D#). While they are more accurate, calculations involving double precision numbers are the slowest.

The precision of constants as well as variables can be declared and will then determine the precision of the calculations in which they are used. For example,

PRINT 2/3

produces

.6666667

while

PRINT 2#/3#

produces

.6666666666666667

Variables and constants not specifically declared otherwise are assumed to be single precision floating point.

ASCII Code—ASCII Character Conversions

Earlier in this chapter, the ASCII code was described as a method by which the computer converts information in the form of strings into numbers. Commands exist to convert strings into ASCII values and vice versa.

Function Format	Operation
X = ASC(P$)	Converts only the first character of the string P$ to its ASCII code number.
P$ = CHR$(X)	Assigns the character with the ASCII code number of X to P$, which now contains only one character.
P$ = STRING$(X, Y)	Generates a string, P$, of length X composed of characters all having the ASCII code number Y.
A = SCREEN(R, C)	Assigns A the ASCII code of the character on the screen at position R, C.

PROGRAM 9.1

This program demonstrates the use of the ASCII character conversions.

```
1 REM     C$ = CHARACTER INPUT
2 REM     A = ASCII VALUE OF C$
3 REM     K$ = NEW STRING
4 REM     Y$ = INDICATOR
5 REM
6 REM
10 INPUT "ENTER ANY CHARACTER";C$
20 A = ASC(C$)
30 PRINT "THE ASCII VALUE OF '";C$;"' IS:"A
40 K$ = STRING$(17,A)
50 PRINT "'";CHR$(A);"' REPEATED 17 TIMES LOOKS LIKE THIS: ";
60 PRINT K$
70 INPUT "WOULD YOU LIKE TO RUN THIS AGAIN";Y$
80 IF ASC(Y$) = 89 THEN 10
Ok
RUN
ENTER ANY CHARACTER? R
THE ASCII VALUE OF 'R' IS: 82
'R' REPEATED 17 TIMES LOOKS LIKE THIS: RRRRRRRRRRRRRRRRR
WOULD YOU LIKE TO RUN THIS AGAIN? N
Ok
```

REVIEW

1. Write a program that will allow the user to input a letter. Have the computer print that letter's ASCII code and then print the letter that comes two letters after it in the alphabet. If Y or Z is the letter input, then A or B should be returned respectively.

```
RUN
A LETTER FROM THE ALPHABET PLEASE? R
THE ASCII OF 'R' IS 82
TWO LETTERS AFTER 'R' IS 'T'
A LETTER FROM THE ALPHABET PLEASE? Y
THE ASCII OF 'Y' IS 89
TWO LETTERS AFTER 'Y' IS 'A'
A LETTER FROM THE ALPHABET PLEASE?
Break in 10
Ok
```

String Manipulation Functions

Strings can be manipulated with the following functions:

Function	Operation
D$ = DATE$	Assigns D$ a string representing the current date.
I = INSTR(N,A$,B$)	Assigns I the starting location of the substring B$ in A$. The search starts at the Nth character of A$.
I$ = INKEY$	Assigns I$ a one character string which is not printed when entered. The ENTER key need not be struck to input the character.
L$ = LEFT$(A$,N)	Assigns L$ a substring of the string A$ from the leftmost character to and including the Nth character.
L = LEN(A$)	Assigns L a value equal to the number of characters in the string A$, including blank spaces.
M$ = MID$(A$,N)	Assigns M$ a substring of the string A$ from the Nth character to the rightmost character of the string.
M$ = MID$(A$, N1, N2)	Assigns M$ a substring of the string A$, starting with the character N1 and being N2 characters long.
MID$(A$, N1, N2) = R$	Replaces N2 characters of A$, starting at character N1, with the first N2 characters of R$.
R$ = RIGHT$(A$,N)	Assigns R$ a substring of the string A$ consisting of the rightmost N characters.

S$ = SPACE$(N)	Assigns S$ a string of N blank spaces.
S$ = STR$(X)	Converts X into a string of numeric characters and assigns it to S$.
SWAP A$, B$	Exchanges the contents of A$ and B$.
SWAP X, Y	SWAP can also be used to exchange the contents of numeric variables X and Y.
T$ = TIME$	Assigns T$ a string representing the current time.
V = VAL(A$)	Converts the first set of numeric characters in the string A$ into a numeric value that is assigned to V. Non-numeric characters are ignored.

PROGRAM 9.2

This program will input a ten character string without an ENTER and manipulate it to show the use of string functions.

```
1 REM      T$ = TARGET STRING
2 REM
3 REM
100 REM     STRING INPUT SECTION USING INKEY$
110 WHILE LEN(T$) < 10
120     T$ = T$ + INKEY$
130 WEND
140 PRINT T$
150 REM
160 REM
200 REM     STRING MANIPULATION SECTION
220 PRINT "'";T$;"' BACKWARDS IS: ";
230 FOR X = 10 TO 1 STEP -1
240     PRINT MID$(T$,X,1);
250 NEXT X
260 PRINT
270 PRINT "THE VALUE OF '";T$;"' IS:";VAL(T$)
280 PRINT "THIS IS THE YEAR ";RIGHT$(DATE$,4)
300 PRINT "'";VAL(T$);"' BACKWARDS IS: ";
310 FOR X = LEN(STR$(VAL(T$))) TO 1 STEP -1
320     PRINT MID$(STR$(VAL(T$)),X,1);
330 NEXT X
340 PRINT
350 PRINT "THE LETTER 'Q' IS ";
360 IF INSTR(1,T$,"Q") = 0 THEN PRINT "NOT TO BE FOUND ";
                              ELSE PRINT "CHARACTER #";INSTR(1,T$,"Q");
370 PRINT "IN YOUR STRING."
380 PRINT "AFTER REPLACING THE FOURTH CHARACTER WITH 'Z',"
390 PRINT "THE STRING BECOMES: ";
400 MID$(T$,4,1) = "Z"
410 PRINT T$
Ok
```

```
RUN
145RTLMJDQ
'145RTLMJDQ' BACKWARDS IS: QDJMLTR541
THE VALUE OF '145RTLMJDQ' IS: 145
THIS IS THE YEAR 1982
' 145 ' BACKWARDS IS: 541
THE LETTER 'Q' IS CHARACTER # 10 IN YOUR STRING.
AFTER REPLACING THE FOURTH CHARACTER WITH 'Z',
THE STRING BECOMES: 145ZTLMJDQ
Ok
```

Unlike INPUT, INKEY$ does not wait for data from the keyboard. When INKEY$ is executed, the computer checks immediately to see if a key is being pressed. If not, the computer proceeds to the next program line. The WHILE-WEND loop at lines 110-130 will be continuously executed until ten characters have been entered.

PART A

1. Enter a string A$, and use a loop to print the ASCII number of each of its characters.

2. Input three letters, add their ASCII numbers, find the INT of one third of their sum, and print the character corresponding to the result. Is there any meaning to this process?

3. Using properly selected ASCII numbers on a DATA line, print the sentence "ASCII DID THIS!"

4. Using ASCII numbers 45 and 46 and the PRINT TAB statement, print the following figure.

5. Enter the string THREE!@#$%STRING!@#$%FUNCTIONS. Use LEFT$, MID$, and RIGHT$ to print the phrase "THREE STRING FUNCTIONS".

6. Enter a string A$ of any length. Print the length of A$ and the ASCII number of its first and last characters.

7. Write a program where you input a name and then have the computer print the ASCII number of the most common letter in the name.

8. Let A$="2598". Have the computer apply VAL to those parts of A$ whose sum is 123.

9. Enter the words "QUEEN", "LENGTH", and "REMEMBER". Print each word with all E's removed.

10. Use the computer or a hand calculator to find the binary equivalents of the decimal values given below.

   89, 74, 80, 107, 255, 129, 28, 39, 29, 24, 43

11. Use the computer or a hand calculator to find the decimal equivalents for the binary values given below.

   1011, 10100, 1111, 1110, 1010011, 110011, 1011100,
   1101111, 11000000, 10000111

12. Input a string A$ which consists of the digits 0 to 9, inclusive, each to be used only once (e.g., 1956472038). Use string functions to obtain from A$ two numbers N1 and N2, N1 being the number represented by the first three digits of A$ and N2 the number represented by the last three digits. Print the sum of N1 and N2.

13. Let A$ consist of the first twelve letters of the alphabet. Using A$, construct the right triangle shown at the right.

```
RUN
A
AB
ABC
ABCD
ABCDE
ABCDEF
ABCDEFG
ABCDEFGH
ABCDEFGHI
ABCDEFGHIJ
ABCDEFGHIJK
ABCDEFGHIJKL
Ok
```

14. As a young boy Franklin Roosevelt signed his letters to his mother backwards: TLEVESOOR NILKNARF. Write a program that accepts a person's name and prints it backwards.

15. Using the ASCII chart given in the text, determine the output for the following program. Check by running the program.

```
10 FOR A = 1 TO 4
20    READ A$
30    PRINT ASC(A$)
40 NEXT A
50 DATA "W","H","7","625"
60 END
```

16. The output of the following program is Foxy Moxie's message to Jimmy Band. What is the message? Check by running the program.

```
10 FOR W = 1 TO 6
20    READ A$,B$,C$
30    PRINT LEFT$(A$,1);MID$(B$,2,2);RIGHT$(C$,1)
40 NEXT W
50 END
60 REM    DATA SECTION
70 DATA FGT,LOXK,NTY
80 DATA SFJ,DAYT,GES
90 DATA HWT,QELM,BIP
100 DATA WJM,WILS,WZL
110 DATA CDE,HOMV,PSE
120 DATA SOA,AOOC,TZN
```

17. Choose fifteen random integers from 65 to 90, inclusive, to serve as ASCII code numbers. Convert these fifteen integers to the fifteen characters for which they stand, and print the results.

18. Write a program which produces a sentence containing twenty nonsense words. Each word can contain from two to five letters. Use random numbers and the ASCII code to produce the words.

```
RUN
DIPLN FHDI OHHXR AR GPBV CPCL XLPVG FC RKN PY ZO DD HH TTQ KXHO
BQHT RQKT VBOH TPF IUXEC
Ok
```

19. Using random numbers and the ASCII code numbers from 32 to 126, inclusive, have the computer generate a string of 100 characters, allowing repetitions. Tabulate how many characters are letters, numbers, or miscellaneous characters. Print the results.

20. Using string functions, write a program to play a word guessing game. Ask the player to guess a secret word. Search through each guess to see if the guess contains any correct letters. If any letter is correct, have the computer print the ones that are. If the entire word is guessed, type "YOU GUESSED IT!!"

```
RUN
GUESS A WORD? SUE
GUESS A WORD? HARRIET
H IS IN THE WORD
A IS IN THE WORD
GUESS A WORD? BASEBALL
A IS IN THE WORD
A IS IN THE WORD
GUESS A WORD? GRUMP
G IS IN THE WORD
M IS IN THE WORD
GUESS A WORD? HANGMAN
YOU GUESSED IT!!
Ok
```

21. You are a spy who will use the computer to produce a secret code.
(a) Input a short message, and have the computer type back what appears to be nonsense words. To produce the coded words, convert each letter of the original message into its corresponding ASCII code number, add two to each number, and convert to characters to produce the message. Keep all spaces between the words in their original places, and understand that the letters Y and Z are to be converted to A and B.
(b) Write a program that will decode the message.

```
NCYTGPEGXKNNG
UEJQQN
```

22. When the following program is run the output is:

$$A = 1500 \qquad B = 999.9764$$

Explain in a clear, brief manner why the value of B is not exactly 1000, and why the value of A is exactly 1500.

```
10 FOR X = 1 TO 3000
20    A = A + 1/2
30    B = B + 1/3
40 NEXT X
50 PRINT "A =";A, "B =";B
60 END
```

23. Often, literary critics argue over the true identity of the author of some ancient manuscript. To resolve such disputes, it is helpful to show similarities between the anonymous text and a text by a known author. Write a program which tabulates the occurrences of each article ("a", "an", and "the"), each adverb (check for "ly"), and of each mark of punctuation (".", ",", "!", "?", ";", ":").

24. Create bizarre "sentences" by having the computer print the words of a real sentence in reverse order. Your program should NOT reverse the order of the letters in each word.

25. Last night you were informed that your aunt had left you several million dollars. You decide to start your own corporation. In the tradition of DEC, GTE, RCA, IBM, and other great corporate conglomerates, you want your corporate name to be composed of as many initials as you like, each standing for a word (e.g., Radio Corporation of America becomes RCA). Write a program which accepts up to ten words and then prints a block of letters composed of the first letters of each word. For example, given "WE AWAIT SILENT TRYSTERO'S EMPIRE", the program should return "WASTE".

26. Write a program which prints a triangle made up of parts of the word "triangle". The triangle should be obtuse, and the program should ask for its height, how far to indent the bottom edge, and where the bottom edge ends.

```
RUN
A, B, AND C? 18,24,36
T
  I
   AN
    NGL
     LET
      ETRI
       TRIAN
        IANGL
         ANGLET
          NGLETRI
           LETRIAN
            ETRIANGL
             TRIANGLET
              IANGLETRI
               ANGLETRIAN
                NGLETRIANGL
                 LETRIANGLET
                  ETRIANGLETRI

Ok
```

27. Enter a positive integer N$ as it would be expressed in binary form. That is, enter a string of ones and zeros. Have the computer print the equivalent of N$ as it is expressed in the decimal system.

10 SEQUENTIAL FILES

A computer file is analagous to a filing cabinet which stores information that can be recalled and cross referenced. As such, the computer file provides the means for storing large quantities of data indefinitely.

The computer utilizes two different file types: sequential and random-access. The sequential file is best adapted to situations requiring data to be recalled in the same order as it was originally stored in the file. Proceeding line-by-line from the beginning, the computer reads the file sequentially until all the desired information has been retrieved. If information is to be retrieved from a random location in the file (for example, a single entry in a mailing list), random-access files are better suited. Since they are more difficult to use, random-access files will be discussed separately in the next chapter.

It is suggested that before proceeding to learn the use of files, the programmer should first read Appendix B in order to become familiar with the special aspects of Disk BASIC.

OPEN

The OPEN statement establishes a line of communication between a program and a file and prepares the file for use. The OPEN statement must include the name of a file, and a channel designator; it also must specify the mode of access desired. A file name is a unique label used by the computer to identify each file and program stored on a disk. A channel designator is an integer from 1 to 15, and not larger than the number of files specified when the system was initialized. It indicates the channel to be used as a line of communication between the program and the file.

The four modes of access are:

O: Sequential Output. The computer will output data to the file starting at the beginning. If the file does not already exist, it will automatically be created, otherwise the new data will be *written over any previously existing data* stored in the file.

I: Sequential Input. The computer will input data from the file to the computer starting at the beginning. If the file does not already exist, it will print FILE NOT FOUND.

A: Sequential Output at End of File. The data will be output from the computer and appended to the end of the file. Previously stored data will be added to, not lost. If it does not already exist, the file be created.

R: Random Input and Output. This option is discussed in Chapter 11.

The general format for the OPEN statement is:

OPEN "<mode>", <channel>, "<file name>"

It is important to note that the mode and the file name must be enclosed in quotation marks. For example,

10 OPEN "I", 2, "PAYROLL.TXT"

will open a file named PAYROLL.TXT for sequential input on channel 2. Remember that files and programs must not have the same name.

CLOSE

Any file previously opened must be closed. This procedure is necessary in order to break the line of communication between a program and a file that was originally established by the OPEN command. A file is closed by using the command CLOSE followed by the channel designator that was specified when the file was opened. For example,

100 CLOSE 2

will close the file previously opened on channel two. Closing a file insures that all its information is properly retained. One should never remove a disk from a drive on which files are open. There is no way to guarantee that all of the data has been written to the file until it is closed, thus removing a disk prematurely may result in loss of data.

WRITE

While the OPEN statement establishes a line of communication between a program and a file, the WRITE# command is used to place data in the file. Its form is:

WRITE #<channel>, <variable>, <variable> . . .

Information contained in the variables mentioned in the WRITE# statement will be placed in the file associated with the specified channel. The WRITE# statement automatically places quotation marks around string data and commas between both numeric and string data in the file. The commas and quotation marks act as markers so that the computer can tell the different items of data apart when reading them from the file.

PROGRAM 10.1

This program, named CREATE.BAS, opens a sequential file named WORK.TXT on the disk in drive one. In it are stored the names of four employees, their hourly wages and the number of hours they have worked. Note the structure of line 60.

```
1 REM      EMPLOYEE$ = Employee name
2 REM      WAGE = Wage
3 REM      HOURS = Hours worked
4 REM
5 REM
10 OPEN "O", 1, "B:WORK.TXT"
20 FOR EMPLOYEE = 1 TO 4
30     INPUT "NAME";EMPLOYEE$
40     INPUT "WAGE";WAGE
50     INPUT "HOURS WORKED";HOURS
60     WRITE #1, EMPLOYEE$,WAGE,HOURS
70     PRINT
80 NEXT EMPLOYEE
90 CLOSE 1
Ok
RUN
NAME? LESTER WATERS
WAGE? 4.45
HOURS WORKED? 39

NAME? JULIE COOK
WAGE? 4.75
HOURS WORKED? 42

NAME? ELI HUROWITZ
WAGE? 5.10
HOURS WORKED? 36.75

NAME? DIANE BARRY
WAGE? 4.95
HOURS WORKED? 27.5

Ok
```

REVIEW

1. Write a program named CALENDAR.BAS that will create the sequential file MONTHS.TXT containing the names of the months of the year.

INPUT#

The INPUT# statement is used to read information from a sequential file. Its format is similar to the WRITE# statement.

$$INPUT \#<channel>, <variable>, <variable> \ldots$$

It is necessary that the order in which the variables are listed in the INPUT# statement be the same as the order of the WRITE# statement that created the file. For example, a program that reads the data from WORK.TXT created by Program 10.1 would have to input the data in the order EMPLOYEE$, WAGE, HOURS. After the file has been closed the same channel designator need not be used to access it at a later time. For example, a program accessing the file created by Program 10.1 might use channel 3.

PROGRAM 10.2

This program, named SHOW.BAS, will open the file WORK.TXT created by Program 10.1 and print the names and hours worked for the four employees.

```
1 REM     EMPLOYEE$ = Employee name
2 REM     WAGE = Wage
3 REM     HOURS = Hours worked
4 REM
5 REM
10 OPEN "I", 2, "B:WORK.TXT"
20 PRINT "NAME";TAB(25);"HOURS WORKED"
30 FOR EMPLOYEE = 1 TO 4
40     INPUT #2, EMPLOYEE$,WAGE,HOURS
50     PRINT EMPLOYEE$;TAB(25);HOURS
60 NEXT EMPLOYEE
70 CLOSE 1
Ok
RUN
NAME                     HOURS WORKED
LESTER WATERS            39
JULIE COOK               42
ELI HUROWITZ             36.75
DIANE BARRY              27.5
Ok
```

Note that line 10 specifies the access mode as "I" because the program will input data from the file to the computer.

The data in the file WORK.TXT appears as follows:

> LESTER WATERS, 4.45 , 39
> JULIE COOK, 4.75 , 42
> ELI HUROWITZ, 5.1 , 36.75
> DIANE BARRY, 4.95 , 27.5

Notice that the variable WAGE is read in the input line but is not printed. The computer has an internal pointer that indicates the next item of information that is to be transferred from the file by the INPUT# statement. When the INPUT# statement is executed, the pointer is moved across the data line as each item is read. To insure that the data in the file is read in the correct sequence, it is important that all of the necessary variables be included in the INPUT# statement, even if some of them are not used by the program.

REVIEW

2. Write a program named RETRIEVE.BAS that will retrieve the name of a selected month of the year from the file MONTHS.TXT.

Updating Sequential Files

Specifying the (A)ppend mode allows the user to append new information to the end of an existing file. When an OPEN command is executed with either the (O)utput or the (I)nput mode, the computer opens the file and prepares either to write to it or read from it starting at the beginning of the file. If a programmer uses the (O)utput mode, the new information added will be written over that which was at the beginning of the file, thus destroying the old information. To avoid this loss of data, the "A" mode instructs the computer to write new information at the end of the file.

PROGRAM 10.3

This program, named UPDATE.BAS, will update the old WORK.TXT file created by Program 10.1 so that it includes information on two new employees just hired.

```
1 REM    EMPLOYEE$ = Employee name
2 REM    WAGE = Wage
3 REM    HOURS = Hours worked
4 REM
5 REM
10 OPEN "A", 1, "B:WORK.TXT"
20 FOR EMPLOYEE = 1 TO 2
30     INPUT "NAME";EMPLOYEE$
40     INPUT "WAGE";WAGE
50     INPUT "HOURS WORKED";HOURS
60     WRITE #1, EMPLOYEE$,WAGE,HOURS
70     PRINT
80 NEXT EMPLOYEE
90 CLOSE 1
Ok
RUN
NAME? ERMA MCCONNELL
WAGE? 4.60
HOURS WORKED? 44.25

NAME? JEREMY LEADER
WAGE? 4.80
HOURS WORKED? 41.5

Ok
```

After changing the FOR. . .NEXT loop in Program 10.2 the program can be re-run to show that the new information is now in the file WORK.TXT.

```
RUN
NAME                      HOURS WORKED
LESTER WATERS             39
JULIE COOK                42
ELI HUROWITZ              36.75
DIANE BARRY               27.5
ERMA MCCONNELL            44.25
JEREMY LEADER             41.5
Ok
```

There is no single command that will remove or alter outdated information in a sequential file. To change such a file, the information to be kept must be transferred to a new file along with the new or corrected information. After the transfer, the old file can be deleted and the new file given an appropriate name.

PROGRAM 10.4

When an employee retires, this program named REMOVE.BAS will remove the employee's name from the file WORK.TXT. All of the data is read sequentially from WORK.TXT and the information that is to be retained is placed in the file WORK.TMP. After the program has finished building the new file WORK.TMP, the KILL and NAME commands are used to delete the old WORK.TXT and rename WORK.TMP as WORK.TXT.

```
1 REM    EMPLOYEE$ = Employee name
2 REM    WAGE = Wage
3 REM    HOURS = Hours worked
4 REM    RETIRED$ = Retired employee's name
5 REM
6 REM
10 INPUT "WHO HAS RETIRED";RETIRED$
20 OPEN "I", 1, "B:WORK.TXT"
30 OPEN "O", 2, "B:WORK.TMP"
40 FOR EMPLOYEE = 1 TO 6
50     INPUT #1, EMPLOYEE$,WAGE,HOURS
60     IF EMPLOYEE$ = RETIRED$ THEN 80
70     WRITE #2, EMPLOYEE$,WAGE,HOURS
80 NEXT EMPLOYEE
90 CLOSE 1,2
100 KILL "B:WORK.TXT"
110 NAME "B:WORK.TMP" AS "B:WORK.TXT"
120 PRINT "THE INFORMATION ON ";RETIRED$;" HAS BEEN REMOVED."
Ok
RUN
WHO HAS RETIRED? JEREMY LEADER
THE INFORMATION ON JEREMY LEADER HAS BEEN REMOVED.
Ok
```

This program works well in this limited example, but the technique it uses is not always practical. The FOR. . .NEXT loop between lines 40 and 80 prevents the program from attempting to read past the end of the data file. However, this method was used because the length of the file WORK.TXT was known. Otherwise, a loop using a GOTO statement must be used to insure that the entire file is read. The file will then be sequentially read until the program comes to the file's end. At this point an INPUT PAST END error will occur, and the program will be halted. If this occurs, files will be left open and important data may be lost. To prevent this error, the EOF function is used in conjunction with a WHILE. . .WEND loop.

EOF

The EOF function has the form

$$EOF (<channel>)$$

It returns a logical true (-1) when the end of the file has been reached, otherwise a logical false (0) is returned.

PROGRAM 10.5

This program, named REMOVE2.BAS, is a revision of Program 10.4 which allows the file WORK.TXT to be of any length.

```
1 REM     EMPLOYEE$ = Employee name
2 REM     WAGE = Wage
3 REM     HOURS = Hours worked
4 REM     RETIRED$ = Retired employee's name
5 REM     FLAG = Indicator to test for data
6 REM
7 REM
10 FLAG = 0
20 INPUT "WHO HAS RETIRED";RETIRED$
30 OPEN "I", 1, "B:WORK.TXT"
40 OPEN "O", 2, "B:WORK.TMP"
50 WHILE EOF(1) = 0
60    INPUT #1, EMPLOYEE$,WAGE,HOURS
70    IF EMPLOYEE$ = RETIRED$ THEN FLAG = -1
                            ELSE WRITE #2, EMPLOYEE$,WAGE,HOURS
80 WEND
90 CLOSE 1,2
100 IF FLAG = 0 THEN PRINT "THERE IS NO ";RETIRED$;" ON THE PAYROLL." :
                        KILL "B:WORK.TMP" : END
110 KILL "B:WORK.TXT"
120 NAME "B:WORK.TMP" AS "B:WORK.TXT"
130 PRINT "THE INFORMATION ON ";RETIRED$;" HAS BEEN REMOVED."
Ok
RUN
WHO HAS RETIRED? SANDRA COOK
THRE IS NO SANDRA COOK ON THE PAYROLL.
Ok
```

Program 10.5 demonstrates two major improvements over Program 10.4. First, the program informs the user if a name has been entered that is not in the file. The variable FLAG is used as an indicator. If the name is in the file, FLAG becomes -1; if not, it remains 0. Second, the EOF function and a WHILE. . .WEND loop are utilized to read the entire file. This technique is recommended for reading most sequential files.

LINE INPUT and PRINT#

In transferring data from a file to a program, the INPUT# statement recognizes commas placed in the file by the WRITE# statement as data separators. Therefore, these statements can not be used when the data contains embedded commas. This is only a problem when dealing with strings. The PRINT# statement places a carriage return after each item of data to separate it from the next without using a comma or quotation marks. This allows the data to contain embedded commas. Its form is:

PRINT #<channel>, <string variable>

When inputting data from the keyboard that contains embedded commas the INPUT statement cannot be used since it recognizes all commas as data separators. The LINE INPUT statement allows data containing commas to be input from the keyboard. Its form is:

LINE INPUT <string variable>

PROGRAM 10.6

This program can be used to build a series of files containing form letters used by a publishing company. Each file has a name corresponding to the type of letter it contains.

```
1 REM    LETTER$ = Form letter
2 REM    LENGTH = Number of lines in letter
3 REM    TEXT$ = Input text
4 REM
5 REM
10 INPUT "WHICH LETTER WILL THIS BE";LETTER$
20 LETTER$ = "B:" + LETTER$ + ".TXT"
30 OPEN "O", 1, LETTER$
40 INPUT "HOW MANY LINES WILL THIS BE";LENGTH
50 FOR LN = 1 TO LENGTH
60    LINE INPUT TEXT$
70    PRINT #1, TEXT$
80 NEXT LN
90 CLOSE 1
Ok
RUN
WHICH LETTER WILL THIS BE? REJECT
HOW MANY LINES WILL THIS BE? 6
     THANK YOU FOR YOUR MANUSCRIPT, "BELLING THE MOUSE".  IT
WAS VERY GOOD, BUT WE ALREADY HAVE OVER TWO HUNDRED WORKS WITH
THAT TITLE.  WE ARE SORRY, BUT YOUR MATERIAL DOES NOT FILL OUR
CURRENT NEEDS.

                         FILTHY RAG PUBLISHERS

Ok
```

LINE INPUT#

The INPUT# statement cannot be used to read data from a file that has embedded commas, since it recognizes commas as data separators. The LINE INPUT# statement recognizes the carriage return placed by the PRINT# statement after each string of data as a separator. The form of the LINE INPUT# statement is:

LINE INPUT #<channel>, <string variable>

It is important not to confuse the use of LINE INPUT# and PRINT# with INPUT# and WRITE#.

PROGRAM 10.7

This program, named MAIL.BAS, will read one of several form letters and personalize it for mailing to several people.

```
1 REM     N = Number of letters
2 REM     RECIPIENT$() = Recipient's name
3 REM     LETTER$ = Form letter
4 REM
5 REM
100 REM     Input data
110 INPUT "WHICH LETTER";LETTER$
120 LETTER$ = "B:" + LETTER$ + ".TXT"
130 INPUT "HOW MANY RECIPIENTS";N
140 DIM RECIPIENT$(N)
150 FOR R = 1 TO N
160    PRINT "RECIPIENT #";R;
170    INPUT RECIPIENT$(R)
180 NEXT R
190 REM
200 REM     Produce letters
210 FOR L = 1 TO N
220    PRINT
230    OPEN "I", 1, LETTER$
240    PRINT "DEAR ";RECIPIENT$(L)
250    WHILE EOF(1) = 0
260       LINE INPUT #1, L$
270       PRINT L$
280    WEND
290    CLOSE 1
300    PRINT
310 NEXT L
Ok
RUN
WHICH LETTER? REJECT
HOW MANY RECIPIENTS? 2
RECIPIENT # 1 ? MR. STEINBECK
RECIPIENT # 2 ? MS. CHRISTIE
```

```
DEAR MR. STEINBECK
     THANK YOU FOR YOUR MANUSCRIPT, "BELLING THE MOUSE".   IT
WAS VERY GOOD, BUT WE ALREADY HAVE OVER TWO HUNDRED WORKS WITH
THAT TITLE.   WE ARE SORRY, BUT YOUR MATERIAL DOES NOT FILL OUR
CURRENT NEEDS.


                         FILTHY RAG PUBLISHERS


DEAR MS. CHRISTIE
     THANK YOU FOR YOUR MANUSCRIPT, "BELLING THE MOUSE".   IT
WAS VERY GOOD, BUT WE ALREADY HAVE OVER TWO HUNDRED WORKS WITH
THAT TITLE.   WE ARE SORRY, BUT YOUR MATERIAL DOES NOT FILL OUR
CURRENT NEEDS.


                         FILTHY RAG PUBLISHERS

Ok
```

Demonstration Programs

The following programs illustrate applications for the material covered in this chapter. They consist of a series of examples concerning the record keeping process of a sporting goods manufacturer.

PROGRAM 10.8

This program, named ACME.BAS, will produce a file named SALES.TXT that contains the sales records of all salespeople working for the Acme Sporting Goods Company. Each salesperson sells baseball bats, balls and helmets.

```
1 REM     STAFF = Number of salespersons
2 REM     PERSON$ = Name of salesperson
3 REM     BATS, BALLS, HELMETS = Bats, balls and helmets sold
4 REM
5 REM
10  OPEN "O", 1, "B:SALES.TXT"
20  INPUT "HOW MANY SALESPERSONS DO YOU HAVE";STAFF
30  PRINT
40  FOR EMPLOYEE = 1 TO STAFF
50      INPUT "SALESPERSON";PERSON$
60      INPUT "BATS SOLD";BATS
70      INPUT "BALLS SOLD";BALLS
80      INPUT "HELMETS SOLD";HELMETS
90      WRITE #1, PERSON$,BATS,BALLS,HELMETS
100     PRINT
110 NEXT EMPLOYEE
120 CLOSE 1
130 PRINT "THE INFORMATION IS IN THE FILE."
Ok
RUN
HOW MANY SALESPERSONS DO YOU HAVE? 5
SALESPERSON? AUSTIN WILMERDING
BATS SOLD? 32
BALLS SOLD? 17
HELMETS SOLD? 23

SALESPERSON? DON KIDDER
BATS SOLD? 4
BALLS SOLD? 10
HELMETS SOLD? 5

SALESPERSON? FIONA L'HUILLIER
BATS SOLD? 29
BALLS SOLD? 34
HELMETS SOLD? 52

SALESPERSON? ROBERT OAKLEY
BATS SOLD? 45
BALLS SOLD? 17
HELMETS SOLD? 39

SALESPERSON? BROOKES WALSH
BATS SOLD? 26
BALLS SOLD? 32
HELMETS SOLD? 12

THE INFORMATION IS IN THE FILE.
Ok
```

PROGRAM 10.9

This program, named ACME2.BAS, will update the sales records for an individual salesperson.

```
1 REM     PERSON$ = Name of salesperson
2 REM     BATS, BALLS, HELMETS = Bats, balls and helmets sold
3 REM     CHANGE$ = Salesperson whose sales have changed
4 REM
5 REM
10 OPEN "I", 1, "B:SALES.TXT"
20 OPEN "O", 2, "B:SALES.TMP"
30 INPUT "WHOSE SALES HAVE CHANGED";CHANGE$
40 WHILE EOF(1) = 0
50    INPUT #1, PERSON$,BATS,BALLS,HELMETS
60    IF PERSON$ = CHANGE$ THEN INPUT "NEW SALES";BATS,BALLS,HELMETS
70    WRITE #2, PERSON$,BATS,BALLS,HELMETS
80 WEND
90 CLOSE 1,2
100 KILL "B:SALES.TXT"
110 NAME "B:SALES.TMP" AS "B:SALES.TXT"
120 PRINT CHANGE$;"'S RECORDS HAVE BEEN UPDATED."
Ok
RUN
WHOSE SALES HAVE CHANGED? BROOKES WALSH
NEW SALES? 30,38,22
BROOKES WALSH'S RECORDS HAVE BEEN UPDATED.
Ok
```

When the computer has found the right salesperson (at line 60) it prompts the user for data from the keyboard. The new information is then placed in the new file SALES.TMP at line 70.

PROGRAM 10.10

This program, named ACME3.BAS, will write a personalized letter of congratulations to all salespersons who have sold 75 units or more.

```
1 REM     PERSON$ = Name of salesperson
2 REM      BATS, BALLS, HELMETS = Bats, balls and helmets sold
3 REM      FLAG = Indicator to see if anyone qualified
4 REM
5 REM
10 OPEN "I", 1, "B:SALES.TXT"
20 FLAG = 0
30 WHILE EOF(1) = 0
40     INPUT #1, PERSON$,BATS,BALLS,HELMETS
50     IF BATS + BALLS + HELMETS >= 75 THEN GOSUB 100
60 WEND
70 CLOSE 1
80 IF FLAG <> 0
        THEN PRINT FLAG;"SALESPERSONS WILL RECEIVE A BONUS."
        ELSE PRINT "NO ONE SOLD ENOUGH.  THEY NEED A PEP TALK."
90 END
100 PRINT
110 PRINT "DEAR ";PERSON$;","
120 PRINT "      CONGRATULATIONS, YOU ARE ONE OF OUR TOP"
130 PRINT "SALES PERSONS.  YOUR BONUS CHECK IS IN THE MAIL."
140 PRINT
150 PRINT TAB(29);"YOUR BOSS"
160 PRINT
170 FLAG = FLAG + 1
180 RETURN
Ok
RUN

DEAR FIONA L'HUILLIER,
     CONGRATULATIONS, YOU ARE ONE OF OUR TOP
SALES PERSONS.  YOUR BONUS CHECK IS IN THE MAIL.

                            YOUR BOSS


DEAR ROBERT OAKLEY,
     CONGRATULATIONS, YOU ARE ONE OF OUR TOP
SALES PERSONS.  YOUR BONUS CHECK IS IN THE MAIL.

                            YOUR BOSS


DEAR BROOKES WALSH,
     CONGRATULATIONS, YOU ARE ONE OF OUR TOP
SALES PERSONS.  YOUR BONUS CHECK IS IN THE MAIL.

                            YOUR BOSS


 3 SALESPERSONS WILL RECEIVE A BONUS.
Ok
```

1. Store 50 random numbers between 0 and 20 in a sequential file. Use a second program to retrieve the numbers, add them, and print the sum.

2. Store in a sequential file the names and prices of five different desserts served at MADGE'S DINER. With a second program add two additional desserts. Have a third program retrieve and print the information.

3. (a) Establish a sequential file name SEQ.TXT which contains the members of the following sequence: 1001, 1002, 1003, . . . 1128.
   (b) Write a program to retrieve any member of the sequence from SEQ.TXT and print it when its place in the sequence (i.e. third number, eighth number, etc.) is inputted.

4. Store ten different first names of friends in a sequential file. A second program is to print all the names in the file which begin with the letters D, E, F, G and H or a message if none are found.

5. (a) Write a program that will create a sequential file FRAT.TXT which contains the names, fraternities, and ages of thirty college students.
   (b) Write a program that will access FRAT.TXT and create a sequential file SIGMA.TXT which contains the names and ages of only students who live in Sigma Chi.

(c) Write a program that accesses the file FRAT.TXT and randomly selects twenty-five students for seats in a classroom of five rows, five seats to a row. Have the computer print the seating plan for the class, placing each student's name at the correct seat location.

6. (a) Create a sequential payroll file called PAY.TXT to store each of ten person's names (last name first), his or her hourly pay rate, the number of dependents, and deductions for medical and life insurance for each week. Supply appropriate data.
(b) Use PAY to prepare the payroll data sheet (supply the number of hours (H) each person worked during the week). The sheet should list the name, hours worked, gross pay, three deductions, and net pay. Assume a tax rate of 25%, with 2% being subtracted from this rate for each dependent.

```
RUN
MENACE DENNIS
---- --- --- ---- --- --- ---- ---

HOURS WORKED                        40
GROSS PAY:                    $ 40
TAX:                          $ 10
MEDICAL INSURANCE:            $ 2
LIFE INSURANCE:               $ 14
NET:                          $ 27

BEAVER LEAVITTO
---- --- --- ---- --- --- ---- ---

HOURS WORKED                        37.1
GROSS PAY:                    $ 83.48
TAX:                          $ 20.87
MEDICAL INSURANCE:            $ 1
LIFE INSURANCE:               $ 16
NET:                          $ 60.61
```

7. (a) Two persons, NIT and WIT, measured the Fahrenheit temperature (F) outside on Feb. 12 at various times (T) during a ten hour period. Their results are recorded here. Set up two sequential files, NIT.TXT and WIT.TXT, one for each person's data.

NIT	T	F	WIT	T	F
	0.0	18.1		1.0	20.9
	2.1	24.0		1.9	23.3
	3.8	27.2		3.5	26.1
	6.0	29.3		6.0	28.8
	8.0	26.6		8.2	26.2
	9.0	16.1		10.0	16.0

(b) Write a program that will merge the two files into one sequential file named MERGE.TXT. The times should be sequentially in order. However, when a value of (T) occurs both in NIT.TXT and WIT.TXT the average of the two values of (F) should be placed in MERGE.TXT.

(c) Retrieve and print the contents of MERGE.TXT.

8. There are twenty seats (numbered 1-20) in a classroom which will be used to administer the College Board Examination. The computer is to select seats randomly for each student taking the examination and store the student's name in a sequential file named SEATS.TXT.

(a) Write a program that will create and zero (place a blank space in for each name) the sequential file SEATS.TXT.

(b) Write a program that will randomly assign a seat to each of twenty students whose names are in a data statement and then store the name in SEATS.TXT with the appropriate seat number. Make sure no repeats occur.

(c) List the contents of the file SEATS.TXT.

9. (a) The Drama Club has decided to use the computer to print out tickets for a play it will perform in the school's auditorium. To reserve a seat a student runs a program called DRAMA.BAS, and types in the name and the row and seat number he would like. There are ten rows with five seats to a row. His ticket will appear as below. Have the program open a file named SHOW.TXT which stores the seat assignments. Make sure that a seat may not be chosen more than once.

```
DRAMA CLUB SHOW
MICHAEL JONES HAS
RESERVED ROW 4
SEAT 3 FOR
JULY 4, 1983
```

(b) Write a program which will list the empty seats giving their row and seat numbers.

(c) Write a program that will print a seating plan giving the names of the seat holders in their correct location.

RANDOM-ACCESS FILES

A random-access file is structured like a collection of drawers in a filing cabinet, each holding a block of data that may be accessed individually. This filing system offers advantages to the one "drawer" structure of sequential files. To read the last line of data in a sequential file, every line of data preceding it must be read in sequence. However, any "drawer" in a random-access file can be opened without opening any of the others. Updating a random-access file is easier than updating a sequential file since the contents of one "drawer" can be updated without accessing the rest of the file. Unlike a sequential file, which is opened for a specific mode, a random-access file can be both written to and read from simultaneously.

In the random-access file each "drawer", called a record, consists of space reserved to store information. The length of the records in a file, i.e., the amount of information each one can hold, is specified when a random-access file is created and is the same for all of the records within a given file. When the system is initialized the computer assumes the maximum length of a record to be 128 characters unless otherwise instructed. The user may define records to be of any length up to the maximum specified at start up.

A single record need not hold simply one item of data but many pieces, as long as they do not require more space than the specified size of the record.

To utilize the potential offered by random-access files, it is necessary to understand how the computer stores information. For file processing, the computer could have been designed to put each small item of information on the disk as soon as that information was made available. Since accesssing the disk is time consuming, however, it is more efficient to transfer information to the disk in complete records. This requires the computer to have a temporary storage space called a buffer, where information is stored until a record is complete.

With sequential files the user has no control over the interaction between the buffer and the disk. Instead, the computer automatically determines when the buffer is full and then transfers its contents to the disk. Random-access files, however, give the user complete control over both the structure of the buffer's contents and its transfer to the disk.

The process of transferring data between a program and a random-access file involves the following series of steps:

1. Using the OPEN statement, the file must be created, opened, and a buffer made ready to receive data.

2. Using the FIELD statement, the buffer must be partitioned to fit the structure of each record.

3. Data has to be transferred from the program to the buffer using the LSET and RSET commands.

4. Data has to be transferred from the buffer to the file using the PUT command.

5. To retrieve data from the file for use in the program, the GET command is used.

Each of these steps is presented separately and should be read carefully so that the reader understands how each interacts with the others.

OPEN

Like sequential files, random-access files use the OPEN statement. The format for opening random-access files is

OPEN "R", <channel>, "<file name>", <record length>

For example,

20 OPEN "R", 3, "KAZOO", 50

will open a file named KAZOO for random-access on channel three, with each record in the file containing fifty characters, and will assign it a buffer.

FIELD

Unlike sequential files, random-access files store all information as strings. This requires numeric data to be converted to strings before being stored. The commands used in performing these conversions are discussed later in this chapter.

After the OPEN statement assigns a buffer to a file, the FIELD statement is used to organize the buffer so that data can be sent through it from the program to the file and vice versa. The FIELD statement partitions the buffer into regions where each holds a string and is referenced by a specific string variable. Its simplest form is

FIELD <channel>, <length> AS <string variable>

For example,

$$10 \text{ OPEN "R", 2, "DATA", 50}$$
$$20 \text{ FIELD 2, 50 AS A\$}$$

After the file has been opened at line 10, the FIELD statement at line 20 reserves the entire fifty characters in the buffer for the string variable A$. It is possible to partition the buffer to hold more than one string.

$$20 \text{ FIELD 2, 20 AS A\$, 30 AS B\$}$$

will reserve the first twenty characters of the buffer for the contents of A$ and the last thirty characters for the contents of B$.

LSET and RSET

The FIELD statement reserves a certain number of spaces for string variables in a buffer, but it does not transfer the strings to the buffer. To do this, it is necessary to use the LSET and RSET commands. The form for both is

LSET
   or   <string variable defined in FIELD> = <string to be transferred to buffer>
RSET

For example,

$$20 \text{ FIELD 1, 24 AS N1\$}$$
$$30 \text{ LSET N1\$ = "TWENTY-FOUR CHARACTERS!!"}$$

or

$$20 \text{ FIELD 1, 24 AS N1\$}$$
$$30 \text{ RSET N1\$ = "TWENTY-FOUR CHARACTERS!!"}$$

Besides transferring strings to the buffer, these commands also change the strings to make sure that they properly fit the space allotted in the FIELD statement. For example, if N1$ contains 15 characters, 9 blank characters have to be added to bring the total to 24. If N1$ contains more than 24 characters, it must be truncated to 24. These operations are performed by either the LSET or RSET commands.

The LSET command left justifies a string by adding needed blank characters to the right end of the string. If N1$ contains 15 characters, LSET will add 9 blank characters on the right end. RSET justifies by adding the 9 blank characters on the left end. Both LSET and RSET will truncate excess characters from the right end of a string which is larger than the space specified in the FIELD statement.

PROGRAM 11.1

This program demonstrates how LSET and RSET change strings to ready them for storage in a random-access file.

```
10 OPEN "R", 1, "B:SUNSET", 30
20 FIELD 1, 5 AS A$, 10 AS B$, 5 AS C$, 10 AS D$
30 LSET A$ = "ABCDEFG"
40 LSET B$ = "ABCDEFG"
50 RSET C$ = "ABCDEFG"
60 RSET D$ = "ABCDEFG"
70 PRINT "THIS IS HOW THE 30 CHARACTERS APPEAR IN THE"
80 PRINT "BUFFER, EXCLUDING THE PARENTHESES:"
90 PRINT TAB(3);"A$";TAB(12);"B$";TAB(22);"C$";TAB(31);"D$"
100 PRINT "(";A$;")(";B$;")(";C$;")(";D$;")"
110 CLOSE 1
Ok
RUN
THIS IS HOW THE 30 CHARACTERS APPEAR IN THE
BUFFER, EXCLUDING THE PARENTHESES:
  A$        B$         C$        D$
(ABCDE)(ABCDEFG    )(ABCDE)(    ABCDEFG)
Ok
```

Notice that the FIELD statement at line 20 has set aside 5 characters for A$, but since the string in line 30 is longer than 5 characters, the LSET command in line 30 has truncated the last two. Since 10 characters were set aside for B$, the LSET command in line 40 has added 3 spaces to the right of the string to make it 10 characters long. As only 5 spaces were allotted to C$, the RSET command in line 50 truncated the excess characters from the right. The RSET command in line 60 has added 3 spaces to the left of B$ so that it fills up the space allotted by the FIELD statement.

PUT

The LSET and RSET commands only transfer information from the program to the buffer, but do not transfer the contents of the buffer to the disk. The PUT statement is used to transfer the data in the buffer to a record in the file. Each record is numbered sequentially, from one to the number of records in the file.

The form of the PUT statement is:

PUT <channel>, <record number>

If the record number is not specified, the data is transferred to the record immediately following the last record accessed by the program. For example,

20 PUT 2, 4

instructs the computer to transfer the contents of the buffer to the fourth record of the file open on channel 2. It is important to note that if the next PUT statement executed after the above example does not specify a record number, the data in the buffer will be transferred to the fifth record in the file.

PROGRAM 11.2

This program, named PEOPLE.BAS, creates the file ADDRESS.TXT and will allow the names and addresses for five people to be placed in the file.

```
1 REM    PERSON$,P$ = Name (15 characters)
2 REM    ADDRESS$,A$ = Address (25 characters)
3 REM
4 REM
10   OPEN "R", 1, "B:ADDRESS.TXT", 40
20   FIELD 1, 15 AS PERSON$, 25 AS ADDRESS$
30   FOR X = 1 TO 5
40      INPUT "NAME";P$
50      INPUT "ADDRESS";A$
60      LSET PERSON$ = P$
70      LSET ADDRESS$ = A$
80      PUT 1
90      PRINT
100 NEXT X
110 CLOSE 1
Ok
RUN
NAME? C. MAHAN
ADDRESS? 186 BLUE SPRUCE DR.

NAME? G. MANDEL
ADDRESS? 338 OPOSSUM AVE.

NAME? R. MACPHERSON
ADDRESS? 116 FRANKLIN CORNER RD.

NAME? C. JENKINS
ADDRESS? 12 NEWPORT RD.

NAME? D. RIMMER
ADDRESS? 1 SANDBURG DR.

Ok
```

The variable names used in the INPUT statements and in the FIELD statements must not be the same if the program is to transfer data correctly to the file.

REVIEW

1. Write a program, named CALEN2.BAS, that will create a random-access file MONTHS.TXT and will place the name of each month of the year in order in a separate record.

GET

The GET statement performs the opposite function of the PUT statement. It is used to transfer information in a record on the disk to the buffer associated with the file. Again, a FIELD statement must be employed in order to partition the buffer for the data that is to be transferred into it. The form of the GET statement is:

GET <channel>, <record number>

Like the PUT statement, the GET statement will transfer data from the record following the last record accessed if no record number is specified. For example,

20 GET 3, 12

will transfer the contents of record number 12 to the buffer associated with channel 3.

PROGRAM 11.3

This program, named PEOPLE2.BAS, will retrieve and print the name and address of any person stored in the file ADDRESS.TXT.

```
1 REM     PERSON$ = Name (15 characters)
2 REM     ADDRESS$ = Address (25 characters)
3 REM     RECORD = Record number
4 REM
5 REM
10 PRINT "ENTER A NEGATIVE NUMBER TO STOP THE PROGRAM"
20 OPEN "R", 2, "B:ADDRESS.TXT", 40
30 FIELD 2, 15 AS PERSON$, 25 AS ADDRESS$
40 INPUT "WHICH RECORD";RECORD
50    IF RECORD <= 0 THEN 100
60    GET 2, RECORD
70    PRINT PERSON$ : PRINT ADDRESS$
80    PRINT
90 GOTO 40
100 CLOSE 2
Ok
```

```
RUN
ENTER A NEGATIVE NUMBER TO STOP THE PROGRAM
WHICH RECORD? 3
R. MACPHERSON
116 FRANKLIN CORNER RD.

WHICH RECORD? 1
C. MAHAN
186 BLUE SPRUCE DR.

WHICH RECORD? -1
Ok
```

REVIEW

2. Write a program, named LOOKUP.BAS, that will retrieve the name of a selected month from the file MONTHS.TXT.

Converting Numbers Into Strings

Since random-access files can only store strings, it is necessary to convert numeric data into a string before it is stored. The following functions perform this operation:

Function	Operation
N$ = MKI$(N%)	Converts an integer (N%) into a two character string (N$).
N$ = MKS$(N!)	Converts a single-precision number (N!) into a four character string (N$).
N$ = MKD$(N#)	Converts a double-precision number (N#) into an eight character string (N$).

Converting Strings Into Numbers

When converted numeric data is retrieved from a random-access file, it may be converted back to numeric data using the following functions:

Function	Operation
N% = CVI(N$)	Converts a two character string (N$) into an integer (N%).
N! = CVS(N$)	Converts a four character string (N$) into a single-precision number (N!).
N# = CVD(N$)	Converts an eight character string (N$) into a double-precision number (N#).

LOC

The LOC function is useful when working with random-access files. The LOC function returns the record number used in the last GET or PUT executed on a particular channel. The statement

$$N = LOC(3)$$

will assign to the variable N the record number used in the last GET or PUT operation performed on channel 3. The LOC function will return zero until a GET or PUT is executed.

If a GET statement attempts to read a record past the end of a file, the buffer associated with that file is filled with null characters (CHR$ (0)). This information can be used to determine the number of records in a random-access file. Proceeding sequentially, all of the records in a file can be read and counted until null records are found.

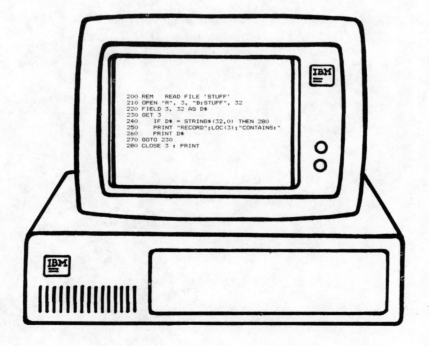

PROGRAM 11.4

This program illustrates the use of LOC and the method for finding the end of a file.

```
1 REM      N,R = Number of records in file
2 REM      D$,I$ = Data (32 characters)
3 REM
4 REM
10   REM   CREATE FILE 'STUFF' AND ALLOW USER TO PLACE
              DATA IN THAT FILE
30   OPEN "R", 1, "B:STUFF", 32
40   FIELD 1, 32 AS D$
50   INPUT "HOW MANY RECORDS DO YOU WANT IN THE FILE";N
60   FOR R = 1 TO N
70      INPUT "ENTER DATA";I$
80      LSET D$ = I$ : PUT 1, R
90      PRINT "THAT WAS PLACED IN RECORD";LOC(1);"OF STUFF"
100 NEXT R
110 CLOSE 1 : PRINT
120 REM
130 REM
200 REM    READ FILE 'STUFF'
210 OPEN "R", 3, "B:STUFF", 32
220 FIELD 3, 32 AS D$
230 GET 3
240    IF D$ = STRING$(32,0) THEN 280
250    PRINT "RECORD";LOC(3);"CONTAINS:"
260      PRINT D$
270 GOTO 230
280 CLOSE 3 : PRINT
Ok
RUN
HOW MANY RECORDS DO YOU WANT IN THE FILE? 3
ENTER DATA? HOW'S THIS FOR DATA?
THAT WAS PLACED IN RECORD 1 OF STUFF
ENTER DATA? O.K. LET'S PUT THIS IN # 2
THAT WAS PLACED IN RECORD 2 OF STUFF
ENTER DATA? THAT'S ALL FOLKS...
THAT WAS PLACED IN RECORD 3 OF STUFF

RECORD 1 CONTAINS:
HOW'S THIS FOR DATA?
RECORD 2 CONTAINS:
O.K. LET'S PUT THIS IN # 2
RECORD 3 CONTAINS:
THAT'S ALL FOLKS...

Ok
```

3. Write a program, named SIZE.BAS, that will determine the length of the file MONTHS.TXT and place that information in the first record of a new file called LENGTH.TXT.

Demonstration Programs

The following series of programs establishes a file named GRADES.TXT which contains the names and grades of a number of students and then demonstrates how the file can be used.

PROGRAM 11.5

This program, named SCHOOL.BAS, will store students' names and the course names and grades for four courses in which they are enrolled in a file named GRADES.TXT. In each case the student's I.D. number is used as the record number.

```
1 REM     STUDENT$,S$ = Student's name (20 characters)
2 REM     CRS1$,CRS2$,CRS3$,CRS4$,C$ = Courses (20 characters)
3 REM     GRD1$,GRD2$,GRD3$,GRD4$,G = Grades (2 characters each)
4 REM     ID = Student's ID number
5 REM
6 REM
10    OPEN "R", 1, "B:GRADES.TXT", 108
20    FIELD 1, 20 AS STUDENT$, 20 AS CRS1$, 2 AS GRD1$,
              20 AS CRS2$, 2 AS GRD2$, 20 AS CRS3$,
              2 AS GRD3$, 20 AS CRS4$, 2 AS GRD4$
30    INPUT "NUMBER OF STUDENTS";S
40    FOR ID = 1 TO S
50        INPUT "STUDENT'S NAME";S$ : LSET STUDENT$ = S$
60        INPUT "COURSE NAME";C$ : LSET CRS1$ = C$
70        INPUT "GRADE";G : LSET GRD1$ = MKI$(G)
80        INPUT "COURSE NAME";C$ : LSET CRS2$ = C$
90        INPUT "GRADE";G : LSET GRD2$ = MKI$(G)
100       INPUT "COURSE NAME";C$ : LSET CRS3$ = C$
110       INPUT "GRADE";G : LSET GRD3$ = MKI$(G)
120       INPUT "COURSE NAME";C$ : LSET CRS4$ = C$
130       INPUT "GRADE";G : LSET GRD4$ = MKI$(G)
140       PRINT "THAT STUDENT HAS BEEN ASSIGNED ID #";ID
150       PUT 1
160       PRINT
170   NEXT ID
180 CLOSE 1
Ok
```

```
RUN
NUMBER OF STUDENTS? 10
STUDENT'S NAME? APRIL BARRY
COURSE NAME? ENGLISH
GRADE? 87
COURSE NAME? PSYCHOLOGY
GRADE? 83
COURSE NAME? ART HISTORY
GRADE? 96
COURSE NAME? EUROPEAN HISTORY
GRADE? 79
THAT STUDENT HAS BEEN ASSIGNED ID # 1

STUDENT'S NAME? HENRY BECK
COURSE NAME? PHYSICS
GRADE? 82
COURSE NAME? CALCULUS
GRADE? 78
COURSE NAME? ENGLISH
GRADE? 80
COURSE NAME? DRAFTING
GRADE? 73
THAT STUDENT HAS BEEN ASSIGNED ID # 2

                    •
                    •
                    •

STUDENT'S NAME? KIM FORD
COURSE NAME? AP BIOLOGY
GRADE? 93
COURSE NAME? ENGLISH
GRADE? 84
COURSE NAME? COMPUTING II
GRADE? 96
COURSE NAME? ECONOMICS
GRADE? 79
THAT STUDENT HAS BEEN ASSIGNED ID # 10

Ok
```

(A COMPLETE RUN IS NOT SHOWN.)

PROGRAM 11.6

This program, named REPORT.BAS, will read and print a particular student's grades and computed grade average. Note the method used to check for nonexistent I.D. numbers.

```
1 REM     STUDENT$,S$ = Student's name (20 characters)
2 REM     CRS1$,CRS2$,CRS3$,CRS4$,C$ = Courses (20 characters)
3 REM     GRD1$,GRD2$,GRD3$,GRD4$,G = Grades (2 characters each)
4 REM     ID = Student's ID number
5 REM     AVERAGE = Student's average
6 REM
7 REM
10   PRINT "ENTER A NEGATIVE NUMBER TO STOP."
20   OPEN "R", 1, "B:GRADES.TXT", 108
30   FIELD 1, 20 AS STUDENT$, 20 AS CRS1$, 2 AS GRD1$,
              20 AS CRS2$, 2 AS GRD2$, 20 AS CRS3$,
              2 AS GRD3$, 20 AS CRS4$, 2 AS GRD4$
40   INPUT "STUDENT'S ID#";ID
50      IF ID <= 0 THEN 130
60      GET 1, ID
70      IF STUDENT$ = STRING$(20,0) THEN PRINT "BAD ID#" :
                                    GOTO 40
80      AVERAGE = (CVI(GRD1$) + CVI(GRD2$) + CVI(GRD3$) +
                CVI(GRD4$))/4
90      PRINT TAB(5);CVI(GRD1$);TAB(10);CVI(GRD2$);TAB(15);
100     PRINT CVI(GRD3$);TAB(20);CVI(GRD4$);TAB(30);
110     PRINT "AVE. =";AVERAGE : PRINT
120 GOTO 40
130 CLOSE 1
Ok
RUN
ENTER A NEGATIVE NUMBER TO STOP.
STUDENT'S ID#? 7
     84    80    78    81        AVE. = 80.75

STUDENT'S ID#? 4
     83    76    82    90        AVE. = 82.75

STUDET'S ID#? -1
Ok
```

PROGRAM 11.7

This program, named CORRECT.BAS, will allow a teacher to correct a mistake in a student's grades.

```
1 REM     STUDENT$,S$ = Student's name (20 characters)
2 REM     CRS1$,CRS2$,CRS3$,CRS4$,C$ = Courses (20 characters)
3 REM     GRD1$,GRD2$,GRD3$,GRD4$,G = Grades (2 characters each)
4 REM     ID = Student's ID number
5 REM
6 REM
10   PRINT "ENTER A NEGATIVE NUMBER TO STOP."
20   OPEN "R", 1, "B:GRADES.TXT", 108
30   FIELD 1, 20 AS STUDENT$, 20 AS CRS1$, 2 AS GRD1$,
              20 AS CRS2$, 2 AS GRD2$, 20 AS CRS3$,
               2 AS GRD3$, 20 AS CRS4$, 2 AS GRD4$
40   INPUT "STUDENT'S ID#";ID
50      IF ID <= 0 THEN 210
60      GET 1, ID
70      IF STUDENT$ = STRING$(20,0) THEN PRINT "BAD ID#" :
                                    GOTO 40
80      PRINT "ENTER NEW GRADES"
90      PRINT CRS1$,
100     INPUT G : LSET GRD1$ = MKI$(G)
110     PRINT CRS2$,
120     INPUT G : LSET GRD2$ = MKI$(G)
130     PRINT CRS3$,
140     INPUT G : LSET GRD3$ = MKI$(G)
150     PRINT CRS4$,
160     INPUT G : LSET GRD4$ = MKI$(G)
170     PUT 1, ID
180     PRINT "THE RECORDS ON ";STUDENT$;" HAVE BEEN UPDATED."
190     PRINT
200 GOTO 40
210 CLOSE 1
Ok
RUN
ENTER A NEGATIVE NUMBER TO STOP.
STUDENT'S ID#? 5
ENTER NEW GRADES
PHYSICS                   ? 87
AMERICAN HISTORY          ? 75
INDEPENDENT STUDY         ? 78
STATISTICS                ? 84
THE RECORDS ON LESTER WATERS        HAVE BEEN UPDATED.

STUDENT'S ID#? -1
Ok
```

PROGRAM 11.8

This program, named NEWKIDS.BAS, allows new students to be added to the file by creating new records at the end of the file.

```
1 REM     STUDENT$,S$ = Student's name (20 CHARACTERS)
2 REM     CRS1$,CRS2$,CRS3$,CRS4$,C$ = Courses (20 characters)
3 REM     GRD1$,GRD2$,GRD3$,GRD4$,G = Grades (2 characters each)
4 REM     ID = Student's ID number
5 REM
6 REM
10  OPEN "R", 1, "B:GRADES.TXT", 108
20  FIELD 1, 20 AS STUDENT$, 20 AS CRS1$, 2 AS GRD1$,
            20 AS CRS2$, 2 AS GRD2$, 20 AS CRS3$,
            2 AS GRD3$, 20 AS CRS4$, 2 AS GRD4$
30  REM
40  REM
100 REM     FIND LENGTH OF FILE
110 GET 1
120 IF STUDENT$ <> STRING$(20,0) THEN 40
130 REM
140 REM
200 REM     INPUT DATA ON NEW STUDENTS
210 INPUT "NUMBER OF NEW STUDENTS";S
220 FOR ID = LOC(1) TO LOC(1) + S - 1
230     INPUT "STUDENT'S NAME";S$ : LSET STUDENT$ = S$
240     INPUT "COURSE NAME";C$ : LSET CRS1$ = C$
250     INPUT "GRADE";G : LSET GRD1$ = MKI$(G)
260     INPUT "COURSE NAME";C$ : LSET CRS2$ = C$
270     INPUT "GRADE";G : LSET GRD2$ = MKI$(G)
280     INPUT "COURSE NAME";C$ : LSET CRS3$ = C$
290     INPUT "GRADE";G : LSET GRD3$ = MKI$(G)
300     INPUT "COURSE NAME";C$ : LSET CRS4$ = C$
310     INPUT "GRADE";G : LSET GRD4$ = MKI$(G)
320     PRINT "THAT STUDENT HAS BEEN ASSIGNED ID #";ID
330     PUT 1, ID
340     PRINT
350 NEXT ID
360 CLOSE 1
Ok
```

```
RUN
NUMBER OF NEW STUDENTS? 2
STUDENT'S NAME? SHERRY FRENCH
COURSE NAME? ENGLISH
GRADE? 87
COURSE NAME? PHILOSOPHY
GRADE? 83
COURSE NAME? ASTRONOMY
GRADE? 81
COURSE NAME? COMPUTER SCIENCE
GRADE? 67
THAT STUDENT HAS BEEN ASSIGNED ID # 11

STUDENT'S NAME? LISA HUROWITZ
COURSE NAME? CHEMISTRY
GRADE? 81
COURSE NAME? STATISTICS
GRADE? 82
COURSE NAME? ENGLISH
GRADE? 77
COURSE NAME? BOTANY
GRADE? 78
THAT STUDENT HAS BEEN ASSIGNED ID # 12

Ok
```

PROGRAM 11.9

This program, named EXTRA.BAS, creates a random-access file named ACTIVI-TY.TXT which will contain the extracurricular activities and athletic teams in which students are involved.

```
1 REM     ACTIV1$,ACTIV2$,A$ = Activities (20 characters each)
2 REM     TEAM$,T$ = Athletic team (15 characters)
3 REM     ID = Student's ID#
4 REM
5 REM
10   PRINT "ENTER STUDENT ID#, TWO ACTIVITIES AND ATHLETIC TEAM"
20   PRINT "ENTER A NEGATIVE NUMBER TO STOP."
30   OPEN "R", 1, "B:ACTIVITY.TXT", 55
40   FIELD 1, 20 AS ACTIV1$, 20 AS ACTIV2$, 15 AS TEAM$
50   INPUT "ID#";ID
60      IF ID <= 0 THEN 130
70      INPUT "FIRST ACTIVITY";A$ : LSET ACTIV1$ = A$
80      INPUT "SECOND ACTIVITY";A$ : LSET ACTIV2$ = A$
90      INPUT "ATHLETIC TEAM";T$ : LSET TEAM$ = T$
100     PUT 1, ID
110     PRINT
120 GOTO 50
130 CLOSE 1
Ok
RUN
ENTER STUDENT ID#, TWO ACTIVITIES AND ATHLETIC TEAM
ENTER A NEGATIVE NUMBER TO STOP
ID#? 1
FIRST ACTIVITY? THEATER
SECOND ACTIVITY? GLEE CLUB
ATHLETIC TEAM? TENNIS

ID#? 2
FIRST ACTIVITY? DEBATING CLUB
SECOND ACTIVITY? CHESS CLUB
ATHLETIC TEAM? FOOTBALL
```

(A COMPLETE RUN IS NOT SHOWN.)

Accessing Multiple Files

It is possible to work with two or more random-access files simultaneously within a single program. When this is done the programmer should not confuse the variables associated with each specific file. Note how the channel numbers are used to keep the information in each file separate within the program.

PROGRAM 11.10

This program, named FOOTBALL.BAS, opens the files GRADES.TXT and ACTIVITY.TXT and prints the names and grade averages for each member of the football team. The same record number indicates the same student in both files.

```
1  REM    STUDENT$,S$ = STUDENT'S NAME (20 CHARACTERS)
2  REM    CRS1$,CRS2$,CRS3$,CRS4$,C$ = Courses (20 characters)
3  REM    GRD1$,GRD2$,GRD3$,GRD4$,G = Grades (2 characters each)
4  REM    ACTIV1$,ACTIV2$,A$ = Activities (20 characters each)
5  REM    TEAM$,T$ = Athletic team (15 characters)
6  REM    ID = Studen ID number
7  REM
8  REM
10   OPEN "R", 1, "B:GRADES.TXT", 108
20   OPEN "R", 2, "B:ACTIVITY.TXT", 55
30   FIELD 1, 20 AS STUDENT$, 20 AS CRS1$, 2 AS GRD1$,
               20 AS CRS2$, 2 AS GRD2$, 20 AS CRS3$,
               2 AS GRD3$, 20 AS CRS4$, 2 AS GRD4$
40   FIELD 2, 20 AS ACTIV1$, 20 AS ACTIV2$, 15 AS TEAM$
50   ID = ID + 1
60      GET 1, ID
70      IF STUDENT$ = STRING$(20,0) THEN 140
80      GET 2, ID
90      IF LEFT$(TEAM$,8) <> "FOOTBALL" THEN 130
100     AVERAGE = (CVI(GRD1$) + CVI(GRD2$) + CVI(GRD3$) +
                CVI(GRD4$))/4
110     PRINT STUDENT$,AVERAGE
120     PRINT
130  GOTO 50
140  CLOSE 1,2
Ok
RUN
HENRY BECK                  78.25

ERIC SLAYTON                80.75

JEREMY LEADER               85.5

Ok
```

EXERCISES

1. Store the 26 letters of the alphabet in a random-access file in order. Have a program pick five random numbers from 1 to 26 and use these numbers to put together a five letter "word".

2. Store titles of ten books in a random-access file. Use this file to make a sequential file for all the titles beginning with letters from N to Z, inclusive.

3. (a) Establish a random-access file named SAYING.TXT which is to consist of wise sayings. Each sage remark is to consist of up to 128 characters. The number of such utterances is to be determined by the user.
   (b) Write the program required to retrieve and print any one of the wise sayings in SAYING.TXT.

WISE MEN SAY, TO NOT TRY TO FIND THE
ANSWER, ONLY TO UNDERSTAND QUESTION.

4. (a) Create a random-access file named ACCOUNTS.TXT that will contain the customer name and current balance for twenty-five savings accounts.
   (b) Write a program that will update the file ACCOUNTS.TXT whenever an individual makes a deposit or withdrawal.
   (c) Write a program using the file ACCOUNTS.TXT that sends a letter of warning to the holders of all overdrawn accounts, or a letter of congratulations to the holders of

accounts with $500 or more informing them that they will be receiving a toaster in the mail.

5. (a) Create a random-access file named CARS.TXT to record how many full-sized, mid-sized and compact cars a dealer sells each month for a twelve month period.
(b) Write a program that will retrieve information from the file CARS.TXT for a specific month and then print a bar graph comparing the sales of the three sizes of cars for that month.

6. (a) Write a program that will create a random-access file FRAT.TXT which contains the names, fraternities, and ages of thirty college students.
(b) Write a program that will access FRAT.TXT and create a sequential file SIGMA.TXT which contains the names and ages of the students who live in Sigma Chi.
(c) Write a program that accesses the file FRAT.TXT and randomly selects fifteen students for seats in a classroom of three rows, five seats to a row. Have the computer print a seating plan for the class, placing each student's name at the correct seat location.

7. Open four separate random-access files named NAME.TXT, SALARY.TXT, AGESEX.TXT, and AUTO.TXT, and store in them the data listed. All information is stored under a person's identification number, assumed for convenience to run from 1 to 10.

File 1 (NAME.TXT)

NAME	ADDRESS	STATE
1. BOWMAN	CANAAN	CT
2. BROOKS	SYOSSET	NY
3. CHRISTIAN	HARDWICK	VT
4. CUMMINGS	TRENTON	NJ
5. EDWARDS	MONTGOMERY	AL
6. HALEY	WESTFIELD	NJ
7. HALPERN	NEW YORK	NY
8. REYNOLDS	HOUSTON	TX
9. SCOTT	SHERIDAN	WY
10. WALKER	NEWARK	NJ

File 2 (SALARY.TXT)		File 3 (AGESEX.TXT)	
SALARY	SAVINGS	AGE	SEX
1. 18,000	4,200.	1. 48	M
2. 27,000	3,600.	2. 39	F
3. 59,000	2,200.	3. 46	M
4. 78,000	500.	4. 71	M
5. 25,000	7,800.	5. 29	M
6. 45,000	12,000.	6. 38	F
7. 9,000	400.	7. 51	M
8. 21,000	3,200.	8. 62	F
9. 33,000	4,700.	9. 22	F
10. 40,000	3,900.	10. 32	M

File 4 (AUTO.TXT)

AUTO	YR
1. BUICK	79
2. OLDS	72
3. CHEV	80
4. CHEV	73
5. FORD	78
6. CHEV	76
7. FORD	73
8. CAD	74
9. VW	79
10. FORD	69

By performing the correct file searches, find the following:

(a) Names and addresses of men over 30 years old who own a Ford and have an income over twenty thousand dollars a year.

(b) Names of men and women who drive a Chevrolet, Ford, or Volkswagen and have a salary above fifteen thousand dollars a year and savings below two thousand dollars.

(c) The F.B.I. is looking for a young man (under 35) who drives a Ford with New Jersey plates. Have the computer print his name and address.

8. (a) Write a program that will create a random-access file named SAVE.TXT that can be used by a bank to store information about ten depositors. Each depositor's name, social security number, complete address (number and street, city, state, and zip code), and account balance are to be included. The file SAVE.TXT is structured as shown below.

Variable	Variable name	Space allotment
Name	N$	20
Social Security Number	SS$	11
Street Address	A$	25
City	C$	15
State	S$	2
ZIP Code	Z$	5
Balance	B$	4

(b) Write a single program which allows any of the information, including the balance of the account, to be changed or updated.

```
RUN
DEPOSITOR'S ACCOUNT NUMBER? 2
NAME: MARY ANN WILSON
            (1) CHANGE NAME
            (2) CHANGE SOCIAL SECURITY NUMBER
            (3) CHANGE ADDRESS
            (4) CHANGE BALANCE

OPTION? 4
OLD BALANCE: 134.58
NEW BALANCE? 159.58
Ok
```

(c) The bank gives its depositors 1/2% interest per month compounded monthly. Write a program which is run at the end of each month to add 1/2% to the balance of each account.

9. The computer is to be used to store information on charge account customers at the Buy Low Department Store in a random access file named CHARGE.TXT. The information on each customer is to be stored in a single record with the record number serving as the customer's charge account number.

(a) Create the file CHARGE.TXT and store in it the name, street address, city, state, zip code, and total unpaid balance for each of ten charge customers.

(b) Write a program that will daily update the balances as new charges are made and bills are paid.

```
RUN
ENTER A NEGATIVE NUMBER TO STOP THE PROGRAM
ACCOUNT #? 1
BALANCE STANDS AT $ 0
CHARGE OR PAYMENT? C
AMOUNT? 487.23
NEW BALANCE IS $ 487.23

ACCOUNT #? -1
Ok
```

(c) Write a program that will send each customer a bill at the end of each month. If the total due exceeds $800, the message YOUR ACCOUNT EXCEEDS YOUR CHARGE LIMIT, PAY IMMEDIATELY is printed at the bottom of the bill.

```
RUN
FROM: BUY LOW DEPARTMENT STORE
TO: LIZ KANE
ACCOUNT # 1

YOU HAVE CHARGED $ 487.23 AGAINST YOUR
ACCOUNT.   THIS AMOUNT IS NOW DUE.

                        THANK YOU


FROM: BUY LOW DEPARTMENT STORE
TO: PAUL JOHNSON
ACCOUNT # 2

YOU HAVE CHARGED $ 874.12 AGAINST YOUR
ACCOUNT.   THIS AMOUNT IS NOW DUE.

YOUR ACCOUNT EXCEEEDS YOUR CHARGE LIMIT.
PAY IMMEDIATELY!

                        THANK YOU


Ok
```

(d) Write a program that will close the account of a customer who has paid his or her balance and is moving away. (Hint: Place all blanks in the record.)

```
RUN
WHICH ACCOUNT IS BEING CLOSED? 2
ACCOUNT # 2 HAS BEEN CLOSED.
Ok
```

(e) Write a program that opens an account for a new customer. Have the computer search the existing records and use one that is empty. If no empty record is found, add a new one.

```
RUN
NAME? SARA JONES
STREET ADDRESS? 75 GEORGE DYE RD.
CITY? TRENTON
STATE? NJ
ZIP CODE? 08690
THIS PERSON WILL BE ASSIGNED ACCOUNT # 2
Ok
```

11.22

12 BUSINESS APPLICATIONS

This chapter presents a series of programs which illustrate how the computer can be used by a small business. Since all statements used in this chapter have been previously explained the programs are presented with little explanation. These programs are meant to serve only as an outline of those that a business would actually use. The programmer should be able to adapt and expand these programs to tailor them to his or her specific needs.

Programs are presented which maintain an inventory and produce the payroll for a small company.

INVENTORY PROGRAMS

PROGRAM 12.1

When this program, named UPDATE.BAS, is initially run it creates the file IN-VNTRY.TXT and allows the user to store information on products in the company's current inventory. On subsequent runs of the program discontinued items can be removed and new items added to the inventory. It uses a complete record to store information on each item in inventory. The record number serves as the item's product identification number and the record holds nine separate pieces of information about the item. Each of these is identified in the REM statements at the beginning of the program. Notice that seven of the pieces of information require two variables, the first for the INPUT statement and the second for the LSET statement. Since SOLD$ and STARTDATE$ do not require input data, only one variable is used.

```
1    REM    ITEM = Product ID#
2    REM    D$,DESC$ = Product description (28 characters)
3    REM    P,PRICE$ = Retail price (4 characters)
4    REM    C,COST$ = Wholesale price (4 characters)
5    REM    S,STOCK$ = Number of units in stock (2 characters)
6    REM    L$,LOCAT$ = Stockroom shelf location (2 characters)
7    REM    M,MINSTOCK$ = Minimum stock size (2 characters)
8    REM    F,FULLSTOCK$ = Optimal stock size (2 characters)
9    REM    SOLD$ = Total units sold to date (2 characters)
10   REM    STARTDATE$ = First date of sale (10 characters)
11   REM    QUERY$ = Miscellaneous user input
12   REM           .
13   REM
100  REM    This program is used to add a new product to be sold
            or discontinue an old one
110  OPEN "R", 1, "B:INVNTRY.TXT", 56
120  FIELD 1, 28 AS DESC$, 4 AS PRICE$, 4 AS COST$, 2 AS STOCK$,
            2 AS LOCAT$, 2 AS MINSTOCK$, 2 AS FULLSTOCK$,
            2 AS SOLD$, 10 AS STARTDATE$
130  PRINT "'A' TO ADD A PRODUCT, 'D' DISCONTINUE, OR 'E' END";
140  INPUT QUERY$
150  IF ASC(QUERY$) = 65 THEN 200
                      ELSE IF ASC(QUERY$) = 68 THEN 400
                                      ELSE 600
160  REM    ASC("A") = 65, ASC("D") = 68
170  REM
180  REM
200  REM    Add a new product
210  GET 1
220  IF DESC$ <> STRING$(28,0) AND DESC$ <> STRING$(28,15)
        THEN 210 : REM    Find free record
230  PRINT "THIS WILL BE ITEM #";LOC(1)
240  REM    LOC(1) = NUMBER OF LAST RECORD ACCESSED
250  INPUT "DESCRIPTION";D$ : LSET DESC$ = D$
260  INPUT "PRICE";P : LSET PRICE$ = MKS$(P)
270  INPUT "COST";C : LSET COST$ = MKS$(C)
280  INPUT "HOW MANY IN STOCK";S : LSET STOCK$ = MKI$(S)
290  INPUT "LOCATION CODE";L$ : LSET LOCAT$ = L$
300  INPUT "REORDER POINT";M : LSET MINSTOCK$ = MKI$(M)
310  INPUT "FULL STOCK LEVEL";F : LSET FULLSTOCK$ = MKI$(F)
320  LSET SOLD$ = MKI$(0)
330  LSET STARTDATE$ = DATE$
340  PUT 1, LOC(1)
350  PRINT
360  GOTO 130
370  REM
380  REM
```

```
400 REM    Discontinue a product
410 INPUT "ITEM #";ITEM
420 GET 1, ITEM
430 IF DESC$ = STRING$(28,0) OR DESC$ = STRING$(28,15)
        THEN PRINT "BAD #" : GOTO 410 : REM    NO INFO HERE
440 PRINT : PRINT DESC$ : PRINT
450 INPUT "IS THAT THE CORRECT ITEM";QUERY$
460 IF ASC(QUERY$) <> 89 THEN 410 : REM    ASC("Y") = 89
470 LSET DESC$ = STRING$(28,15) : REM    Replace old information
480 LSET PRICE$ = MKS$(0)       : REM    in record with ASCII
490 LSET COST$ = MKS$(0)        : REM    character 15 & 0's.
500 LSET STOCK$ = MKI$(0)       : REM    This identifies record
510 LSET LOCAT$ = STRING$(2,15) : REM    as available for a new
520 LSET MINSTOCK$ = MKI$(0)    : REM    product's information.
530 LSET FULLSTOCK$ = MKI$(0)
540 LSET SOLD$ = MKI$(0)
550 LSET STARTDATE$ = STRING$(10,15)
560 PUT 1, ITEM
570 GOTO 130
580 REM
590 REM
600 REM    Close file and end program
610 CLOSE 1
620 END
```

Note how line 220 is used to fine a free record to store information about a new product. In this program when a product is discontinued the description, location code, and data sections of its record are filled with characters using CHR$(15). The remaining sections are assigned the string equivalent of zeroes. This is an arbitrary choice, any characters could have been used to fill the record of a discontinued item.

When a new item is to be added to the inventory, the program searches for a record containing CHR$(15) characters in the record's first field. If such a record is found, that record is then used to store information about the new item. If no such record is found, a record containing CHR$(0) characters is then located to indicate the end of the file so that the next record can be used. This technique for locating the end of a file is also demonstrated in Program 11.4.

When an item is to be discontinued, line 430 determines whether its record has been previously emptied or is past the end of the file.

PROGRAM 12.2

This program, named CORRECT.BAS, is used to correct data in the file INVNTRY.TXT. Notice that SOLD$ and STARTDATE$ now use secondary variables to allow input from the keyboard.

```
1    REM      ITEM = Product ID#
2    REM      D$,DESC$ = Product description (28 characters)
3    REM      P,PRICE$ = Retail price (4 characters)
4    REM      C,COST$ = Wholesale price (4 characters)
5    REM      S1,STOCK$ = Number of units in stock (2 characters)
6    REM      L$,LOCAT$ = Stockroom shelf location (2 characters)
7    REM      M,MINSTOCK$ = Minimum stock size (2 characters)
8    REM      F,FULLSTOCK$ = Optimal stock size (2 characters)
9    REM      S2,SOLD$ = Total units sold to date (2 characters)
10   REM      S$,STARTDATE$ = First date of sale (10 characters)
11   REM      QUERY = Miscellaneous user input
12   REM
13   REM
100     REM     This program is used to correct data in the file
                INVNTRY.TXT
110     OPEN "R", 1, "B:INVNTRY.TXT", 56
120     FIELD 1, 28 AS DESC$, 4 AS PRICE$, 4 AS COST$, 2 AS STOCK$,
                2 AS LOCAT$, 2 AS MINSTOCK$, 2 AS FULLSTOCK$,
                2 AS SOLD$, 10 AS STARTDATE$
130     PRINT "ENTER A NEGATIVE NUMBER TO END THE PROGRAM"
140     PRINT
150     REM
160     REM
200     REM     Get appropriate record and display menu
210     INPUT "ITEM #"; ITEM
220     IF ITEM < 0 THEN 1500
230     GET 1, ITEM
240     IF DESC$ = STRING$(28,0) OR DESC$ = STRING$(28,15)
            THEN PRINT "BAD #" : GOTO 210
250     PRINT DESC$
260     PRINT ,"(1) CHANGE DESCRIPTION"
270     PRINT ,"(2) CHANGE PRICE"
280     PRINT ,"(3) CHANGE COST"
290     PRINT ,"(4) CHANGE STOCK SIZE"
300     PRINT ,"(5) CHANGE LOCATION CODE"
310     PRINT ,"(6) CHANGE REORDER POINT"
320     PRINT ,"(7) CHANGE FULL STOCK LEVEL"
330     PRINT ,"(8) CHANGE TOTAL SOLD TO DATE"
340     PRINT ,"(9) CHANGE STARTING SALES DATE"
350     PRINT ,"(10) SAVE CHANGE(S)"
360     PRINT
370     INPUT "OPTION";QUERY
380     ON QUERY GOTO 500,600,700,800,900,1000,1100,1200,1300,1400
390     REM
400     REM
```

```
500    REM    Change description
510    INPUT "NEW DESCRIPTION";D$ : LSET DESC$ = D$
520    GOTO 360
530    REM
540    REM
600    REM    Change price
610    PRINT "OLD PRICE:";CVS(PRICE$)
620    INPUT "NEW PRICE";P : LSET PRICE$ = MKS$(P)
630    GOTO 360
640    REM
650    REM
700    REM    Change cost
710    PRINT "OLD COST:";CVS(COST$)
720    INPUT "NEW COST";C : LSET COST$ = MKS$(C)
730    GOTO 360
740    REM
750    REM
800    REM    Change stock size
810    PRINT "OLD STOCK SIZE:";CVI(STOCK$)
820    INPUT "NEW STOCK SIZE";S1 : LSET STOCK$ = MKI$(S1)
830    GOTO 360
840    REM
850    REM
900    REM    Change location code
910    PRINT "OLD LOCATION CODE: ";LOCAT$
920    INPUT "NEW LOCATION CODE";L$ : LSET LOCAT$ = L$
930    GOTO 360
940    REM
950    REM
1000 REM    Change reorder point
1010 PRINT "OLD REORDER POINT:";CVI(MINSTOCK$)
1020 INPUT "NEW REORDER POINT";M : LSET MINSTOCK$ = MKI$(M)
1030 GOTO 360
1040 REM
1050 REM
1100 REM    Change full stock level
1110 PRINT "OLD FULL STOCK LEVEL:";CVI(FULLSTOCK$)
1120 INPUT "NEW FULL STOCK LEVEL";F : LSET FULLSTOCK$ = MKI$(F)
1130 GOTO 360
1140 REM
1150 REM
1200 REM    Change total sold to date
1210 PRINT "OLD SALES TOTAL:";CVI(SOLD$)
1220 INPUT "NEW SALES TOTAL";S2 : LSET SOLD$ = MKI$(S2)
1230 GOTO 360
1240 REM
1250 REM
1300 REM    Change starting sales date
1310 PRINT "OLD STARTING DATE: ";STARTDATE$
1320 INPUT "NEW STARTING DATE";S$ : LSET STARTDATE$ = S$
1330 GOTO 360
1340 REM
1350 REM
```

```
1400 REM    Save changes
1410 PUT 1, ITEM
1420 PRINT
1430 GOTO 210
1440 REM
1450 REM
1500 REM    Close file and end program
1510 CLOSE 1
1520 END
```

PROGRAM 12.3

This program, named DAILY.BAS, updates the current stock levels in the file INVNTRY.TXT as items are sold.

```
1   REM    ITEM = Product ID#
2   REM    DESC$ = Product description (28 characters)
3   REM    PRICE$ = Retail price (4 characters)
4   REM    COST$ = Wholesale price (4 characters)
5   REM    STOCK$ = Number of units in stock (2 characters)
6   REM    LOCAT$ = Stockroom shelf location (2 characters)
7   REM    MINSTOCK$ = Minimum stock size (2 characters)
8   REM    FULLSTOCK$ = Optimal stock size (2 characters)
9   REM    SOLD$ = Total units sold to date (2 characters)
10  REM    STARTDATE$ = First date of sale (10 characters)
11  REM    SOLD = Number of units sold this day
12  REM    QUERY$ = Miscellaneous user input
13  REM
14  REM
100 REM    This program is used to update the inventory levels
           in accordance with daily sales
110 OPEN "R", 1, "B:INVNTRY.TXT", 56
120 FIELD 1, 28 AS DESC$, 4 AS PRICE$, 4 AS COST$, 2 AS STOCK$,
           2 AS LOCAT$, 2 AS MINSTOCK$, 2 AS FULLSTOCK$,
           2 AS SOLD$, 10 AS STARTDATE$
130 PRINT "ENTER A NEGATIVE NUMBER TO END THE PROGRAM" : PRINT
140 REM
150 REM
```

```
200 REM    Update stock level
210 INPUT "ITEM #";ITEM
220 IF ITEM < 0 THEN 400
230 GET 1, ITEM
240 IF DESC$ = STRING$(28,15) OR DESC$ = STRING$(28,0)
       THEN PRINT "BAD #" : PRINT : GOTO 210
250 PRINT DESC$
260 INPUT "IS THAT THE CORRECT ITEM";QUERY$
270 IF ASC(QUERY$) <> 89 THEN PRINT : GOTO 210
280 INPUT "HOW MANY SOLD TODAY";SOLD
290 IF SOLD > CVI(STOCK$) THEN PRINT "NOT THAT MANY IN STOCK" :
       GOTO 280
300 LSET STOCK$ = MKI$(CVI(STOCK$) - SOLD)
310 LSET SOLD$ = MKI$(CVI(SOLD$) + SOLD) : REM # sold to date
320 PUT 1, ITEM
330 PRINT
340 GOTO 210
350 REM
360 REM
400 REM    Close file and end program
410 CLOSE 1
420 END
```

PROGRAM 12.4

This program, named REPORT.BAS, will produce an inventory report on either a single item or the entire inventory. When a full inventory report is produced the user is alerted if any of the items are understocked and given the option to reorder.

```
1    REM    ITEM = Product ID#
2    REM    DESC$ = Product description (28 characters)
3    REM    PRICE$ = Retail price (4 characters)
4    REM    COST$ = Wholesale price (4 characters)
5    REM    STOCK$ = Number of units in stock (2 characters)
6    REM    LOCAT$ = Stockroom shelf location (2 characters)
7    REM    MINSTOCK$ = Minimum stock size (2 characters)
8    REM    FULLSTOCK$ = Optimal stock size (2 characters)
9    REM    SOLD$ = Total units sold to date (2 characters)
10   REM    STARTDATE$ = First date of sale (10 characters)
11   REM    REORDER() = List of items understocked
12   REM    INDEX = Count of items understocked
13   REM    QUERY$ = Miscellaneous user input
14   REM
15   REM
```

```
100 REM     This program will produce an inventory report
110 OPEN "R", 1, "B:INVNTRY.TXT", 56
120 FIELD 1, 28 AS DESC$, 4 AS PRICE$, 4 AS COST$, 2 AS STOCK$,
               2 AS LOCAT$, 2 AS MINSTOCK$, 2 AS FULLSTOCK$,
               2 AS SOLD$, 10 AS STARTDATE$
130 DIM REORDER(100)
140 INPUT "(S)INGLE ITEM OR (F)ULL REPORT";QUERY$
150 IF ASC(QUERY$) = 83 THEN 200
                           ELSE IF ASC(QUERY$) = 70 THEN 400
160 PRINT "INVALID RESPONSE" : GOTO 140
170 REM
180 REM
200 REM     Single item report
210 PRINT "ENTER A NEGATIVE NUMBER TO END THE PROGRAM"
220 PRINT
230 INPUT "ITEM #";ITEM
240 IF ITEM < 0 THEN 600
250 GET 1, ITEM
260 IF DESC$ = STRING$(28,0) OR DESC$ = STRING$(28,15)
       THEN PRINT "BAD #" : PRINT : GOTO 230
270 PRINT DESC$;"  -  PRICE:";CVS(PRICE$);" - ";
280 PRINT CVI(STOCK$);"IN STOCK"
290 PRINT "LOCATION: ";LOCAT$;"  - ";CVI(SOLD$);
300 PRINT "SOLD SINCE ";STARTDATE$
310 GOTO 220
320 REM
330 REM
400 REM     Full report
410 ITEM = ITEM + 1
420 GET 1, ITEM
430 IF DESC$ = STRING$(28,15) THEN 410 : REM     Dropped item &
440 IF DESC$ = STRING$(28,0) THEN 600  : REM     file end check
450 PRINT "#";ITEM;" -  ";DESC$;"  -  PRICE:";CVS(PRICE$)
460 PRINT "IN STOCK:";CVI(STOCK$);" -  LOCATION: ";LOCAT$;
470 PRINT "  - ";CVI(SOLD$);"SOLD SINCE ";STARTDATE$
480 PRINT
490 IF CVI(STOCK$) >= CVI(MINSTOCK$) THEN 410
500 INDEX = INDEX + 1
510 REORDER(INDEX) = ITEM : REM     Record item #
520 GOTO 410
530 REM
540 REM
600 REM     Close file and chain to reorder program if under-
               stocked else end program
610 CLOSE 1
620 IF INDEX = 0 THEN 690
630 PRINT INDEX;"ITEMS ARE UNDERSTOCKED"
640 INPUT "DO YOU WISH TO REORDER";QUERY$
650 IF ASC(QUERY$) <> 89 THEN 690 : REM     ASC("Y") = 89
660 REORDER(0) = INDEX : REM     Pass # of understocked items
670 COMMON REORDER()        : REM     Pass array containing
680 CHAIN "B:REORDER.BAS" : REM     list of understocked items
690 END
```

PROGRAM 12.5

This program, named REORDER.BAS, is chained automatically from Program 12.4 if the user wishes to reorder understocked items. Information on each supplier is stored in the file SUPPLIER.TXT. This information is used to produce order forms for needed items.

```
1   REM     ITEM = Product ID#
2   REM     DESC$ = Product description (28 characters)
3   REM     PRICE$ = Retail price (4 characters)
4   REM     COST$ = Wholesale price (4 characters)
5   REM     STOCK$ = Number of units in stock (2 characters)
6   REM     LOCAT$ = Stockroom shelf location (2 characters)
7   REM     MINSTOCK$ = Minimum stock size (2 characters)
8   REM     FULLSTOCK$ = Optimal stock size (2 characters)
9   REM     SOLD$ = Total units sold to date (2 characters)
10  REM     STARTDATE$ = First date of sale (10 characters)
11  REM     REORDER() = List of items under stock
12  REM     INDEX = Count of items under stock
13  REM     SUPPLIER$ = Name of supplying company (30 characters)
14  REM     STREET$ = Supplier's street address (20 characters)
15  REM     CITY$ = Supplier's home city (15 characters)
16  REM     STATE$ = Supplier's home state (2 characters)
17  REM     ZIP$ = Zip code (5 characters)
18  REM     ID$ = Supplier's own product code (2 characters)
19  REM     QUERY$ = Miscellaneous user input
20  REM
21  REM
100 REM     This program reorders understocked items
110 OPEN "R", 1, "B:INVNTRY.TXT", 56
120 FIELD 1, 28 AS DESC$, 4 AS PRICE$, 4 AS COST$, 2 AS STOCK$,
              2 AS LOCAT$, 2 AS MINSTOCK$, 2 AS FULLSTOCK$,
              2 AS SOLD$, 10 AS STARTDATE$
130 OPEN "R", 2, "B:SUPPLIER.TXT", 74
140 FIELD 2, 30 AS SUPPLIER$, 20 AS STREET$, 15 AS CITY$,
              2 AS STATE$, 5 AS ZIP$, 2 AS ID$
150 FOR INDEX = 1 TO REORDER(0)
160     GET 1, REORDER(INDEX)
170     GET 2, REORDER(INDEX)
180     PRINT "TO: ";SUPPLIER$;TAB(40);"FROM: ACME DISCOUNT"
190     PRINT TAB(5);STREET$;TAB(46);"17 MAIN ST."
200     PRINT TAB(5);CITY$;", ";STATE$;TAB(46);"TRENTON, KY."
210     PRINT TAB(5);ZIP$;TAB(46);"41009"
220     PRINT : PRINT
230     PRINT "ID","DESCRIPTION",,,"QUANTITY","PRICE"
240     PRINT STRING$(78,45)
250     PRINT ID$,DESC$,CVI(FULLSTOCK$) - CVI(STOCK$),CVS(COST$)
260     PRINT : PRINT TAB(62);"TOTAL = $";
270     PRINT (CVI(FULLSTOCK$) - CVI(STOCK$))*CVS(COST$)
280     PRINT : PRINT : PRINT
290 NEXT INDEX
300 CLOSE 1,2
310 END
```

PROGRAM 12.6

This program, named ORDINFO.BAS, is used to create and update the file SUP-PLIER.TXT.

```
1 REM     SUPPLIER$ = Name of supplying company (30 characters)
2 REM     STREET$ = Supplier's street address (20 characters)
3 REM     CITY$ = Supplier's home city (15 characters)
4 REM     STATE$ = Supplier's home state (2 characters)
5 REM     ZIP$ = Zip code (5 characters)
6 REM     ID$ = Supplier's own product code (2 characters)
7 REM
8 REM
100 REM     This program is used to build and maintain the
            file SUPPLIER.TXT
110 OPEN "R", 1, "B:SUPPLIER.TXT", 74
120 FIELD 1, 30 AS SUPPLIER$, 20 AS STREET$, 15 AS CITY$,
            2 AS STATE$, 5 AS ZIP$, 2 AS ID$
130 PRINT "ENTER A NEGATIVE NUMBER TO END THE PROGRAM"
140 PRINT
150 INPUT "ITEM";ITEM
160    IF ITEM < O THEN 260
170    INPUT "SUPPLIER";S1$ : LSET SUPPLIER$ = S1$
180    INPUT "STREET";S2$ : LSET STREET$ = S2$
190    INPUT "CITY";C$ : LSET CITY$ = C$
200    INPUT "STATE";S3$ : LSET STATE$ = S3$
210    INPUT "ZIP CODE";Z$ : LSET ZIP$ = Z$
220    INPUT "SUPPLIER'S PRODUCT CODE";I$ : LSET ID$ = I$
230    PUT 1, ITEM
240    PRINT
250 GOTO 150
260 CLOSE 1
270 END
```

PAYROLL PROGRAMS

PROGRAM 12.7

When initially run this program, named PAYUPD.BAS, creates the file PAYROLL.TXT. When subsequently run it is used to update the file as employees are added and deleted. Note that an employee's wage can be stored either at an hourly or weekly rate.

```
1    REM     ID = Employee identification number
2    REM     N$,EMP$ = Employee name (20 characters)
3    REM     S1$,STRT$ = Employee's street address (20 characters)
4    REM     C$,CITY$ = Home city (15 characters)
5    REM     S2$,STATE$ = Home state (2 characters)
6    REM     Z$,ZIP$ = Zip code (5 characters)
7    REM     T$,TEL$ = Telephone number (12 characters)
8    REM     W,WAGE$ = Weekly/hourly wage (4 characters)
9    REM     S3$,SS$ = Social Security number (11 characetsrs)
10   REM     B,BC$ = Blue Cross/Blue Shield payment (4 characters)
11   REM     P,PENS$ = Pension plan (4 characters)
12   REM     F1,FINC$ = Federal witholding tax (4 characters)
13   REM     S,SINC$ = State witholding tax (4 characters)
14   REM     F2,FICA$ = Social Security deduction (4 characters)
15   REM     QUERY$ = Miscellaneous user input
16   REM
17   REM
100  REM     This program is used to update payroll records when
             employees are hired and fired
110  OPEN "R", 1, "B:PAYROLL.TXT", 109
120  FIELD 1, 20 AS EMP$, 20 AS STRT$, 15 AS CITY$, 2 AS STATE$,
             5 AS ZIP$, 12 AS TEL$, 4 AS WAGE$, 11 AS SS$, 4 AS BC$,
             4 AS PENS$, 4 AS FINC$, 4 AS SINC$, 4 AS FICA$
130  INPUT "ENTER (N)EW DATA, REMOVE (O)LD DATA OR (E)ND";QUERY$
140  IF ASC(QUERY$) = 78 THEN 200
                         ELSE IF ASC(QUERY$) = 79 THEN 500
                                                  ELSE 800
150  REM     ASC("N") = 78, ASC("O") = 79
160  REM
170  REM
200  REM     Add data on a new employee
210  GET 1
220  IF EMP$ <> STRING$(20,0) AND EMP$ <> STRING$(20,15)
         THEN 210 : REM   Find free record
230  PRINT "THIS WILL BE EMPLOYEE #";LOC(1)
240  INPUT "NAME";N$ : LSET EMP$ = N$
250  INPUT "ADDRESS: STREET";S1$ : LSET STRT$ = S1$
260  INPUT "CITY";C$ : LSET CITY$ = C$
270  INPUT "STATE";S2$ : LSET STATE$ = S2$
280  INPUT "ZIP CODE";Z$ : LSET ZIP$ = Z$
290  INPUT "TELEPHONE";T$ : LSET TEL$ = T$
300  INPUT "WAGE (ENTER AS A NEGATIVE NUMBER IF HOURLY)";W :
             LSET WAGE$ = MKS$(W)
310  INPUT "SOCIAL SECURITY NUMBER";S3$ : LSET SS$ = S3$
320  INPUT "BLUE CROSS/BLUE SHIELD PAYMENT";B : LSET BC$ = MKS$(B)
330  INPUT "PENSION RATE";P : LSET PENS$ = MKS$(P)
340  INPUT "FEDERAL WITHOLDING RATE";F1 : LSET FINC$ = MKS$(F1)
350  INPUT "STATE WITHOLDING RATE";S : LSET SINC$ = MKS$(S)
360  INPUT "FICA";F2 : LSET FICA$ = MKS$(F2)
370  PUT 1, LOC(1)
380  PRINT
390  GOTO 130
400  REM
410  REM
```

```
500 REM    Remove data on an old employee
510 INPUT "EMPLOYEE #";ID
520 GET 1, ID
530 IF EMP$ = STRING$(20,0) OR EMP$ = STRING$(20,15)
         THEN PRINT "BAD ID" : GOTO 510
540 PRINT : PRINT EMP$ : PRINT
550 INPUT "IS THAT THE CORRECT EMPLOYEE";QUERY$
560 IF ASC(QUERY$) <> 89 THEN 510
570 LSET EMP$ = STRING$(20,15)  : REM    Replace old information
580 LSET STRT$ = STRING$(20,15) : REM    in record with innocuous
590 LSET CITY$ = STRING$(15,15) : REM    characters & O's.
600 LSET STATE$ = STRING$(2,15) : REM    This identifies record
610 LSET ZIP$ = STRING$(5,15)   : REM    as available for a new
620 LSET TEL$ = STRING$(12,15)  : REM    employee's information.
630 LSET WAGE$ = MKS$(O)
640 LSET SS$ = STRING$(11,15)
650 LSET BC$ = MKS$(O)
660 LSET PENS$ = MKS$(O)
670 LSET FINC$ = MKS$(O)
680 LSET SINC$ = MKS$(O)
690 LSET FICA$ = MKS$(O)
700 PUT 1, ID
710 GOTO 130
720 REM
730 REM
800 REM    Close file and end program
810 CLOSE 1
820 END
```

PROGRAM 12.8

Based on the information stored in the file PAYROLL.TXT this program, named PAYCHECK.BAS, computes the bi-weekly wages for each employee and then prints his or her paycheck.

```
1   REM    ID = Employee identification number
2   REM    EMP$ = Employee name (20 characters)
3   REM    STRT$ = Employee's street address (20 characters)
4   REM    CITY$ = Home city (15 characters)
5   REM    STATE$ = Home state (2 characters)
6   REM    ZIP$ = Zip code (5 characters)
7   REM    TEL$ = Telephone number (12 characters)
8   REM    WAGE,WAGE$ = Weekly/hourly wage (4 characters)
9   REM    SS$ = Social Security number (11 characetsrs)
10  REM    BC$ = Blue Cross/Blue Shield payment (4 characters)
11  REM    PENS$ = Pension plan (4 characters)
12  REM    FINC$ = Federal witholding tax (4 characters)
13  REM    SINC$ = State witholding tax (4 characters)
14  REM    FICA$ = Social Security deduction (4 characters)
15  REM    HOURS = Time worked if hourly employee
16  REM    PENS = Individual pension deduction
17  REM    PENTOT = Total pension deductions
18  REM    FINC = Individual federal witholding
```

```
19 REM     FINCTOT = Total federal witholding
20 REM     SINC = Individual state witholding
21 REM     SINCTOT = Total state witholding
22 REM     FICA = Individual Social Security deduction
23 REM     FICATOT = Total Social Security deductions
24 REM     AMOUNT() = Net employee pay
25 REM     PAYTO$() = Check recipient
26 REM     CHECK = Check index
27 REM
28 REM
100 REM     This program computes bi-weekly paychecks.  Hourly
            employees are assumed to work a 40 hour week.
110 OPEN "R", 1, "B:PAYROLL.TXT", 109
120 FIELD 1, 20 AS EMP$, 20 AS STRT$, 15 AS CITY$, 2 AS STATE$,
            5 AS ZIP$, 12 AS TEL$, 4 AS WAGE$, 11 AS SS$, 4 AS BC$,
            4 AS PENS$, 4 AS FINC$, 4 AS SINC$, 4 AS FICA$
130 DIM PAYTO$(100), AMOUNT(100) : REM    Dimension must always
                                          be greater or equal to
                                          size of payroll
140 REM
150 REM
200 REM     Compute paycheck amounts
210 GET 1
220 IF EMP$ = STRING$(20,15) THEN 210 : REM    Fired employee &
230 IF EMP$ = STRING$(20,0) THEN 400  : REM     file end check
240 WAGE = CVS(WAGE$)
250 IF WAGE > 0 THEN 300
260 PRINT LOC(1);"- ";EMP$
270 INPUT "NUMBER OF HOURS WORKED THIS PAY PERIOD";HOURS
280 PRINT
290 IF HOURS <= 80 THEN WAGE = -1*WAGE*HOURS
                  ELSE WAGE = -1*WAGE*80 + -1.5*WAGE*(HOURS-80)
300 BCTOT = BCTOT + CVS(BC$)
310 PENS = CVS(PENS$)/100*WAGE : PENTOT = PENTOT + PENS
320 FINC = CVS(FINC$)/100*WAGE : FINCTOT = FINCTOT + FINC
330 SINC = CVS(SINC$)/100*WAGE : SINCTOT = SINCTOT + SINC
340 FICA = CVS(FICA$)/100*WAGE : FICATOT = FICATOT + FICA
350 AMOUNT(LOC(1)) = WAGE - CVS(BC$) - PENS - FINC - SINC - FICA
360 PAYTO$(LOC(1)) = EMP$
370 GOTO 210
380 REM
390 REM
400 REM     Produce final report
410 PRINT
420 PRINT "DEPOSIT";PENTOT;"INTO PENSION FUND"
430 PRINT "PAY";SINCTOT;"TO STATE FOR WITHOLDING"
440 PRINT "PAY";FINCTOT;"TO IRS FOR WITHOLDING"
450 PRINT "PAY";FICATOT;"TO SOCIAL SECURITY ADMINISTRATION"
460 PRINT
470 REM
480 REM
```

```
500 REM    Print paychecks
510 FOR CHECK = 1 TO LOC(1) - 1
520    IF PAYTO$(CHECK) = "" THEN 630
530    PRINT "ACME DISCOUNT";TAB(35);DATE$
540    PRINT "LAST NATIONAL BANK"
550    PRINT "ACCT: 3-1415-927"
560    PRINT
570    PRINT "PAY TO THE"
580    PRINT "ORDER OF: ";PAYTO$(CHECK);TAB(35);"$";AMOUNT(CHECK)
590    PRINT
600    PRINT TAB(33);STRING$(13,95)
610    PRINT TAB(35);"Treasurer"
620    PRINT : PRINT : PRINT
630 NEXT CHECK
640 REM
650 REM
700 REM    Close file and end program
710 CLOSE 1
720 END
```

PROGRAM 12.9

This program, named PAYSHEET.BAS, alphabetizes the payroll list using a bubble sort and then prints a payroll report. A bubble sort compares consecutive items of data. If they are out of order they are switched. Repeating this process many times will result in an alphabetized list.

```
1    REM    ID = Employee identification number
2    REM    EMP$ = Employee name (20 characters)
3    REM    STRT$ = Employee's street address (20 characters)
4    REM    CITY$ = Home city (15 characters)
5    REM    STATE$ = Home state (2 characters)
6    REM    ZIP$ = Zip code (5 characters)
7    REM    TEL$ = Telephone number (12 characters)
8    REM    WAGE$ = Weekly/hourly wage (4 characters)
9    REM    SS$ = Social Security number (11 characetsrs)
10   REM    BC$ = Blue Cross/Blue Shield payment (4 characters)
11   REM    PENS$ = Pension plan (4 characters)
12   REM    FINC$ = Federal witholding tax (4 characters)
13   REM    SINC$ = State witholding tax (4 characters)
14   REM    FICA$ = Social Security deduction (4 characters)
15   REM    INDEX = Employee name & ID index
16   REM    FLAG = Indicator to check for swap on last sort pass
17   REM    P = Sort pointer
18   REM    PU1$,PU2$,PU$ = PRINT USING format
19   REM
20   REM
```

```
100 REM    This program produces a sorted payroll sheet
110 OPEN "R", 1, "B:PAYROLL.TXT", 109
120 FIELD 1, 20 AS EMP$, 20 AS STRT$, 15 AS CITY$, 2 AS STATE$,
          5 AS ZIP$, 12 AS TEL$, 4 AS WAGE$, 11 AS SS$, 4 AS BC$,
          4 AS PENS$, 4 AS FINC$, 4 AS SINC$, 4 AS FICA$
130 DIM LN$(100), ID(100) : REM    Must always be greater or
                                    equal to size of payroll
140 REM
150 REM
200 REM    Place all employeee last names in an array
210 GET 1
220 IF EMP$ = STRING$(20,15) THEN 210 : REM    Fired employee &
230 IF EMP$ = STRING$(20,0) THEN 280  : REM     file end check
240 INDEX = INDEX + 1
250 LN$(INDEX) = RIGHT$(EMP$,LEN(EMP$) - INSTR(1,EMP$," "))
260 ID(INDEX) = LOC(1)
270 GOTO 210
280 ID(0) = INDEX
290 REM
300 REM
400 REM    Sort list using bubble sort technique
410 FLAG = -1
420 WHILE INDEX > 1 AND FLAG <> 0
430     FLAG = 0
440     FOR P = 1 TO INDEX - 1
450         IF LN$(P) > LN$(P+1) THEN SWAP LN$(P), LN$(P+1) :
                              SWAP ID(P), ID(P+1) :
                              FLAG = -1
460     NEXT P
470     INDEX = INDEX - 1
480 WEND
490 REM
500 REM
600 REM    Print payroll sheet
610 PRINT "    NAME          SS#        WAGE     ";
620 PU1$ = "\          \ \           \ \      \ "
630 PRINT "PENSION BC/BS    FED     STATE    FICA  "
640 PU2$ = "###.##  ###.##  ###.##  ###.##  ###.##"
650 PU$ = PU1$ + PU2$
660 FOR INDEX = 1 TO ID(0)
670 GET 1, ID(INDEX)
680 IF CVS(WAGE$) < 0 THEN W$ = RIGHT$(STR$(CVS(WAGE$)),
                              LEN(STR$(CVS(WAGE$)))-1) +
                              "(H)" : GOTO 700
690 W$ = RIGHT$(STR$(CVS(WAGE$)),
        LEN(STR$(CVS(WAGE$)))-1) + "(W)"
700 PRINT USING PU$;LN$(INDEX),SS$,W$,CVS(PENS$),CVS(BC$),
                CVS(FINC$),CVS(SINC$),CVS(FICA$)
710 NEXT INDEX
720 REM
730 REM
800 REM    Close file and end program
810 CLOSE 1
820 END
```

APPENDIX

A

USING THE EDITOR

The IBM-PC has an editor which helps the programmer correct a program currently in the computer's memory. The programmer can best learn the use of the editor by spending time to become familiar with its different functions. A short outline of the edit commands is presented here.

EDIT

Any program line displayed on the screen can be edited by simply using the appropriate edit keys. To edit a line that is not on the screen, type EDIT followed by the line number to be edited. For example,

EDIT 50

will instruct the computer to display line 50 and place the cursor beneath the first digit of the line number. If the line to be edited is already on the screen, this step can be omitted.

Pressing the RETURN key (←⎯) while editing a line causes the computer to record any changes made in that line.

Key	Function
HOME	Moves the cursor to the upper left hand corner of the screen.
CTRL - HOME	Clears the screen and moves the cursor to the upper left hand corner.
↑	Moves the cursor up one line.
↓	Moves the cursor down one line.

[←]	Moves the cursor to the left one space.
[→]	Moves the cursor to the right one space.
CTRL- [→]	Moves the cursor to the right to the next key word.
CTRL- [←]	Moves the cursor to the left to the previous key word.
[END]	Moves the cursor to the end of the line.
CTRL - [END]	Erases to the end of the line from the current position.
[Del]	Deletes one character from the current position.
[←] (delete key)	Deletes one character from the left of the cursor.
[ESC]	Erases the entire current line from the screen.
CTRL - [Break]	Causes the computer to leave the EDIT mode without recording any changes made in the line.

APPENDIX

B

DISK BASIC FEATURES

Program and File Names

Every program and file on a disk is identified by a unique name. The general format for a program or file name is:

<name> . <extension>

The name may be from one to eight characters long, the first character of which must be a letter. The extension, which is optional, may be from one to three characters, starting with a letter. It is useful to standardize extensions by employing .BAS for BASIC programs and .TXT for files. This allows the user to easily distinguish between programs and files. Only the following characters are allowed as part of a name or extension.

```
A, B,  ... Z
0, 1,  ... 9
< > ( ) { }
@ # $ % ^ & !
- _ ' ` ~ \ ¦
```

The following examples are valid program or file names:

MAIL.BAS
CODES.TXT
POTATOES

SAVE

The SAVE command is used to store a program on a disk. Its form is:

SAVE "<disk drive> : <program name>"

For example,

SAVE "B:MYPROG.BAS"

will save the program currently in memory on the disk in drive B and give it the name MYPROG.BAS. If no disk drive is specified the computer assumes drive A. Note that the program name must be enclosed in quotation marks. If no extension is specified, .BAS will be assumed.

If a P option is specified, the program will be saved in a coded format on the disk. For example,

SAVE "B:MYPROG.BAS",P

While the program will still run as before, any attempt to list or edit it will result in an "Illegal function call" message. It is not possible to unprotect a program.

LOAD

Programs previously saved on a disk may be recalled using the LOAD command. For example,

LOAD "B:MYPROG.BAS"

will load MYPROG.BAS into memory from the disk in drive B.

KILL

Unwanted programs and files currently stored on a disk can be removed using the kill command. Its form is

KILL "<program or file name>"

The command

KILL "B:MYPROG.BAS"

will delete MYPROG.BAS from the disk in drive B.

FILES

The FILES command displays the directory of a disk. For example,

FILES

will display the directory of the disk in drive A.

FILES "B:*.*"

will display the directory of the disk in drive B.

RENUM

The RENUM command is used to renumber the line numbers of a program currently in the computer's memory. Its form is:

RENUM <newline> , <startline> , <increment>

Newline is the new line number of the first line of the program to be renumbered. When not specified, the computer will assume 10.

Startline is the line number of the original program where renumbering is to begin. When not specified, renumbering begins with the first line in the program and then renumbers the entire program.

Increment specifies the difference between successive renumbered program lines. If omitted, the computer assumes 10.

For example, the command:

RENUM 100,,20

will renumber the entire program currently in memory, so that the first line number is 100, the second 120, the third 140, and so on. Note that startline was not specified in this example.

The RENUM command will also change the line numbers used within statements so that they correspond with the new line numbers of the program.

MERGE

The MERGE command is used to combine a program in memory with one that has been previously stored on a disk. Its form is:

MERGE "<program name>"

For example,

MERGE "B:ADDENDUM.BAS"

will combine the program in memory with the program ADDENDUM.BAS on the disk in drive B. If any line numbers in the program in memory match line numbers in the program from the disk, the lines in memory will be replaced by those from the disk.

Programs are usually stored on a disk in a coded format which will not allow them to be merged with a program in memory. To be merged, the program on disk must be stored in ASCII format. This is accomplished with the command:

SAVE "B:MYPROG.BAS",A

NAME

The NAME command is used to change the name of a program or file stored in a disk. Its form is

NAME "<old name>" AS "<new name>"

For example,

NAME "B:CAT.BAS" AS "B:HARRY.BAS"

will give the program CAT.BAS on the disk in drive B the new name HARRY.BAS.

CHAIN and COMMON

The CHAIN command enables one program to pass control to another. Its form is:

CHAIN "<program name>",<line>, ALL

'Program name' is the name of the program to be chained to. Line is the line number where execution will start. If not specified, execution will start at the first line of the program. Specifying the ALL option instructs the computer to pass the values of all of the variables used by the first program to the chained program. To use the value of a variable from the first program in the second, the variable must be given the same name in both programs.

50 CHAIN "MYPROG.BAS",60,ALL

will pass program execution to line 60 of MYPROG.BAS and pass the values of all variables.

50 CHAIN "MYPROG.BAS",,ALL

will pass program execution to the first line of MYPROG.BAS and pass the values of all variables.

If the ALL option is not specified, the COMMON statement may be used to pass the values of selected variables to the chained program. The COMMON statement must be executed before a CHAIN statement. Its form is:

COMMON <variable list>

For example,

20 COMMON Q, Z(), R$

Note the format used to specify the subscripted variable Z. Z() should be dimensioned only in the original program.

SYSTEM

When running BASIC, the SYSTEM command is used to return to the DOS.

APPENDIX C — DISK OPERATING SYSTEM

Starting the System—

To start the computer in the disk operating mode, place a copy of the DOS disk in drive A (the left hand drive if two are available) and then turn on the computer. After a few seconds, the computer will respond by asking a series of questions.

Current date is Tue 1-01-1980
Enter new date:

Enter the date in the form requested (e.g. 6-22-1982).

Current time is 0:00:15.72
Enter new time:

Enter the time in the form requested (e.g. 14:32:10). Note that the computer uses a 24 hour clock. The computer will now respond

The IBM Personal Computer DOS
Version 1.10 (c) Copyright IBM Corp

A>

BASIC

If the user wishes to leave the DOS and work with BASIC, the command BASIC is used. Its simplest form is

BASIC
or
BASICA

BASIC instructs the computer to load the standard Disk BASIC supplied with the DOS. BASICA instructs the computer to load the optional Advanced BASIC if available. A more complete form of the BASIC command is:

BASIC/F:<files>/S:<buffer size>/M:<max workspace>

or

BASICA/F:<files>/S:<buffer size>/M:<max workspace>

/F:<files> sets the maximum number of files that may be opened simultaneously by one program (up to 15). If the option is not specified, the computer will allow three files to be opened simultaneously.

/S:<buffer size> sets the maximum allowable record length for use with random-access files, up to 32767 characters. If not specified, records may be up to 128 characters long.

/M:<max workspace> sets the maximum amount of memory that can be used for programs and data by BASIC, up to 65536 bytes. If not specified, BASIC uses all of the available memory up to 65536 bytes. For example,

BASICA/F:5/S:512

will allow five files to be opened simultaneously and random-access files to have a maximum record length of 512 characters.

COPY

The COPY command is used to duplicate a file or program. Its simplest form is:

COPY <original>

For example,

$$\text{COPY PAYROLL.TXT SAFETY.TXT}$$

will cause the computer to make an exact copy of PAYROLL.TXT and place it in a new file named SAFETY.TXT on the same disk.

$$\text{COPY B:MYPROG.BAS   A:}$$

will make an exact copy of the program MYPROG.BAS on the disk in drive B and place it on the disk in drive A, naming it also MYPROG.BAS.

The COPY command can also be used to append two or more files. This is done by specifying two or more source files separated by plus signs (+). For example,

$$\text{COPY FILE1.TXT + FILE 2.TXT   FILE3.TXT}$$

will place the contents of both FILE1.TXT and FILE2.TXT in FILE3.TXT. If a duplicate file name is not specified, the appended file will be placed in the first file mentioned. For example,

$$\text{COPY FILE1.TXT + FILE2.TXT}$$

will place the combined contents of both FILE1.TXT and FILE2.TXT in FILE1.TXT.

DIR

To produce a catalogue of a disk, type

$$\text{DIR <d>:}$$

which will list the directory of the disk in the specified drive (A or B).

RENAME

It is possible to change the name of files and programs using the RENAME command. Its form is

$$\text{RENAME <old name> <new name>}$$

For example,

$$\text{RENAME B:PAYROLL.BAS B:SALARY.BAS}$$

will give the program PAYROLL.BAS on the disk in drive B the new name SALARY.BAS.

ERASE

The ERASE command is used to remove unwanted files and programs from a disk. For example,

ERASE B:OLDFILE.TXT

will remove the file OLDFILE.TXT from the disk in drive B.

FORMAT

New disks must be initialized, or "formatted" before the IBM-PC can use them. The form of the FORMAT command is:

FORMAT <d>:

For example,

FORMAT B:

The computer will respond

Insert new diskette for drive B:
and strike any key when ready

After the new disk has been inserted, the computer will format the disk and print a status report when finished.

DISKCOPY

The DISKCOPY command is used to copy an entire disk at one time. Its form is:

DISKCOPY <original disk>: <backup>:

For example,

DISKCOPY A: B:

will copy the contents of the disk in drive A onto the disk in drive B. For systems with only one drive follow the computer's instructions after typing DISKCOPY.

If the disk being copied to has not been previously formatted, DISKCOPY will format it automatically.

APPENDIX D

FORMATTING OUTPUT

There are many instances when a programmer will want to have the computer's output produced in some special form. This is especially true when charts or tables are to be printed in some specific format. The PRINT USING statement is usually employed to produce formatted output.

PRINT USING

The PRINT USING statement allows an entire line of output to be formatted into zones of variable length. These zones may contain a series of numbers, strings, or a combination of both. The general form of PRINT USING is:

PRINT USING "<format>"; <variables or expressions>

The format must be a string variable or a string enclosed within quotation marks. Its purpose is to inform the computer of the format which will be employed in printing the variables or expressions. The variables or expressions must be preceded by a semicolon and separated from each other by commas.

PROGRAM D.1

This program demonstrates some simple applications of PRINT USING.

```
10 A = 25.68 : B = 3.21 : C = 2.4
20 PRINT USING "##.#    #.#      #"; A, B, C
30 PRINT
40 PRINT USING "##.##     #.#      #.#"; 3.798, 2.78, 3.55
Ok
RUN
25.7    3.2    2

 3.80    2.8    3.6
Ok
```

Notice how either variables or expressions may be used in the PRINT USING statement and also how numbers are rounded off to the desired number of decimal places.

The following table shows the valid formats that may be used in a PRINT USING statement.

Symbol	Use	Examples
#	Reserve space for one digit.	### ##
.	Indicate location of decimal point within number sign (#) field.	#.### ###.##
,	Specify location of one or more commas within a # field.	##,###.## #,###
+	Display the sign of the number being printed. The + may be placed before or after the # field.	+###.# ####.##+
−	Display a leading or trailing minus sign regardless of the sign of the number.	−###.## ###−
$$	Display a single dollar sign just prior to the leftmost digit of a # field.	$$###.## $$#,###
**	Replace any leading blanks in a # field with asterisks.	**####.## **##.##
**$	This combines ** and $$ such that a single dollar sign will be displayed just prior to the leftmost digit in a # field. Any leading spaces remaining will be filled with asterisks.	**$###.## **$#.##

^^^^	Output a number in scientific notation.	#.### ^^^^
!	Output only the first character of a string.	!
\\	Output only the first two characters of a string.	\\
\<n-2 spaces>\	Output the first n characters of a string.	\　　\
_	Any single character preceded by an underscore will be printed.	_#
&	Allows a string of any length to be inserted in the output where specified.	&
<any other char>	Output any characters not in this table as though they were in a normal print statement.	ABCD Q12R

PROGRAM D.2

This program demonstrates the use of the different symbols given in the table.

```
10 PRINT USING "   ###"; 657
20 PRINT USING "   ###.###"; 63.2867
30 PRINT USING "   #,###.##"; 1287.53
40 F$ = "Over ### contributed to the goal of ##,###,###.##"
45 C = 212 : PRINT USING F$; C, 23967000.92#
50 PRINT USING "    +###.#      #.####+"; -42.3, 8.9172
60 PRINT USING "    ###.#+     +#.####"; -42.3, 8.9172
70 PRINT USING "We can format numbers such as +##.#"; 18.37
80 PRINT USING "   $$####.##"; 201.76
90 A = 4201.67
100 PRINT USING "Amount is: **$#,###.## of budget."; A
110 PRINT USING "Mr. Dandy gave **$####.## to charity."; 43.1
120 PRINT
Ok
RUN
  657
   63.287
   1,287.53
Over 212 contributed to the goal of 23,967,000.92
    -42.3      8.9172+
    42.3-     +8.9172
We can format numbers such as +18.4
    $201.76
Amount is: **$4,201.67 of budget.
Mr. Dandy gave ****$43.10 to charity.

Ok
```

It is possible to place the format portion of the PRINT USING statement into a string. For example,

$$10 \text{ F\$} = \text{``\#\#.\#} \qquad \text{\#\#} \qquad \backslash \qquad \backslash\text{''}$$

can be used later in a PRINT USING statement.

$$70 \text{ PRINT USING F\$, A, B, N\$}$$

This technique is especially useful in formatting columns in a table so that they line up with their appropriate headings. The headings are typed in the line directly above the line containing the format string. By lining up the quotation marks in each of the lines, it is easy to produce the correct format. Program D.3 demonstrates this procedure.

PROGRAM D.3

```
10 PRINT "Key     Description      Cost       Qty        Total         In stock?"
20 F2$ = " !    \                \   $$##.##    ###     **$#,###.##        &"
30 FOR L = 1 TO 6
40     READ K$, L$, C, Q, Y$
50     PRINT USING F2$; K$, L$, C, Q, C*Q, Y$
60     T = T + C*Q : Q2 = Q2 + Q
70 NEXT L
80 PRINT : J$= "### items were sold raising **$###,###.## today"
90 PRINT USING J$; Q2, T
100 DATA D, Diskettes, 5.95, 20, Yes,  K, Cleaner, 2.29, 16, No
110 DATA B, I/O Manual, 17.95, 100, No,  R, Ribbon, 1.99, 50, Yes
120 DATA W, CPU Cables, 55.00, 48, Yes,  Z, Games Pkg., 49.95, 12, No
Ok
RUN
Key     Description      Cost       Qty        Total         In stock?
 D      Diskettes       $5.95        20     ****$119.00         Yes
 K      Cleaner         $2.29        16     *****$36.64         No
 B      I/O Manual     $17.95       100     **$1,795.00         No
 R      Ribbon          $1.99        50     *****$99.50         Yes
 W      CPU Cables     $55.00        48     **$2,640.00         Yes
 Z      Games Pkg.     $49.95        12     ****$599.40         No

246 items were sold raising ***$5,289.54 today
Ok
```

REVIEW ANSWERS

CHAPTER ONE

1. ```
10 X = 5
20 Y = 5*X + 7
30 PRINT Y
```

2. ```
10 A$ = "HARRY"
20 B$ = "SHERRY"
30 PRINT "HELLO "; A$
40 PRINT B$; " IS LOOKING FOR YOU."
```

3. ```
10 READ X
20 Y = 3*X + 5
30 PRINT Y;
40 GOTO 10
50 DATA 3, 5, 12, 17, 8
```

4. ```
5 PRINT "NAME", "FIRST GRADE"
10 READ N$, A, B, C, D
30 PRINT N$, A
40 GOTO 10
50 DATA WATERS,83,95,86,80,FRENCH,42,97,66,89,MIKAN,61,83,42,90
```

5. ```
10 INPUT "WHAT IS X"; X
20 Y = 5 * X
30 PRINT "5*X="; Y
40 PRINT "X/5="; X/5
50 GOTO 10
```
```

```
6.  10 INPUT "WHAT IS YOUR NAME"; N$
    20 INPUT "WHAT IS YOUR FRIEND'S NAME"; F$
    30 PRINT F$; " IS A FRIEND OF "; N$
    40 PRINT
    50 GOTO 10
```

CHAPTER TWO

```
1.  10 INPUT "ENTER TWO NUMBERS"; A,B
    20 IF A > B THEN PRINT A : PRINT B : GOTO 10
    30 PRINT B : PRINT A : GOTO 10
```

```
2.  10 INPUT "ENTER TWO LAST NAMES"; A$,B$
    20 IF A$ < B$ THEN PRINT A$ : PRINT B$ : GOTO 10
    30 PRINT B$ : PRINT A$ : GOTO 10
```

```
3.  10 INPUT "ENTER A NUMBER";N
    20 IF N > 25 AND N < 112 THEN PRINT N;"IS BETWEEN 25 AND 112"
                            ELSE PRINT N;"IS OUT OF RANGE"
    30 GOTO 10
```

```
4.  10 INPUT "ENTER N$";N$
    20 IF N$ < "GARBAGE" OR N$ > "TRASH" THEN PRINT "YES"
                                ELSE PRINT "NO"
    30 GOTO 10
```

```
5.  10 FOR X = 1 TO 25
    20    PRINT X;
    30 NEXT X
```

```
6.  10 FOR S = 20 TO 10 STEP -2
    20    PRINT S;
    30 NEXT S
    40 PRINT
```

```
7.  10 INPUT "STEP VALUE";N
    20 FOR X = 8 TO 20 STEP N
    30    PRINT X;
    40 NEXT X
    50 PRINT
```

CHAPTER THREE

```
1.  10 RANDOMIZE 111
    20 D1 = INT(101 * RND + 50)
    30 D2 = INT(101 * RND + 50)
    40 PRINT D1;"multiplied by";D2;"is";D1 * D2
```

```
2.  1 REM    W = NUMBER OF WRONG GUESSES
    10 RANDOMIZE
    20 PRINT "I'm thinking of a random number between 1 & 50."
    30 R = INT(50*RND + 1)
    40 FOR W = 1 TO 5
    50      INPUT "What is your guess";G
    60      IF G = R THEN PRINT "Correct!!!" : END
    70      IF G < R THEN PRINT "Too Low!"
                     ELSE PRINT "Too High!"
    80 NEXT W
    90 PRINT "You've had 5 guesses now."
    100 PRINT "The number was";R
```

```
3.  1 REM    R = RANDOM NUMBER BETWEEN 0 AND 9
    2 REM    X = NUMBER OF NUMBERS RESULTING BETWEEN 0 & 4
    3 REM    Y = NUMBER OF NUMBERS RESULTING BETWEEN 5 & 9
    4 REM    L = LOOP VARIABLE TO GENERATE 50 RANDOM NUMBERS
    10 RANDOMIZE 1001
    20 FOR L = 1 TO 50
    30     R = INT(10 * RND)
    40     IF R < 5 THEN X = X + 1  ELSE Y = Y + 1
    50 NEXT L
    60 PRINT "There were"; X; "numbers between 0 and 4."
    70 PRINT "There were"; Y; "numbers between 5 and 9."
```

```
4.  1 REM    L = LOOP FOR ENTERING TEN NUMBERS FROM KEYBOARD
    2 REM    N = ARBITRARY VALUE ENTERED FROM KEYBOARD
    3 REM    E = NUMBER OF EVEN NUMBERS ENTERED
    4 REM    10 - E = NUMBER OF ODD NUMBERS ENTERED
    10 FOR L = 1 TO 10
    20      INPUT "ENTER A NUMBER"; N
    30      IF (N/2) = INT(N/2) THEN E = E + 1
    40 NEXT L
    50 PRINT E; "EVEN; "; 10-E ; "ODD"
```

CHAPTER FOUR

1.
```
10 FOR X = 20 TO 24
20      PRINT "Outer Loop:"; X
30      FOR Y = 1 TO 3
40          PRINT "Inner:"; Y,
50      NEXT Y
60      PRINT
70 NEXT X
```

2.
```
10 REM Input three numbers from keyboard
20 FOR I = 1 TO 3
30      INPUT N(I)
40 NEXT I
50 REM Output the three numbers in reverse order
60 FOR K = 3 TO 1 STEP -1
70      PRINT N(K)
80 NEXT K
```

3.
```
10 RANDOMIZE -1734 : REM Any 'ol number will do...
20 REM Read six words
30 FOR X = 1 TO 6
40      INPUT W$(X)
50 NEXT X
60 REM Randomly select 4 words as a sentence
70 FOR R = 1 TO 4
80      A = INT(RND*6)+1
90      PRINT W$(A); " ";
100 NEXT R
110 PRINT "."
```

```
 0 RANDOMIZE -1734 : REM Any 'ol number will do...
 ) REM Read six words from keyboard
   FOR X = 1 TO 6
        INPUT W$(X)
   NEXT X
   EM Randomly select 4 words as a sentence.
    OR R = 1 TO 4
        A = INT(RND*6)+1
        IF W$(A) = "" THEN 80 : REM Already chosen?
        PRINT W$(A); " ";
        W$(A) = "" : REM Indicate chosen
      T R
        NT "." : REM Period indicates end of sentence
```

```
5.    10 REM Read 6 numbers from keyboard
      20 FOR K = 1 TO 6
      30     INPUT X(K)
      40 NEXT K
      50 REM Print numbers in a column
      60 FOR K = 1 TO 6
      70     PRINT X(K)
      80 NEXT K
      90 REM Print numbers on a single line
      100 FOR K = 1 TO 6
      110     PRINT X(K);
      120 NEXT K
      130 PRINT


6.    10 DIM X$(5,3)
      20 REM Read in X$(,)
      30 FOR I = 1 TO 5
      40     FOR J = 1 TO 3
      50         READ X$(I,J)
      60     NEXT J
      70 NEXT I
      80 REM Output X$(,) making rows as coulmns
      90 FOR I = 1 TO 3
      100     FOR J = 1 TO 5
      110         PRINT X$(J,I); " ";
      120     NEXT J
      130     PRINT
      140 NEXT I
      150 DATA A,B,C,D,E,F,G,H,I,J,K,L,M,N,O
```

CHAPTER FIVE

```
1A.   10 INPUT "Are you COMING or GOING";A$
      20 IF A$="COMING" THEN PRINT "HELLO"
                         ELSE PRINT "GOOD-BYE"
      30 END
```

```
1B.  1 REM    Shellsort of the list of club members
     10 INPUT "How many names in the list";N
     20 FOR X = 1 TO N
     30     INPUT "Member";M$(X)
     40 NEXT X
     50 S=N
     60 S=INT(S/1.5) : Q=S
     70 F=0
     80 FOR X=1 TO N
     90     Q=X+S
     100    IF Q > N THEN 130
     110    IF M$(X) > M$(Q) THEN T$ = M$(X) : M$(X) = M$(Q)
                                 : M$(Q) = T$ : F = 1

     120 NEXT X
     130 IF S > 1 THEN 60
     140 IF F = 1 THEN 70
     150 FOR X=1 TO N
     160     PRINT M$(X)
     170 NEXT X
     180 END
```

2A. The problem with 2a is very easy to correct. The FOR-TO-NEXT loop in line 20 is missing the STEP command. Line 20 should read:

20 FOR X =10 TO 1 STEP -1

2B. The product in line 30 is always positive. Therefore, the program need not check for a negative product. The best way to correct this error in logic would be to eliminate line 40 and replace it with:

40 PRINT "THE PRODUCT IS POSITIVE"

CHAPTER SIX

1. X=-2

```
2. 10 INPUT N
   20 X = ABS(N - FIX(N))
   30 Y = INT(X * 100 + .5) / 100
   40 PRINT "INPUT:"; N, "OUTPUT:"; Y
```

```
3.  10 DEF FNR(D) = D * 3.14159 / 180
    20 DEF FND(R) = R * 180 / 3.14159
    30 INPUT "DEGREES";A
    40 PRINT "That is"; FNR(A); "radians."
    50 PRINT
    60 INPUT "RADIANS";B
    70 PRINT "That is"; FND(B); "degrees."
```

CHAPTER SEVEN

```
1.  10 INPUT "Name"; N$
    20 PRINT N$
    30 IF N$ = "DONALD" THEN GOSUB 100
    40 GOTO 10
    100 PRINT "——————"
    110 RETURN
```

```
2.  10 RANDOMIZE
    20 FOR C = 1 TO 5
    30      S = INT(RND*4) + 1 : REM Suit
    40      F = INT(RND*13) + 1 : REM Face Value
    50      PRINT "Card"; C; "is the"; F; "of ";
    60      ON S GOTO 100,200,300,400
    100     PRINT "Spades"
    110     GOTO 500
    200     PRINT "Diamonds"
    210     GOTO 500
    300     PRINT "Clubs"
    310     GOTO 500
    400     PRINT "Hearts"
    500 NEXT C
```

CHAPTER EIGHT

```
1.  10 INPUT "Word"; W$
    20 SCREEN 0,1 : COLOR 17,12,6
    30 LOCATE 12,17
    40 PRINT W$
```

```
2.  10 SCREEN 1,0 : COLOR 1,0
    20 LINE (120,85) - (120,115),3
    30 LINE  - (180,115),3
    40 LINE  - (120,85),3


3.  10 SCREEN 1,0 : COLOR 4,0
    20 LINE (135,75) - (185,125),1,BF


4.  10 INPUT "A,B,R"; A,B,R
    20 SCREEN 2
    30 CIRCLE (A,B),R,1
```

CHAPTER NINE

```
1.  10 INPUT "A LETTER FROM THE ALPHABET PLEASE";A$
    20 PRINT "THE ASCII OF '";A$;"' IS";ASC(A$)
    30 C = ASC(A$) + 2
    40 IF C > 90 THEN C = C - 26
    50 PRINT "TWO LETTERS AFTER '";A$;"' IS '";CHR$(C);"'"
    60 GOTO 10
```

CHAPTER TEN

```
1.  10 OPEN "O",1,"B:MONTHS.TXT"
    20 FOR I = 1 TO 12
    30    READ MONTH$
    40    WRITE #1,MONTH$
    50 NEXT I
    60 CLOSE 1
    100 DATA JANUARY,FEBRUARY,MARCH,APRIL,MAY,JUNE,JULY
    110 DATA AUGUST,SEPTEMBER,OCTOBER,NOVEMBER,DECEMBER


2.  10 INPUT "WHAT NUMBER MONTH DO YOU WANT";N
    20 OPEN "I",1,"B:MONTHS.TXT"
    30 FOR I = 1 TO N
    40    INPUT #1,N$
    50 NEXT I
    60 CLOSE 1
    70 PRINT "MONTH";N;"IS ";N$
```

CHAPTER ELEVEN

```
1.  1 REM     M$,M1$ = MONTH (9 CHARACTERS)
    2 REM
    3 REM
    10 OPEN "R",1,"B:MONTHS.TXT"
    20 FIELD 1, 9 AS M$
    30 FOR M = 1 TO 12
    40     READ M1$
    50     LSET M$ = M1$
    60     PUT 1
    70 NEXT M
    80 CLOSE 1
    90 REM
    100 DATA JANUARY,FEBRUARY,MARCH,APRIL,MAY,JUNE,JULY
    110 DATA AUGUST,SEPTEMBER,OCTOBER,NOVEMBER,DECEMBER


2.  10 OPEN "R",1,"B:MONTHS.TXT",9
    20 FIELD 1, 9 AS N$
    30 INPUT "WHAT NUMBER MONTH";N
    40 GET 1, N
    50 PRINT "MONTH";N;"IS ";N$
    60 CLOSE 1


3.  1 REM     M$ = MONTH (9 CHARACTERS)
    2 REM     L$ = LENGTH OF FILE 'MONTHS.TXT' (2 CHARACTERS)
    3 REM
    4 REM
    10 OPEN "R",1,"B:MONTHS.TXT",9
    20 FIELD 1, 9 AS M$
    30 OPEN "R",2,"B:LENGTH.TXT",2
    40 FIELD 2, 2 AS L$
    50 GET 1
    60 IF M$ <> STRING$(9,0) THEN 50
    70 LSET L$ = MKI$(LOC(1) - 1)
    80 PUT 2,1
    90 CLOSE 1,2
```

CHAPTER ONE

1. ```
   10 PRINT "A"
   20 PRINT " B"
   30 PRINT "  C"
   40 PRINT "ABCD"
   ```

3. ```
   RUN
   THE VALUE OF B
    19
   Ok
   ```

5. ```
   10 READ A,B
   20 PRINT "THE SUM IS";A + B
   30 GOTO 10
   40 DATA 12,8,9,5
   ```

7. ```
   10 INPUT "PRICE, NUMBER OF LOAVES";P,N
   20 PRINT "TOTAL SPENT = $";P*N/100
   ```

9. ```
   10 INPUT X,Y
   20 PRINT "X=";X,"Y=";Y,"X*Y=";X*Y
   30 GOTO 10
   ```

11. ```
    RUN
     300            510
     .3     .51
    Ok
    ```

```
13.   PRINT "AAA";111,222;"AAA","333";"   ";16-3*2
      AAA 111          222 AAA          333    10
      Ok


15.   RUN
      ABCDXYZ
      ABCD 7
       7 XYZ
      -4 XYZ
      Ok


17.   10 PRINT 2 + 3 + 4 + 5


19.   10 READ X,Y
      20 A = 12 * X + 7 * Y
      30 PRINT A
      40 GOTO 10
      50 DATA 3,2,7,9,12,-4


21.   10 INPUT "LENGTH, WIDTH, HEIGHT";L,W,H
      20 PRINT "VOLUME IS";L*W*H


23.   10 INPUT "HEIGHT"; H
      20 INPUT "WIDTH"; W
      30 INPUT "LENGTH"; L
      40 INPUT "PRESENCE"; P
      50 PRINT "YOUR OBJECT USES";H*W*L*P;"TESSERACTS IN FOUR SPACE"


25.   10 INPUT "HOW MANY BOOKS HAVE YOU BORROWED";B
      20 INPUT "HOW MANY DAYS LATE ARE THEY";L
      30 PRINT "YOU OWE $";.1*B*L


27.   10 INPUT "WHAT IS THE PLAYER'S NAME";P$
      20 PRINT "WHAT IS ";P$;"'S";" WAGE";
      30 INPUT W
      40 T = W * .44
      50 PRINT P$;" WOULD KEEP $";W-T
      60 PRINT "HE WOULD PAY $";T;"IN TAXES."


29.   10 INPUT "WHAT IS THE BASE";B
      20 INPUT "WHAT IS THE ALTITUDE";A
      30 PRINT
      40 PRINT "THE AREA IS"; A * B * .5
```

```
31.  10  READ S1,G1,S2,G2,S3,G3,S4,G4,S5,G5
     20  S = S1 + S2 + S3 + S4 + S5
     30  G = G1 + G2 + G3 + G4 + G5
     40  T = S + G
     50  PRINT "SLOTH'S TOTAL VOTE WAS"; S
     60  PRINT "HIS TOTAL PERCENTAGE WAS"; 100 * S / T
     70  PRINT
     80  PRINT "GRAFT'S TOTAL VOTE WAS"; G
     90  PRINT "HIS TOTAL PERCENTAGE WAS"; 100 * G / T
    100  DATA 528,210,313,721,1003,822,413,1107,516,1700


33.  10  INPUT "MONTH, DAY, AND YEAR OF BIRTH"; M1, D1, Y1
     20  D9 = Y1 * 365 + M1 * 30 + D1
     30  INPUT "TODAY'S MONTH, DAY, AND YEAR"; M2, D2, Y2
     40  D8 = Y2 * 365 + M2 * 30 + D2
     50  S = 8 * (D8-D9)
     60  PRINT "YOU HAVE SLEPT ABOUT";S;"HOURS."
```

CHAPTER TWO

```
1.  10  INPUT A,B
    20  IF A < B THEN 60
    30  IF A > B THEN 80
    40  PRINT A;"IS EQUAL TO";B
    50  GOTO 10
    60  PRINT A;"IS LESS THAN";B
    70  GOTO 10
    80  PRINT A;"IS GREATER THAN";B
    90  GOTO 10


3.  10  INPUT A$
    20  IF A$ > "MIDWAY" THEN PRINT A$


5.  10  INPUT A$,B$ : PRINT A$,B$ : PRINT B$,A$


7.  10  INPUT A$
    20  IF A$ > "DOWN" AND A$ < "UP" THEN PRINT "A$ IS BETWEEN"


9.  10  INPUT X
    20  IF X <= 25 OR X >= 75 THEN PRINT "NOT IN THE INTERVAL"
                                ELSE PRINT "IN THE INTERVAL"
    30  GOTO 10
```

```
11.  10 FOR I = 11 TO -11 STEP -2
     20    PRINT I^3
     30 NEXT I


13.  10 FOR I = 1 TO 40
     20    PRINT "*";
     30 NEXT I


15.  10 FOR I = 10 TO 97 STEP 3
     20    PRINT I;
     30 NEXT I


17.  10 INPUT "CREATURE";X$
     20 RESTORE
     30 FOR I = 1 TO 6
     40    READ C$,W$ : REM GET CREATURE AND WEAPON
     50    IF C$ = X$ THEN 90
     60 NEXT I
     70 PRINT "CREATURE ";X$;" NOT FOUND."
     80 GOTO 10
     90 PRINT "YOU CAN KILL A ";C$;" WITH A ";W$
     100 GOTO 10
     110 DATA LICH,FIRE BALL,MUMMY,FLAMING TORCH
     120 DATA WEREWOLF,SILVER BULLET,VAMPIRE,WOODEN STAKE
     130 DATA MEDUSA,SHARP SWORD,TRIFFID,FIRE HOSE


19.  LINE:  10 20 30 40 50 60 10 20 30 40 50 60 10 20 30 40 50 60


21.  10 FOR I = 1 TO 10
     20    PRINT : PRINT "-----------------------------"
     30    PRINT "   HAPPY HOLIDAY MOTEL"
     40    PRINT "        ROOM";I
     50    PRINT "-----------------------------"
     60 NEXT I


23.  10 PRINT " X","X^2","X^3"
     20 PRINT
     30 FOR I = 2 TO 10 STEP 2
     40    PRINT I,I^2,I^3
     50 NEXT I
```

```
25.  10  INPUT N
     20  FOR H = 1 TO N : REM H IS HIEGHT THE TRIANGLE IS
     30     IF W = H THEN 70 : REM W IS WIDTH
     40     PRINT "*";
     50     W = W + 1
     60     GOTO 30
     70     PRINT : W = 0 : REM RESET WIDTH FOR EACH H
     80  NEXT H


27.  10  FOR I = 1 TO 5
     20     READ N$,P : REM GET NAME, PERFORMANCE
     30     IF P >= 75 THEN 110
     40     PRINT : PRINT "DEAR ";N$;","
     50     PRINT "   I AM SO SORRY THAT I MUST FIRE YOU."
     60     PRINT "YOU HAVE BEEN SUCH A FINE EMPLOYEE"
     70     PRINT "WITH A PERFORMANCE RATING OF";P;"%"
     80     PRINT "I'M SURE YOU'LL HAVE NO TROUBLE"
     90     PRINT "FINDING ANOTHER JOB." : PRINT TAB(20);"SINCERELY,"
     100    PRINT : PRINT TAB(20);"GEORGE SHWABB":PRINT
     110 NEXT I
     120 DATA OAKLEY,69,HOWE,92,ANDERSON,96,WOLLEY,88,GOERZ,74


29.  10  INPUT "HOURS WORKED";H
     20  INPUT "HOURLY WAGE";W
     30  M = W * H
     40  IF H > 40 THEN M = M + .5 * W * (H-40)
     50  PRINT "THE WAGE FOR THE WEEK IS $";M


31.  1 REM    A = AMOUNT OF MONEY LEFT
     10 A = 200 : REM INITIAL AMOUNT
     20 INPUT "HOW MUCH DOES THE ITEM COST";C
     25 IF C = 0 THEN END
     30 A = A - 1.05 * C : REM 1.05*C IS COST WITH TAX
     35 IF A < 0 THEN PRINT "YOU DONT HAVE ENOUGH"
                 : A = A + 1.05*C : GOTO 20
     40 PRINT "YOUR TOTAL IS NOW $";A
     50 PRINT
     60 GOTO 20
```

CHAPTER THREE

1. ```
   10 RANDOMIZE
   20 FOR I = 1 TO 10
   30    N = RND
   40     IF N > .5 THEN PRINT N;
   50 NEXT I
   ```

3. ```
   10 INPUT N
   20 IF N = INT(N) THEN PRINT N
   30 GOTO 10
   ```

5. ```
   10 RANDOMIZE
   20 N = INT(4 * RND + 2)
   30 D = INT(4 * RND + 1)
   40 Q = INT(4 * RND)
   50 F = .05*N + .1*D + .25*Q : REM TOTAL AMOUNT FOUND
   60 PRINT "YOU FOUND $";F
   70 IF F >= 1 THEN PRINT "YOU CAN BUY LUNCH."
                   ELSE PRINT "SORRY, YOU CAN'T BUY LUNCH."
   ```

7. ```
   1 REM    A = AMOUNT IN BANK
   2 REM    I = WEEK NUMBER
   10 A = 11
   20 FOR I = 1 TO 4
   30    PRINT "WEEK";I;", HOW MANY PENNIES DO YOU HAVE";
   40    INPUT N
   50    A = A + N
   60    PRINT "YOUR TOTAL IS NOW $";A/100
   70 NEXT I
   ```

9. ```
   10 CLS
   20 FOR I = 1 TO 24
   30    LOCATE I,2*I-1
   40    PRINT "*"
   50 NEXT I
   ```

11A. ```
   RUN
      1
       2
        3
         4
                        1
                        2
                        3
                        4

      Ok
   ```

11B. RUN
```
   123.4           123.5
   123.45          123.46
Ok
```

13.   X   Y
```
      -                -
      1*               5*
      2                0
                       2
                       1
                       -1
      3*               2*
```

      * - THIS SHOULD BE CIRCLED.

15.
```
10 FOR I = 13 TO 147 STEP 2
20    S = S + I
30 NEXT I
40 PRINT "THE SUM =";S
```

17.
```
10 RANDOMIZE 111
20 FOR I = 1 TO 1000
30    N = INT(9*RND + 1)
40 IF N / 2 = INT(N / 2) THEN E = E + 1
                        ELSE O = O + 1
50 NEXT I
60 PRINT "THERE WERE";O;"ODD INTEGERS."
70 PRINT "THERE WERE";E;"EVEN INTEGERS."
```

19.
```
10 Y = 1983 : B = 1000
20 PRINT "DATE","BALANCE"
30 Y = Y + 1
40 B = B * 1.05
50 PRINT "JAN 1,";Y,INT(100*B+.5)/100
60 IF B > 2000 THEN END
70 GOTO 30
```

21.
```
10 READ V
20 PI = 3.14159
30 R = (.75 * V / PI) ^ (1/3)
40 R = INT(R*100 + .5)/100
50 PRINT "RADIUS IS";R
60 GOTO 10
70 DATA 690,720,460
```

```
23.   10 PRINT TAB(15);"*"
      20 FOR I = 1 TO 5
      30    PRINT TAB(15-I);"*";TAB(15+I);"*"
      40 NEXT I
      50 PRINT TAB(9);"*************"


25A.  5 RANDOMIZE 86
      10 CLS : LOCATE 3,1
      20 PRINT TAB(10);"-------------------------"
      30 FOR Z = 1 TO 4 : PRINT TAB(10);"!";TAB(30);"!" : NEXT Z
      40 PRINT TAB(10);"!";TAB(18);"------";TAB(30);"!"
      50 FOR Z = 1 TO 4
      60    PRINT TAB(10);"!";TAB(18);"!";
      70    PRINT TAB(22);"!";TAB(30);"!";
      80 NEXT Z
      90 PRINT TAB(10);"!";TAB(18);"------";TAB(30);"!"
      100 FOR Z = 1 TO 4 : PRINT TAB(10);"!";TAB(30);"!" : NEXT Z
      110 PRINT TAB(10);"-------------------------"
      120 FOR S = 1 TO 10
      130    X = INT(25 * RND + 1)
      140    Y = INT(40 * RND + 1)
      150    LOCATE X,Y
      160    PRINT "*";
      170 NEXT S
      180 LOCATE 24,1


25B.  5 RANDOMIZE 86
      10 CLS : LOCATE 3,1
      20 PRINT TAB(10);"-------------------------"
      30 FOR Z = 1 TO 4 : PRINT TAB(10);"!";TAB(30);"!" : NEXT Z
      40 PRINT TAB(10);"!";TAB(18);"------";TAB(30);"!"
      50 FOR Z = 1 TO 4
      60    PRINT TAB(10);"!";TAB(18);"!";
      70    PRINT TAB(22);"!";TAB(30);"!";
      80 NEXT Z
      90 PRINT TAB(10);"!";TAB(18);"------";TAB(30);"!"
      100 FOR Z = 1 TO 4 : PRINT TAB(10);"!";TAB(30);"!" : NEXT Z
      110 PRINT TAB(10);"-------------------------"
      120 FOR S = 1 TO 10
      130    X = INT(25 * RND + 1)
      140    Y = INT(40 * RND + 1)
      150    LOCATE X,Y
      160    PRINT "*";
      170 IF X > 7 AND X < 14 AND Y > 17 AND Y < 23 THEN T = T + 10
             : GOTO 200
      180 IF X > 2 AND X < 19 AND Y > 9 AND Y < 31 THEN T = T + 4
             : GOTO 200
      190 T = T - 1
      200 NEXT S
      210 LOCATE 24,1 : PRINT "SCORE IS";T
```

CHAPTER FOUR

```
1.  10 FOR I = 1 TO 8
    20     FOR J = 1 TO 30
    30        PRINT "*";
    40     NEXT J
    50     PRINT : REM USED TO MOVE TO NEXT LINE
    60 NEXT I
```

```
3.  10 FOR I = 1 TO 6
    20     INPUT "ENTER X(I)";X(I)
    30 NEXT I
    40 FOR I = 1 TO 5 STEP 2
    50     PRINT I,X(I)
    60 NEXT I
    70 FOR I = 2 TO 6 STEP 2
    80     PRINT I,X(I)
    90 NEXT I
```

```
5.  5 DIM A(4,12)
    10 FOR I = 1 TO 4
    20     FOR J = 1 TO 12
    30        A(I,J) = 3*I + J*J
    40     NEXT J
    50 NEXT I
    60 INPUT "N";N
    70 FOR I = 1 TO 12
    80     PRINT A(N,I);
    90 NEXT I
    100 PRINT
    110 GOTO 60
```

```
7A.  RUN
      1              5
      1              6
      2              5
      2              6
      3              5
      3              6
     Ok
```

```
7B.  RUN
      10
      10
      10
      12
      12
      11
      14
      13
      11
     Ok
```

RUN

```
 45                89                35
Ok
```

9.
```
10 FOR X = 40 TO 1 STEP -1
20     FOR Y = 1 TO 10
30         READ N
40          IF N = X THEN PRINT N;
50     NEXT Y
55 RESTORE
60 NEXT X
70 DATA 5,27,37,16,27,8,2,40,1,9
```

11.
```
5 RANDOMIZE
10 DIM N(100)
20 FOR X = 1 TO 100
30     N(X) = INT(99*RND + 1) : REM GET A NEW RANDOM NUMBER
35     REM    LOOP THROUGH ALL PREVIOUS NUMBERS
40     FOR Y = O TO X-1
50          IF N(X) = N(Y) THEN 90 : REM SEE IF ANY DUPLICATES
60     NEXT Y
70 NEXT X
80 END
90          PRINT "DUPLICATE AFTER";X;"NUMBERS"
100 FOR I = 1 TO X
110     PRINT N(I);
120 NEXT I
```

13.
```
10 FOR I = 3 TO 30
20     FOR J = I + 1 TO 40 : REM ADD ONE SO NO DUPLICATES
30         FOR K = J + 1 TO 50
40              IF K*K = J*J + I*I THEN PRINT I,J,K
50         NEXT K
60     NEXT J
70 NEXT I
```

15.
```
5 DIM N(20)
10 RANDOMIZE 3456
20 FOR I = 1 TO 20
30     N(I) = INT(90*RND + 10)
40 NEXT I
50 PRINT "ODD INTEGERS:";
60 FOR I = 1 TO 20
70     IF N(I)/2 <> INT(N(I)/2) THEN PRINT N(I);
80 NEXT I
90 PRINT :PRINT "EVEN INTEGERS:";
100 FOR I = 1 TO 20
110     IF N(I)/2 = INT(N(I)/2) THEN PRINT N(I);
120 NEXT I
```

```
17A.   10 DIM N$(5,6)
       20 INPUT "WHAT DAY AND TIME WOULD YOU LIKE";D,T
       30 IF N$(D,T) <> "" THEN PRINT "THAT TIME IS TAKEN ":GOTO 20
       40 INPUT "WHAT IS YOUR NAME ";N$(D,T)
       50 PRINT "THANK YOU SO VERY MUCH."
       60 GOTO 20


17B.   10 DIM N$(5,6)
       20 INPUT "ARE YOU THE DOCTOR ";A$
       30 IF A$ = "YES" THEN 90
       40 INPUT "WHAT DAY AND TIME WOULD YOU LIKE";D,T
       50 IF N$(D,T) <> "" THEN PRINT "THAT TIME IS TAKEN ":GOTO 40
       60 INPUT "WHAT IS YOUR NAME ";N$(D,T)
       70 PRINT "THANK YOU SO VERY MUCH."
       80 GOTO 20
       90 INPUT "WHICH DAY";D
       100 PRINT
       110 PRINT "SCHEDULE FOR DAY";D
       120 PRINT "TIME","PATIENT"
       130 FOR T = 1 TO 6
       140 PRINT T,
       150  IF N$(D,T) = "" THEN PRINT "SANKA BREAK" : GOTO 170
       160 PRINT N$(D,T)
       170 NEXT T
       180 GOTO 20


19.    10 DIM N(100)
       20 RANDOMIZE : R = INT(100 * RND + 1)
       30 FOR X = 1 TO 100
       40    INPUT "GUESS";G
       50    IF G = R THEN 150
       60    FOR Z = 1 TO X-1
       70       IF N(Z) = G THEN 130
       80    NEXT Z
       90    N(X) = G
       100   IF G > R THEN PRINT "LOWER" : GOTO 120
       110    PRINT "HIGHER"
       120 NEXT X
       130 PRINT "WAKE UP! YOU GUESSED THAT NUMBER BEFORE!"
       140 GOTO 40
       150 PRINT "CORRECT"
```

```
21.  1 REM     ARRAY P HOLDS POINT VALUES FOR THE BOARD
     2 REM     ARRAY B = P EXCEPT A ZERO IS ENTERED WHEN A PENNY
               HITS THE BOARD
    10 DIM P(6,6),B(6,6)
    20 REM    SET UP OUTSIDE OF BOARD FOR 1 POINT
    30 FOR I = 1 TO 6
    40    P(1,I) = 1 : P(6,I) = 1 : P(I,6) = 1 : P(I,1) = 1
    50 NEXT I
    60 REM    SET UP BOARD POSITIONS WORTH 2 POINTS
    70 FOR I = 2 TO 5
    80    P(2,I) = 2 : P(5,I) = 2 : P(I,2) = 2 : P(I,5) = 2
    90 NEXT I
   100 REM    SET UP THE THREEE POINT POSITIONS
   110 P(3,3) = 3 : P(3,4) = 3 : P(4,3) = 3 : P(4,4) = 3
   120 REM    SET ARRAY B EQUAL TO ARRAY P
   130 FOR Q = 1 TO 6
   140    FOR W = 1 TO 6
   150       B(Q,W) = P(Q,W)
   160    NEXT W
   170 NEXT Q
   180 REM    NOW GET TEN RANDOM ROWS AND COLUMNS FOR PENNY TOSSES
   190 RANDOMIZE 9876
   200 FOR T = 1 TO 10
   210    R = INT(6 * RND + 1) : C = INT(6 * RND + 1)
   220    B(R,C) = 0 : REM SET HIT POSITIONS TO 0
   230    S = S + P(R,C) : REM    ADD ON POINT VALUE FOR THE HIT
   240 NEXT T
   250 REM    PRINT OUT THE RESULTANT BOARD
   260 FOR R = 1 TO 6
   270    FOR C = 1 TO 6
   280       IF B(R,C) = 0 THEN PRINT " X ";: GOTO 300
   290       PRINT B(R,C);
   300    NEXT C
   310    PRINT
   320 NEXT R
   330 PRINT :PRINT "SCORE IS";S


23.  1 REM    A$() = THE LETTERS OF THE ALPHABET
     2 REM    W$ = THE WORD FORMED
    10 DIM A$(26)
    20 RANDOMIZE 4242
    30 FOR I = 1 TO 26
    40    READ A$(I)
    50 NEXT I
    60 FOR W = 1 TO 15
    70    R = INT(7 * RND + 1) : REM GET RANDOM LENGTH
    80    FOR L = 1 TO R : REM    GET WORD OF LENGTH R
    90       W$ = W$ + A$(INT(26 * RND + 1)) : REM    ADD LETTERS ON
   100    NEXT L
   110    PRINT W$
   120    W$ = "" : REM    BLANK W$ FOR NEXT WORD
   130 NEXT W
   200 REM
   210 DATA A,B,C,D,E,F,G,H,I,J,K,L,M,N,O,P,Q,R,S,T,U,V,W,X,Y,Z
```

```
25.   10 M = 500
      20 FOR X = 1 TO 21
      30     FOR Q = 1 TO 4
      40         M = M + M * .06/4
      50     NEXT Q
      60     PRINT "AT THE END OF YEAR";X;"THERE IS $";M
      70     M = M + 60
      80 NEXT X
```

CHAPTER FIVE

1. a) This program will generate an "Out of DATA in 10" error. Line 10 attempts to read a fourth data element from line 40. A possible correction might read;

    40 DATA 2,3,4,5

    where the value 5 becomes the fourth data element.

    b) This program will endlessly print .5 because no new data is read in. Correct line 40 as follows:

    40 GOTO 10

    c) Lines 20 and and 30 each contain syntax errors. The function "*/" referenced at line 20 is illegal. The statement may be corrected to read:

    20 PRINT A*B+C

    to indicate multiplication, or:

    20 PRINT A/B+C

    to indicate division of A by B. Line 30 may be corrected by placing quotation marks around "D/F=" to read:

    30 PRINT "D/F=";D/F

    In addition, the variables D and F should be defined, or else a division by zero will result in line 30.

    d) The conditional clause at line 20 is incomplete. The user has not specified what variable should be 10. The obvious variable is F, so that line 20 reads:

    20 IF F>5 OR F<10 THEN 40

A comma or a semicolon must be inserted between the variables F and G at line 40 so that the computer understands that they are two separate elements:

40 PRINT F,G

e) The FOR. . .TO. . .NEXT loops are improperly nested:

```
10   FOR X=1 TO 8
20     FOR Y=1 TO 3
30       X=X+Y
40     NEXT X
50   NEXT Y
60   PRINT X
70   END
```

Line 40 and 50 may be corrected as follows:

```
40   NEXT Y
50   NEXT X
```

Also, changing the value of variables used in FOR-TO-NEXT loops is not recommended practice such as at line 30.

f) This program will continuously print the sum of 3 and 6 since new data is not being read at line 10. Correct line 40 as follows:

40 GOTO 10

Also the variable E is undefined (its value is zero) in line 30. Line 10 should be

10 READ C,D,E

3. RUN
```
-6               6
Ok
```

5. a) The computer will return the error "Syntax Error in 20". Since it appears that the variable "X" is intended to contain formula weight, line 20 may be corrected to read:

20 INPUT "FORMULA WEIGHT";X

b) When this program attempts to branch to line 50 at line 35, it will not find line 50, and the error message "Undefined line number in 35" will be printed. Change line 35 to:

35 IF Y=X THEN A=A+1 : GOTO 55

c) Note that both lines 10 and 20 do not contain the same number of closing parentheses as opening parentheses, thereby causing an "Illegal function call in 10". The computer reports the first error encountered so the error in line 20 goes undiscovered. The first opening parenthesis is not necessary in either of these lines.

d) Upon encountering line 30, the computer will print the error message "Syntax Error in 30". The line in question should read:

30 IF X>200 THEN 10

e) When the computer runs this program, it will print "Type mismatch in 20" and terminate the run. The problem arises from trying to add a floating point variable to a string variable. Variables can be of several types. They can be integers (which means they have no decimal places), floating point or real (which means they have decimal places), or string variables. Assuming the intent of this program was to sum all the numbers between 1 and 26, the best way to correct this program is to change all occurrences of "A$" to "A".

$$20 \qquad A=A+X$$
$$40 \quad PRINT\ A$$

f) The error encountered in this example is "String too long in 20". The longest a string may be is 255 characters, therefore, the loop between lines 10 and 30 cannot be executed more than 255 times. Change line 10 to:

10 FOR X = 1 TO 255

7. The computer stores all decimal numbers in binary form. Because of this, small "rounding errors" are introduced into stored numbers. When these errors are compounded as in the large summation at line 30 (100 and 1000 times), it leads to very visible miscalculations as seen when this program is run. In this case the error was small.

CHAPTER SIX

1.
```
10 INPUT N
20 IF N < 0 THEN PRINT "NO NEGATIVE NUMBERS ALLOWED" : GOTO 10
30 PRINT "N =";N," SQUARE ROOTS = + OR -";SQR(N) : GOTO 10
```

```
3A.    PRINT 3^2^3
       729

3B.    PRINT 5 - 4^2
       -11

3C.    PRINT 3 * (5 + 16)
       63

3D.    PRINT 5 + 3 * 6 / 2
       14

3E.    PRINT 640 / 10 / 2 * 5
       160

3F.    PRINT 5 + 3 * 4 - 1
       16

3G.    PRINT 2^3^2
       64

3H.    PRINT 2^(3^2)
       512

3I.    PRINT 64 / 4 * .5 + ((1 + 5) * 2^3) * 1 / (2 * 4)
       14


5.     10 INPUT N
       20 PRINT SGN(N)*N

       THIS PROGRAM RETURNS ABS(N)



7.     10 PRINT "RADIANS","DEGREES"
       20 FOR A = 0 TO 3 STEP .25
       30    PRINT A,A*180/3.141592653#
       40 NEXT A



9.     10 INPUT N
       20 N = N * 3.1415926535#/180
       30 C = COS(N)
       40 S = SIN(N)
       50 T = TAN(N)
       60 IF C > S AND C > T THEN PRINT "COSINE =";C
                       ELSE IF S > T THEN PRINT "SINE =";S
                                   ELSE PRINT "TANGENT =";T
```

```
11.  10 DEF FNF(X) = 9 * X^3 - 7 * X^2 + 4*X - 1
     20 INPUT "A,B";A,B
     30 PRINT FNF(B) - FNF(A)


13.  10 PRINT " X";TAB(9);"LN(X)";TAB(24);"EXP(X)"
     20 PRINT
     30 FOR X = 1 TO 15
     40    PRINT X;TAB(7);LOG(X);TAB(22);EXP(X)
     50 NEXT X


15.  RUN
      5              -4              3              4
     Ok


17.  RUN
     FNF(-4 )  IS NEGATIVE
     FNF(-2 )  IS NEGATIVE
     FNF( 0 )  IS NEGATIVE
     FNF( 2 )  IS ZERO
     FNF( 4 )  IS POSITIVE
     FNF( 6 )  IS POSITIVE
     Ok


19.  RUN
     -3
     -2
     -1
      0
      1
      2
      3
      4
     Ok


21.  10 INPUT "R AND THETA (IN DEGREES) :";R,T
     20 T = T * 3.141592653#/180
     30 X = R * COS(T)
     40 Y = R * SIN(T)
     50 PRINT "(X,Y) = (";X;",";Y;")"


23.  10 FOR X = 1 TO 100
     20    Y = ABS(SIN(X) * 1000)
     30    R = INT(Y)/16 - INT(INT(Y)/16)
     40    PRINT R
     50 NEXT X
```

```
25.  10 FOR N = 0 TO 6.2 STEP .2
     20    U = SIN(N)
     30    PRINT TAB(20 * U + 22);"SHAZAM!"
     40 NEXT N
```

CHAPTER SEVEN

```
1.   10 GOSUB 400
     20 FOR J = 1 TO 40
     30    PRINT "*";
     40 NEXT J
     50 GOSUB 400
     60 FOR J = 1 TO 3
     70    PRINT "!",
     80 NEXT J
     90 GOSUB 400
     100 FOR J = 1 TO 20
     110    PRINT "AB";
     120 NEXT J
     130 END
     400 PRINT
     410 I = I + 1
     420 PRINT "PART";I
     430 RETURN
```

```
3.   10 INPUT "ONE, TWO, THREE, FOUR";X
     20 IF X<>1 AND X<>2 AND X<>3 AND X<>4 THEN 10
     30 ON X GOTO 40,60,80,100
     40 PRINT "DON'T LET YOUR COMPUTER TURN TO TRASH!"
     50 END
     60 PRINT "DON'T LET BUGS GET IN YOUR TRASH."
     70 END
     80 PRINT "STUDY HARD AND YOU WON'T NEED A TRUSS."
     90 END
     100 PRINT "NEVER PLAY WITH TRASH."
     110 END
```

```
5A.  LINE: [10][20][30][70][40][10][20][30][50][40][10]
           [20][30][60][40][10][20][90][100]
```

```
5B.  RUN
     N = 3          Z = 1          P = 4
     Ok
```

```
7.  10 READ A,B,C
    20 GOSUB 200
    30 IF L = 1 THEN 70
    40 R = A * B / 2
    50 PRINT "AREA =";R,"PERIMETER =";A + B + C
    60 GOTO 10
    70 PRINT "NOT A RIGHT TRIANGLE"
    80 GOTO 10
    200 L = 0
    210 IF A + B <= C THEN 250
    220 IF A + C <= B THEN 250
    230 IF B + C <= A THEN 250
    240 IF INT(A^2 + B^2) = INT(C^2) THEN 260
    250 L = 1
    260 RETURN
    270 DATA 3,4,5,0,1,1,2,2,2,12,5,13
    280 END


9.  10 INPUT "WITHDRAWAL(1),DEPOSIT(2), OR CALCULATE INTEREST(3)";D
    15 IF D <> 1 AND D <> 2 AND D <> 3 THEN 10
    20 ON D GOSUB 120,150,180
    30 PRINT "YOUR BALANCE NOW STANDS AT";B;"DOLLARS."
    40 GOTO 10
    115 REM    WITHDRAWAL LOOP
    120 INPUT "HOW MUCH WOULD YOU LIKE TO WITHDRAW";A
    130 IF A >= 0 AND B - A > 0 THEN B = B - A : RETURN
    140 GOTO 120
    145 REM    DEPOSIT LOOP
    150 INPUT "HOW MUCH WOULD YOU LIKE TO DEPOSIT";A
    160 IF A >= 0 THEN B = B + A : RETURN
    170 GOTO 150
    180 INPUT "HOW MANY MONTHS SINCE LAST CALCULATION";M
    190 Q = M / 3
    200 IF Q < 1 THEN PRINT "TOO SOON" : RETURN
    210 FOR C = 1 TO Q
    220    B = B + .0575 / 4 * B
    230 NEXT C
    240 RETURN


11. 10 ON ERROR GOTO 100
    20 FOR X = 20 TO 0 STEP -2
    30    PRINT 10 / LOG(X)
    40 NEXT X
    50 END
    100 IF ERR = 5 THEN PRINT "ILLEGAL USE OF LOG FUNCTION"
    110 RESUME 40
```

CHAPTER EIGHT

1.  ```
    10 SCREEN 1,0 : COLOR 0,0
    20 LINE (38,18) - (107,47),2,BF
    ```

3.  ```
    5 CLS
    10 SCREEN 1,0 : COLOR 0,1
    20 LINE (0,80) - (319,80),3
    30 LINE (140,0) - (140,199),1
    ```

5.  ```
    10 SCREEN 0,1 : COLOR 20,8,2
    20 LOCATE 10,15
    30 PRINT "Today Only!"
    40 PRINT TAB(17); "Uncle Bill's"
    50 PRINT TAB(15); "WHAMBURGERS!"
    60 PRINT TAB(19); "Only $0.79"
    ```

7.  ```
    5 CLS
    10 DIM R(10) : RANDOMIZE
    20 FOR N = 1 TO 200
    30      Q = INT(RND*10) + 1
    40      R(Q) = R(Q) + 1
    50 NEXT N
    60 SCREEN 1,0 : COLOR 0,0
    70 FOR N = 1 TO 10
    80      LOCATE 25,N*3
    90      PRINT N;
    100     C = (N MOD 3) + 1 : REM Color
    110     LINE (N*24+1,182) - (N*24+9,190-R(N)),C,BF
    120     LOCATE 23 - R(N)/8,N*3
    130     PRINT R(N);
    140 NEXT N
    150 LINE (8,185) - (268,185),3
    ```

9.  ```
    10 SCREEN 1,0 : COLOR 8,0 : PI = 3.14159
    20 CIRCLE (160,100),50,2,-5*PI/4,-3*PI/4
    30 CIRCLE (160,72),5,2
    40 PAINT (170,100),3,2
    50 PAINT (0,0),2,2
    60 LINE (105,62) - (215,57),1,BF
    70 LINE (140,57) - (180,45),1,BF
    ```
    ```

```
11. 10 SCREEN 2,0
    20 FOR X = 0 TO .5 STEP .1
    30      CIRCLE (100,100),60,3,,,X
    40 NEXT X


13. 5 CLS
    10 RANDOMIZE : SCREEN 1,0 : COLOR 8,0
    20 FOR C = 1 TO 3
    30      CIRCLE (160,100),C*30,3
    40      PAINT (165+(C-1)*30,100),4-C,3
    50 NEXT C
    60 REM Take 10 shots...
    70 FOR S = 1 TO 10
    80      X = INT(RND*280) + 20
    90      Y = INT(RND*180) + 10
    100     SCORE = SCORE + POINT(X,Y)
    110     CIRCLE (X,Y),3,0
    120     PAINT (X,Y),0,0
    130 NEXT S
    140 PRINT "Score ="; SCORE


15. 5 CLS
    10 SCREEN 1,0 : COLOR 8,0 : PI = 3.14159
    20 FOR A = 0 TO 2*PI STEP 2*PI/7
    30      CIRCLE (100,50),50,2,-A,-(A+2*PI/7)
    40 NEXT A


17A. 10 REM    Towers of Hanoi
     20 REM
     30 REM   Plot the base and pegs in green
     40 REM
     50 CLS : SCREEN 1,0 : COLOR 8,0
     60 LINE (20,150) - (300,165),1,BF : LINE (70,150) - (80,50),1,BF
     70 LINE (155,150) - (165,50),1,BF : LINE (240,150) - (250,50),1,BF
     80 REM    Plot the 5 discs
     100 REM    Plot the 5 discs
     110 FOR D = 1 TO 5
     120      W = CINT((12*D+16)/2) : REM Width
     130      V = 50 + (18*D) : REM Vertical Position
     140      LINE (75-W,V+5) - (75+W,V-5),2,BF
     150 NEXT D
```

```
17B. 10 REM   Towers of Hanoi
     20 REM
     30 REM   Plot the base and pegs in green
     40 REM
     50 CLS : SCREEN 1,0 : COLOR 8,0
     60 LINE (20,150) - (300,165),1,BF : LINE (70,150) - (80,50),1,BF
     70 LINE (155,150) - (165,50),1,BF : LINE (240,150) - (250,50),1,BF
     80 REM    Plot the 5 discs
    100 REM    Plot the 5 discs
    110 FOR D = 1 TO 5
    120      W = CINT((12*D+16)/2) : REM Width
    130      V = 50 + (18*D) : REM Vertical Position
    140      LINE (75-W,V+5) - (75+W,V-5),2,BF
    150      A(1,D) = D : A(2,D) = O : A(3,D) = O
    160 NEXT D
    200 REM Movement of discs
    210 LOCATE 23,1 : PRINT "From Tower, To Tower       ";
    220 LOCATE 23,21 : INPUT T1,T2 : DISC = O
    225 LOCATE 24,1 : PRINT "                            "; : LOCATE 24,1
    230 FOR X = 1 TO 5
    240      IF DISC > O OR A(T1,X) = O THEN 300
    250      DISC = A(T1,X) : XLOC = T1*85 - 10 : REM Tower location
    260      W = CINT((12*DISC+16)/2) : REM Width of disc
    270      V = 50 + (18*X) : REM Vertical pos
    280      LINE (XLOC-W,V+5) - (XLOC+W,V-5),O,BF : REM Wipe out disc
    290      LINE (XLOC-5,V+5) - (XLOC+5,V-5),1,BF : A(T1,X) = O
    300 NEXT X
    310 IF DISC = O THEN PRINT "There is no disk there!"; : GOTO 200
    320 EMPTY = O
    330 FOR X = 5 TO 1 STEP -1
    340      IF EMPTY = O AND A(T2,X) = O THEN EMPTY = X
    350 NEXT X
    360 IF EMPTY = 5 THEN 500
    400 IF A(T2,EMPTY + 1) >= DISC THEN 500
    410 PRINT "You can't do that!"; : T2 = T1 : GOTO 320
    500 REM Plot the disk at A(T2,EMPTY)
    510 XLOC = T2*85 - 10 : V = 50 + (18*EMPTY)
    520 W = CINT((12*DISC+16)/2) : REM Width of disc
    530 LINE (XLOC-W,V+5) - (XLOC + W,V-5),2,BF : REM Plot disc
    540 A(T2,EMPTY) = DISC
    550 IF T2 = 1 OR EMPTY <> 1 THEN 200
    560 PRINT "Good Show Ol' Chap!"
```

CHAPTER NINE

```
1. 10  INPUT "A$";A$
   20  FOR I = 1 TO LEN(A$)
   30     PRINT ASC(MID$(A$,I,1));
   40  NEXT I
```

```
3. 10  READ X%
   20  PRINT CHR$(X%);
   30  GOTO 10
   40  DATA 65,83,67,73,73,32,68,73
   50  DATA 68,32,84,72,73,83,33
```

```
5. 1  REM    A$ = ORIGINAL STRING
   2  REM    L$,M$,R$ = LEFT, MID, RIGHT STRINGS OF ORIGINAL
   3  REM
   4  REM
   10 A$ = "THREE!Ә##$%STRINGӘ##$%FUNCTIONS"
   20 L$ = LEFT$(A$,5) : REM     SETS L$ = "THREE"
   30 M$ = MID$(A$,11,6) : REM     SETS M$ = "STRING"
   40 R$ = RIGHT$(A$,9) : REM     SETS R$ = "FUNCTIONS"
   50 PRINT L$;" ";M$;" ";R$
   60 END
```

```
7. 1  REM    N$ = THE NAME BEING EXAMINED
   2  REM    A() = THE NUMBER OF OCCURRENCES OF EACH LETTER
   3  REM    S = ASCII CODE FOR THE LETTERS IN N$
   4  REM    F = 1 IF THERE IS A TIE BETWEEN LETTERS ELSE F = 0
   5  REM
   6  REM
   10 REM GET THE NAME AND COUNT THE NUMBER OF OCCURRENCES OF EACH LETTER
   20 DIM A(26)
   30 INPUT "NAME";N$
   40 FOR I = 1 TO LEN(N$)
   50    S = ASC(MID$(N$,I,1))
   60    A(S-65) = A(S-65) + 1
   70 NEXT I
   100 REM     NOW LOOK FOR THE MOST COMMMON LETTER
   110 MOST = 1
   120 FOR I = 0 TO 25
   130    IF A(I) = MOST THEN F = 1
   140     IF A(I) > MOST THEN MOST = A(I) : V = I : F = 0
   150 NEXT I
   200 REM     NOW PRINT THE MOST COMMON LETTER
   210 IF F= 0 THEN PRINT CHR$(V+65);" IS THE MOST COMMON LETTER IN ";N$
                     : END
   220 PRINT "THE FOLLOWING LETTERS HAVE AN EQUAL OCCURRENCE : ";
   230 FOR I = 0 TO 25
   240    IF A(I) = MOST THEN PRINT CHR$(I+65);" ";
   250 NEXT I
```

9.
```
1 REM    A$ = A STRING FROM DATA
2 REM    L% = LENGTH OF A STRING
3 REM    B$ = A CHARACTER IN A STRING
4 REM
5 REM
10 READ A$
20 L% = LEN(A$)
30 FOR X% = 1 TO L%
40    B$ = MID$(A$,X%,1) : REM PULL ONE CHARACTER FROM A$
50    IF ASC(B$) = 69 THEN 70
60    PRINT B$;
70 NEXT X%
80 PRINT
90 GOTO 10
100 DATA QUEEN, LENGTH, REMEMBER
```

11.

Binary	Decimal
1011	11
10100	20
1111	15
1110	14
1010011	83
110011	51
1011100	92
1101111	111
11000000	192
10000111	135

13.
```
1 REM    A$ = THE FIRST 12 LETTERS OF THE ALPHABET
2 REM    L% = THE LENGTH OF THE STRING TO BE PRINTED
3 REM
4 REM
10 FOR C% = ASC("A") TO ASC("L")
20    A$ = A$ + CHR$(C%)
30 NEXT C%
40 FOR L% = 1 TO 12
50    PRINT LEFT$(A$,L%)
60 NEXT L%
70 END
```

15.
```
RUN
 87
 72
 55
 54
Ok
```

```
17.   10 RANDOMIZE
      20 FOR X% = 1 TO 15
      30    C% = INT(26*RND + 65)
      40    PRINT CHR$(C%);
      50 NEXT X%
      60 END


19.   10 FOR X = 1 TO 100
      20    A$ = A$ + CHR$(INT(95 * RND + 32))
      30 NEXT X
      40 PRINT : PRINT A$ : PRINT
      50 FOR Y = 1 TO 100
      60    C = ASC(MID$(A$,Y,1))
      70    IF (C>64 AND C<91) OR (C>96 AND C<123) THEN L = L + 1
               ELSE IF (C>47 AND C<58) THEN N = N + 1
                                     ELSE M = M + 1
      80 NEXT Y
      90 PRINT "THERE ARE";L;"LETTERS,";N;"NUMBERS, AND"
      100 PRINT M;"MISCELLANEOUS CHARACTERS."


21A.  10 INPUT "MESSAGE TO ENCODE ";M$
      20 FOR I% = 1 TO LEN(M$)
      30    C% = ASC(MID$(M$,I%,1))
      40    IF C% = 32 THEN 80
      50    IF C% < 65 OR C% > 90 THEN 100
      60    C% = C% + 2
      70    IF C% > 90 THEN C% = C% - 26
      80    A$ = A$ + CHR$(C%)
      90 NEXT I%
      100 PRINT "ENCODED MESSAGE: ";A$
      110 END


21B.  10 INPUT "MESSAGE TO DECODE";M$
      20 FOR I% = 1 TO LEN(M$)
      30    C% = ASC(MID$(M$,I%,1))
      35    IF C% = 32 THEN 70
      40    IF C%<65 OR C%>90 THEN 80
      50    C% = C% - 2
      60    IF C%<65 THEN C% = C% + 26
      70    A$ = A$ + CHR$(C%)
      80 NEXT I%
      90 PRINT "MESSAGE: ";A$
      100 END
```

```
23.  1 REM    S$() = STORES SENTENCES (UP TO 30)
     2 REM    N%() = STORES NUMBER OF OCCURRENCES OF EACH TARGET
     3 REM    R% = RECORDS NUMBER OF OCCURRENCES IN A SENTENCE
     4 REM
     5 REM
     10 DIM S$(30),N%(9)
     20 REM    BEGIN INPUT LOOP AND CONTINUE UNTIL UNTIL THERE IS
                NO SENTENCE INPUT
     30 C% = C% + 1
     40 LINE INPUT "SENTENCE? ";S$(C%)
     50 IF LEN(S$(C%)) = 0 THEN 90
     60 S$(C%) = CHR$(32) + S$(C%) + CHR$(32)
     70 GOTO 30
     90 REM    BEGIN PROGRAM
     100 FOR L% = 1 TO C% - 1
     110     RESTORE
     120     FOR W% = 1 TO 9
     130         READ T$
     140         GOSUB 300
     150         N%(W%) = N%(W%) + R%
     160     NEXT W%
     170 NEXT L%
     180 PRINT "ARTICLES:";N%(1) + N%(2) + N%(3)
     190 PRINT "ADVERBS:";N%(4)
     200 PRINT "PUNCTUATION MARKS:";N%(5)+N%(6)+N%(7)+N%(8)+N%(9)
     210 END
     300 REM    SUBROUTINE TO FIND # OF OCCURRENCES OF TARGET STRING
     310 V = 1 : R% = 0
     320 V = INSTR(V,S$(L%),T$)
     330 IF V <> 0 THEN R% = R% + 1 : V = V + 1 : GOTO 320
     340 RETURN
     400 DATA " A ", " AN "," THE ", "LY ", ".", "!", "?", ";", ","


25.  1 REM    S$ = SENTENCE
     2 REM    F = INDCATOR FOR BEING DONE WITH SENTENCE
     3 REM
     4 REM
     10 LINE INPUT "INPUT SENTENCE OF UP TO TEN WORDS ";S$
     30 WHILE F <> 1
     40     PRINT MID$(S$,V+1,1);
     50     V = INSTR(V+1,S$," ") : IF V = 0 THEN F = 1
     60 WEND
```

```
27.   1 REM     N$ = YOUR NUMBER
      2 REM
      3 REM
      10 INPUT "WHAT IS YOUR BINARY NUMBER";N$
      20 D% = 0
      30 FOR I% = 1 TO LEN(N$)
      40    IF ASC(MID$(N$,I%,1)) = 49 THEN D%=D%+2^(LEN(N$)-I%)
      50 NEXT I%
      60 PRINT "IT'S DECIMAL EQUIVALENT IS";D%
      70 GOTO 10
      80 END
```

CHAPTER TEN

```
1A.   10 RANDOMIZE -432
      20 DIM R(50)
      30 FOR X = 1 TO 50
      40    R(X) = INT(21 * RND)
      50 NEXT X
      60 OPEN "O",1,"B:RANUM.TXT"
      70 REM
      80 REM
      100 REM   NOW WRITE TO THE FILE
      110 FOR I = 1 TO 50
      120    WRITE #1,R(I)
      130 NEXT I
      140 CLOSE 1
```

```
1B.   1 REM     R = THE NUMBER READ FROM THE FILE
      2 REM     S = THE SUM OF ALL R'S
      10 OPEN "I",2,"B:RANUM.TXT"
      20 FOR I = 1 TO 50
      30    INPUT #2,R
      40    S = S + R
      50 NEXT I
      60 CLOSE 2
      70 PRINT "THE SUM IS";S
```

```
3A.   10 OPEN "O",1,"B:SEQ.TXT"
      20 FOR I = 1001 TO 1128
      30    WRITE #1,I
      40 NEXT I
      50 CLOSE 1
```

```
3B.  10 OPEN "I",1,"B:SEQ.TXT"
     20 INPUT "WHICH PLACE IN THE SEQUENCE";P
     30 FOR I = 1 TO P
     40     INPUT #1,N
     50 NEXT I
     60 PRINT "THAT IS";N


5A.  1 REM    N$() = STUDENT NAMES
     2 REM    F$() = FRATERNITY NAMES
     3 REM     A() = AGES
     10 DIM N$(30),F$(30),A(30)
     20 FOR X = 1 TO 30
     30     INPUT "NAME";N$(X)
     40     INPUT "FRATERNITY";F$(X)
     50     INPUT "AGE";A(X)
     60 NEXT X
     70 REM
     100 REM   NOW WRITE TO THE FILE
     110 OPEN "O",1,"B:FRAT.TXT"
     120 FOR I = 1 TO 30
     130    WRITE #1,N$(I),F$(I),A(I)
     140 NEXT I
     150 CLOSE 1


5B.  1 REM    N$() = STUDENT NAMES
     2 REM    F$() = FRATERNITY NAMES
     3 REM     A() = AGES
     10 OPEN "I",1,"B:FRAT.TXT"
     20 OPEN "O",2,"B:SIGMA.TXT"
     30 FOR X = 1 TO 30
     40     INPUT #1,N$,F$,A
     50     IF F$ = "SIGMA CHI" THEN WRITE #2,N$,A
     60 NEXT X
     70 CLOSE 1,2
```

```
5C.  1 REM    N$() = STUDENT NAMES
     2 REM    P()  = A "1" IF STUDENT HAS BEEN SEATED ELSE 0
    10 DIM N$(30),P(30)
    20 OPEN "I",1,"B:FRAT.TXT"
    30 FOR I = 1 TO 30
    40     INPUT #1,N$(I),F$,A
    50 NEXT I
    60 CLOSE 1
    70 PRINT
    80 REM
   100 REM    NOW GET RANDOM SEATING
   110 RANDOMIZE -6455 : REM    CHANGE FOR A NEW SEATING PLAN
   120 FOR X = 1 TO 5
   130    FOR Y = 1 TO 5
   140        R = INT(30 * RND + 1)
   150        IF P(R) = 1 THEN 130 : REM SEE IF STUDENT IS SEATED
   160        PRINT N$(R),
   170    NEXT Y
   175    PRINT
   180 NEXT X


7A.  1 REM    H() = TIME IN HOURS
     2 REM    F() = TEMP IN FAHRENHEIT DEGREES
     3 REM
     4 REM
    10 REM    THIS IS NIT
    20 OPEN "O",1,"B:NIT.TXT"
    30 PRINT "ENTER NIT'S DATA"
    40 FOR A = 1 TO 6
    50     INPUT "TIME";H(A)
    60     INPUT "TEMPERATURE";F(A)
    70 NEXT A : PRINT
    80 REM    NOW PRINT TO THE FILE
    90 FOR B = 1 TO 6
   100     WRITE #1,H(B),F(B)
   110 NEXT B
   120 CLOSE 1
   200 REM    THIS IS WIT
   210 OPEN "O",1,"B:WIT.TXT"
   220 PRINT "ENTER WIT'S DATA"
   230 FOR A = 1 TO 6
   240     INPUT "TIME";H(A)
   250     INPUT "TEMPERATURE";F(A)
   260 NEXT A : PRINT
   270 REM    NOW PRINT TO THE FILE
   280 FOR B = 1 TO 6
   290     WRITE #1,H(B),F(B)
   300 NEXT B
   310 CLOSE 1
```

```
7B.  1 REM     T() = TEMP IN POSITION TIME*10
     2 REM     H = TIME IN HOURS
     3 REM     F = TEMP IN FAHRENHEIT DEGREES
     4 REM
     5 REM
    10 DIM T(100)
    20 OPEN "I",1,"B:NIT.TXT"
    30 OPEN "I",2,"B:WIT.TXT"
    40 OPEN "O",3,"B:MERGE.TXT"
    50 FOR L = 1 TO 6
    60     INPUT #1,H,F : GOSUB 90 : REM    PUT DATA IN ARRAY T
    70     INPUT #2,H,F : GOSUB 90
    80 NEXT L : GOTO 200
    90 REM    IF T(H*10) IS EMPTY THEN PUT THE TEMP IN
   100 REM       ELSE AVERAGE THE VALUES
   110 IF T(H*10) = 0 THEN T(H*10) = F
                        ELSE T(H*10) = (T(H*10)+F)/2
   120 RETURN
   130 REM
   200 REM    NOW PRINT TO THE FILE MERGE.TXT
   210 FOR Z = 0 TO 100
   220    IF T(Z) <> 0 THEN WRITE #3, Z/10, T(Z)
   230 NEXT Z
   240 CLOSE 1,2,3


7C. 10 OPEN "I",1,"B:MERGE.TXT"
    20 WHILE EOF(1) = 0
    30     INPUT #1,H,F
    40     PRINT H,F
    50 WEND
    60 CLOSE 1
    70 END
```

```
9A.  1 REM     X = ROW OF PERSON'S SEAT
     2 REM     Y = COLUMN OF PERSON'S SEAT
     3 REM     S$() = PERSON'S NAME AT SEAT X,Y
     4 REM
     5 REM
     10 DIM S$(10,5)
     20 ON ERROR GOTO 200
     30 OPEN "I",1,"B:SHOW.TXT"
     40 FOR I = 1 TO 51
     50    INPUT #1,X,Y,S$(X,Y)
     60    IF EOF(1) THEN 90
     70 NEXT I
     80 CLOSE 1 : PRINT "I AM SORRY, WE HAVE A PACKED HOUSE." : END
     90 CLOSE 1 : INPUT "YOUR NAME";F$
     100 INPUT "WHAT SEAT WOULD YOU LIKE (ROW, COLUMN)";X1,Y1
     110 IF S$(X1,Y1) <> "" THEN PRINT "THAT SEAT IS TAKEN" : GOTO 100
     120 PRINT "DRAMA CLUB SHOW" : PRINT F$;" HAS"
     130 PRINT "RESERVED ROW";X1 : PRINT "SEAT";Y1;"FOR"
     140 PRINT "JULY 4, 1983" : PRINT
     150 OPEN "A",1,"B:SHOW.TXT" : REM APPEND THE LIST W/NEW PERSON
     160 WRITE #1,X1,Y1,F$
     170 CLOSE 1 : END
     200 REM    IF ERROR OCCURRED THERE MUST BE NO FILE SO MAKE ONE
     210 CLOSE 1 : OPEN "O",1,"B:SHOW.TXT"
     220 WRITE #1,0,0,B
     230 CLOSE 1 : RESUME


9B.  1 REM     X = ROW OF PERSON'S SEAT
     2 REM     Y = COLUMN OF PERSON'S SEAT
     3 REM     S$() = PERSON'S NAME AT SEAT X, Y
     4 REM
     5 REM
     10 DIM S$(10,5)
     20 OPEN "I",1,"B:SHOW.TXT"
     30 WHILE EOF(1) = 0
     40    INPUT #1,X,Y,S$(X,Y)
     50 WEND
     60 CLOSE 1
     100 PRINT "EMPTY SEATS FOR JULY 4TH DRAMA SHOW." : PRINT
     110 FOR R = 1 TO 10
     120    FOR S = 1 TO 5
     130       IF S$(R,S) <> "" THEN 150
     140       PRINT "ROW";R;"SEAT";S
     150    NEXT S
     160 NEXT R
```

```
9C.   1 REM     X = ROW OF PERSON'S SEAT
      2 REM     T = COLUMN OF PERSON'S SEAT
      3 REM     S$() = PERSON'S NAME AT SEAT X,Y
      4 REM
      5 REM
      10 REM    GET DATA
      20 DIM S$(10,5)
      30 OPEN "I",1,"B:SHOW.TXT"
      40 WHILE EOF(1) = 0
      50     INPUT #1,X,Y,S$(X,Y)
      60 WEND
      70 CLOSE 1
      80 REM
      100 REM    NOW PRINT THE SEATING PLAN
      110 FOR R = 1 TO 10
      120     FOR S = 1 TO 5
      130         IF S$(R,S) = "" THEN S$(R,S) = "EMPTY"
      140         PRINT S$(R,S),
      150     NEXT S
      160     PRINT
      170 NEXT R
```

CHAPTER ELEVEN

```
1A.   1 REM     L = ASCII OF LETTER
      2 REM     L$ = LETTER
      3 REM
      10 OPEN "R",1,"B:ALPHABET.TXT",1
      20 FIELD 1,1 AS L$
      30 FOR L = ASC("A") TO ASC("Z")
      40     LSET L$ = CHR$(L)
      50     PUT 1
      60 NEXT L
      70 CLOSE 1
```

```
1B.   1 REM     L$ = LETTER
      2 REM
      3 REM
      10 RANDOMIZE 32767
      20 OPEN "R",1,"B:ALPHABET.TXT",1
      30 FIELD 1, 1 AS L$
      40 FOR L = 1 TO 5
      50     GET 1, INT(RND * 26 + 1)
      60     PRINT L$;
      70 NEXT L
      80 CLOSE 1
```

```
3A.   1 REM    S$,S1$ = SAYING (128 CHARACTERS)
      2 REM    N = NUMBER OF SAYINGS
      10 OPEN "R",1,"B:SAYING.TXT",128
      20 FIELD 1 , 128 AS S$
      30 INPUT "HOW MANY SAYINGS";N
      40 FOR S = 1 TO N
      50    LINE INPUT S1$ : LSET S$ = S1$
      60    PUT 1
      70    PRINT
      80 NEXT S
      90 CLOSE 1


3B.   1 REM    S$ = SAYING
      2 REM    S = NUMBER OF SAYING
      3 REM
      4 REM
      10 OPEN "R",1,"B:SAYING.TXT",128
      20 FIELD 1, 128 AS S$
      30 INPUT "WHICH NUMBER SAYING";S
      40 GET 1,S
      50 IF S$ = STRING$(128,0) THEN PRINT "THERE AREN'T THAT MANY"
                                             :GOTO 30
      60 PRINT S$
      70 CLOSE 1


5A.   1 REM    F ,F$ = FULL-SIZED CARS (2 CHARACTERS)
      2 REM    M, M$ = MID-SIZED CARS  (2 CHARACTERS)
      3 REM    C, C$ = COMPACT CARS    (2 CHARACTERS)
      4 REM    M1,M1$ = MONTH
      5 REM
      6 REM
      10 OPEN "R",1,"B:CARS.TXT",6
      20 FIELD 1 , 2 AS F$, 2 AS M$, 2 AS C$
      30 FOR M1 = 1 TO 12
      40    READ M1$
      50    PRINT M1$;" SALES"
      60    INPUT "FULL-SIZED";F : LSET F$ = MKI$(F)
      70    INPUT "MID-SIZED";M : LSET M$ = MKI$(M)
      80    INPUT "COMPACT";C : LSET C$ = MKI$(C)
      90    PUT 1
      100   PRINT
      110 NEXT M1
      120 CLOSE 1
      130 DATA JANUARY,FEBRUARY,MARCH,APRIL,MAY,JUNE,JULY
      140 DATA AUGUST,SEPTEMBER,OCTOBER,NOVEMBER,DECEMBER
```

```
5B.  1 REM     F$ = FULL-SIZED CARS (2 CHARACTERS)
     2 REM     M$ = MID-SIZED CARS  (2 CHARACTERS)
     3 REM     C$ = COMPACT CARS (2 CAHARACTERS)
     4 REM     M1 = MONTH
     5 REM
     6 REM
     10 OPEN "R",1,"B:CARS.TXT",6
     20 FIELD 1 , 2 AS F$, 2 AS M$, 2 AS C$
     30 PRINT "ENTER A NEGATIVE NUMBER TO STOP"
     40 INPUT "WHICH MONTH (1-12)";M1
     50 IF M1 < 0 THEN 170
     60 CLS
     70 GET 1,M1
     80 PRINT "MONTH";M1
     90 LOCATE 12,1 : PRINT "FULL-SIZED:";
     100 FOR F = 1 TO CVI(F$) : PRINT "*"; : NEXT F : PRINT
     110 LOCATE 13,1 : PRINT " MID-SIZED:";
     120 FOR M = 1 TO CVI(M$) : PRINT "*"; : NEXT M : PRINT
     130 LOCATE 14,1: PRINT "   COMPACT:";
     140 FOR C = 1 TO CVI(C$) : PRINT "*"; : NEXT C : PRINT
     150 PRINT
     160 GOTO 40
     170 CLOSE 1


7A.  1 REM       NAM$ = NAME (9 CHARACTERS)
     2 REM       ADDRESS$ = ADDRESS (10 CHARACTERS)
     3 REM       STATE$ = STATE    (2 CHARACTERS)
     4 REM       SALARY$ = SALARY (4 CHARACTERS)
     5 REM       SAVING$ = SAVINGS (4 CHARACTERS)
     6 REM       AGE$ = AGE (2 CHARACTERS)
     7 REM       SEX$ = SEX (1 CHARACTER)
     8 REM       MODEL$ = MODEL OF THE CAR (5 CHARACTERS)
     9 REM       YEAR$ = YEAR OF THE CAR (2 CHARACTERS)
     10 REM    P() = 1 FOR PEOPLE WE WANT, ELSE P() = 0
     11 REM
     12 REM
     20 OPEN "R",1,"B:AUTO.TXT",7
     30 FIELD 1, 5 AS MODEL$, 2 AS YEAR$
     40 OPEN "R",2,"B:SALARY.TXT",8
     50 FIELD 2, 4 AS SALARY$, 4 AS SAVING$
     60 OPEN "R",3,"B:AGESEX.TXT",3
     70 FIELD 3, 2 AS AGE$, 1 AS SEX$
     80 REM
     100 REM    LOOK FOR PEOPLE WHO MEET THE REQUIREMENTS
     110 FOR ID = 1 TO 10
     120       GET 3,ID
     130     IF SEX$ = "F" OR CVI(AGE$) <= 30 THEN 190
     140     GET 2,ID
     150     IF CVS(SALARY$) <= 20000 THEN 190
     160     GET 1,ID
     170     IF LEFT$(MODEL$,4) <> "FORD" THEN 190
     180     P(ID) = 1 : REM    THESE ARE THE PEOPLE WE WANT
     190 NEXT ID
     200 CLOSE 1,2,3
     210 REM
```

```
300 REM    NOW PRINT OUT THOSE WHO MEET THE REQUIREMENTS
310 OPEN "R",1,"B:NAME.TXT",21
320 FIELD 1, 9 AS NAM$, 10 AS ADDRESS$, 2 AS STATE$
330 FOR I = 1 TO 10
340     GET 1
350      IF P(I) = 1 THEN PRINT NAM$,ADDRESS$,STATE$
360 NEXT I
370 CLOSE 1
```

7B.
```
    1 REM     NAM$ = NAME (9 CHARACTERS)
    2 REM     ADDRESS$ = ADDRESS (10 CHARACTERS)
    3 REM     STATE$ = STATE    (2 CHARACTERS)
    4 REM     SALARY$ = SALARY (4 CHARACTERS)
    5 REM     SAVING$ = SAVINGS (4 CHARACTERS)
    6 REM     MODEL$ = MODEL OF THE CAR (5 CHARACTERS)
    7 REM     YEAR$ = YEAR OF THE CAR (2 CHARACTERS)
    8 REM
    9 REM
   10 OPEN "R",1,"B:NAME.TXT",21
   20 FIELD 1, 9 AS NAM$, 10 AS ADDRESS$, 2 AS STATE$
   30 OPEN "R",2,"B:SALARY.TXT",8
   40 FIELD 2, 4 AS SALARY$, 4 AS SAVING$
   50 OPEN "R",3,"B:AUTO.TXT",7
   60 FIELD 3, 5 AS MODEL$, 2 AS YEAR$
   70 FOR ID = 1 TO 10
   80     GET 2, ID
   90     IF CVS(SALARY$) <= 15000 OR CVS(SAVING$) >= 2000 THEN 140
  100     GET 3, ID
  110     IF MODEL$ <> "CHEV " AND MODEL$ <> "FORD " AND
             MODEL$ <> "VW   " THEN 140
  120     GET 1, ID
  130     PRINT NAM$
  140 NEXT ID
  150 CLOSE 1,2,3
```

```
7C.  1 REM     NAM$ = NAME (9 CHARACTERS)
     2 REM     ADDRESS$ = ADDRESS (10 CHARACTERS)
     3 REM     STATE$ = STATE    (2 CHARACTERS)
     4 REM     AGE$ = AGE (2 CHARACTERS)
     5 REM     SEX$ = SEX ( 1 CHARACTER)
     6 REM     MODEL$ = MODEL OF THE CAR (5 CHARACTERS)
     7 REM     YEAR$ = YEAR OF THE CAR (2 CHARACTERS)
     8 REM
     9 REM
     10 OPEN "R",1,"B:NAME.TXT",21
     20 FIELD 1, 9 AS NAM$, 10 AS ADDRESS$, 2 AS STATE$
     30 OPEN "R",2,"B:AGESEX.TXT",3
     40 FIELD 2, 2 AS AGE$, 1 AS SEX$
     50 OPEN "R",3,"B:AUTO.TXT",7
     60 FIELD 3, 5 AS MODEL$, 2 AS YEAR$
     70 FOR ID = 1 TO 10
     80     GET 2,ID
     90     IF SEX$ = "F" OR CVI(AGE$) >= 35 THEN 150
     100    GET 3, ID
     110    IF MODEL$ <> "FORD " THEN 150
     120    GET 1, ID
     130    IF STATE$ <> "NJ" THEN 150
     140    PRINT NAM$, ADDRESS$, STATE$
     150 NEXT ID
     160 CLOSE 1,2,3


9A.  1 REM     NAM$, N1$ = NAME (20 CHARACTERS)
     2 REM     ADDRESS$, A1$ = STREET ADDRESS (25 CHARACTERS)
     3 REM     CITY$, C1$ = CITY (15 CHARACTERS)
     4 REM     STATE$, S1$ = STATE (2 CHARACTERS)
     5 REM     ZIP$, Z1$ = ZIP CODE (5 CHARACTERS)
     6 REM     B, BAL$ = BALANCE (4 CHARACTERS)
     7 REM     A = ACCOUNT NUMBER
     8 REM
     9 REM
     20 OPEN "R",1,"B:CHARGE.TXT",71
     30 FIELD 1, 20 AS NAM$, 25 AS ADDRESS$, 15 AS CITY$,
                   2 AS STATE$, 5 AS ZIP$, 4 AS BAL$
     40 FOR A = 1 TO 10
     50     PRINT "THIS WILL BE ACCOUNT #";A
     60     INPUT "NAME";N1$ : LSET NAM$ = N1$
     70     INPUT "STREET ADDRESS";A1$ : LSET ADDRESS$ = A1$
     80     INPUT "CITY";C1$ : LSET CITY$ = C1$
     90     INPUT "STATE";S1$ : LSET STATE$ = S1$
     100    INPUT "ZIP CODE";Z1$ : LSET ZIP$ = Z1$
     110    LSET BAL$ = MKS$(0)
     120    PUT 1
     130    PRINT
     140 NEXT A
     150 CLOSE 1
```

```
9B.   1 REM     NAM$ = NAME (20 CHARACTERS)
      2 REM     ADDRESS$ = STREET ADDRESS (25 CHARACTERS)
      3 REM     CITY$ = CITY (15 CHARACTERS)
      4 REM     STATE$ = STATE (2 CHARACTERS)
      5 REM     ZIP$ = ZIP CODE (5 CHARACTERS)
      6 REM     B, BAL$ = BALANCE (4 CHARACTERS)
      7 REM     A = ACCOUNT NUMBER
      8 REM     T$ = TRANSACTION FLAG
      9 REM     A1 = TRANSACTION AMOUNT
     10 REM
     11 REM
     20 OPEN "R",1,"B:CHARGE.TXT",71
     30 FIELD 1, 20 AS NAM$, 25 AS ADDRESS$, 15 AS CITY$,
              2 AS STATE$, 5 AS ZIP$, 4 AS BAL$
     40 PRINT "ENTER A NEGATIVE NUMBER TO STOP THE PROGRAM"
     50 INPUT "ACCOUNT #";A
     60     IF A < 0 THEN 180
     70     GET 1,A
     80     PRINT "BALANCE STANDS AT $";CVS(BAL$)
     90     INPUT "CHARGE OR PAYMENT";T$
    100     INPUT "AMOUNT";A1
    110     B = CVS(BAL$)
    120     IF ASC(T$) = 67 THEN B = B + A1
                        ELSE B = B - A1
    130     PRINT "NEW BALANCE IS $";B
    140     LSET BAL$ = MKS$(B)
    150     PUT 1, A
    160     PRINT
    170 GOTO 50
    180 CLOSE 1
```

```
9C.  1 REM      NAM$ = NAME (20 CHARACTERS)
     2 REM      ADDRESS$ = STREET ADDRESS (25 CHARACTERS)
     3 REM      CITY$ = CITY (15 CHARACTERS)
     4 REM      STATE$ = STATE (2 CHARACTERS)
     5 REM      ZIP$ = ZIP CODE (5 CHARACTERS)
     6 REM      BAL$ = BALANCE (4 CHARACTERS)
     7 REM
     8 REM
    10 OPEN "R",1,"B:CHARGE.TXT",71
    20 FIELD 1, 20 AS NAM$, 25 AS ADDRESS$, 15 AS CITY$,
              2 AS STATE$, 5 AS ZIP$, 4 AS BAL$
    30 GET 1
    40     IF NAM$ = STRING$(20,0) THEN 230
    50     IF NAM$ = STRING$(20,32) THEN 30
    60     IF CVS(BAL$) <= 0 THEN 30
    70     PRINT "FROM: BUY LOW DEPARTMENT STORE"
    80     PRINT "TO: ";NAM$
    90     PRINT "ACCOUNT #";LOC(1)
   100     PRINT
   110     PRINT "YOU HAVE CHARGED $";CVS(BAL$);"AGAINST YOUR"
   120     PRINT "ACCOUNT.  THIS AMOUNT IS NOW DUE."
   130     IF CVS(BAL$) > 800 THEN 190
   140     PRINT
   150     PRINT "                              THANK YOU"
   160     PRINT :PRINT
   170 GOTO 30
   180 END
   190 PRINT
   200 PRINT "YOUR ACCOUNT EXCEEEDS YOUR CHARGE LIMIT."
   210 PRINT "PAY IMMEDIATELY!"
   220 GOTO 140
   230 CLOSE 1
```

```
9D.  1 REM     NAM$ = NAME (20 CHARACTERS)
     2 REM     ADDRESS$ = STREET ADDRESS (25 CHARACTERS)
     3 REM     CITY$ = CITY (15 CHARACTERS)
     4 REM     STATE$ = STATE (2 CHARACTERS)
     5 REM     ZIP$ = ZIP CODE (5 CHARACTERS)
     6 REM     BAL$ = BALANCE (4 CHARACTERS)
     7 REM     A = ACCOUNT NUMBER
     8 REM     BLANK$ = A STRING OF BLANK CHARACTERS
     9 REM
     10 REM
     20 OPEN "R",1,"B:CHARGE.TXT",71
     30 FIELD 1, 20 AS NAM$, 25 AS ADDRESS$, 15 AS CITY$,
               2 AS STATE$, 5 AS ZIP$, 4 AS BAL$
     40 INPUT "WHICH ACCOUNT IS BEING CLOSED";A
     50 BLANK$ = STRING$(25,32)
     60 LSET NAM$ = BLANK$
     70 LSET ADDRESS$ = BLANK$
     80 LSET CITY$ = BLANK$
     90 LSET STATE$ = BLANK$
     100 LSET ZIP$ = BLANK$
     110 LSET BAL$ = MKS$(0)
     120 PUT 1, A
     130 PRINT "ACCOUNT #";A;"HAS BEEN CLOSED."
     140 CLOSE 1


9E.  1 REM     NAM$, N1$ = NAME (20 CHARACTERS)
     2 REM     ADDRESS$, A1$ = STREET ADDRESS (25 CHARACTERS)
     3 REM     CITY$, C1$ = CITY (15 CHARACTERS)
     4 REM     STATE$, S1$ = STATE (2 CHARACTERS)
     5 REM     ZIP$, Z1$ = ZIP CODE (5 CHARACTERS)
     6 REM     BAL$ = BALANCE (4 CHARACTERS)
     7 REM     A = ACCOUNT NUMBER
     8 REM
     9 REM
     20 OPEN "R",1,"B:CHARGE.TXT",71
     30 FIELD 1, 20 AS NAM$, 25 AS ADDRESS$, 15 AS CITY$,
               2 AS STATE$, 5 AS ZIP$, 4 AS BAL$
     40 GET 1
     50 IF NAM$ <> STRING$(20,32) AND NAM$ <> STRING$(20,0) THEN 40
     60 INPUT "NAME";N1$ : LSET NAM$ = N1$
     70 INPUT "STREET ADDRESS";S1$ : LSET ADDRESS$ = S1$
     80 INPUT "CITY";C1$ : LSET CITY$ = C1$
     90 INPUT "STATE";S1$ : LSET STATE$ = S1$
     100 INPUT "ZIP CODE";Z1$ : LSET ZIP$ = Z1$
     110 LSET BAL$ = MKS$(0)
     120 PRINT "THIS PERSON WILL BE ASSIGNED ACCOUNT #";LOC(1)
     130 PUT 1, LOC(1)
     140 CLOSE 1
```

INDEX